Cross-Cultural Pragmatics and Foreign Language Learning

JULIANE HOUSE AND DÁNIEL Z. KÁDÁR

EDINBURGH
University Press

Edinburgh University Press is one of the leading university presses in the UK. We publish academic books and journals in our selected subject areas across the humanities and social sciences, combining cutting-edge scholarship with high editorial and production values to produce academic works of lasting importance. For more information visit our website: edinburghuniversitypress.com

© Juliane House and Dániel Z. Kádár, 2024, 2025

Edinburgh University Press Ltd
13 Infirmary Street
Edinburgh EH1 1LT

First published in hardback by Edinburgh University Press 2024

Typeset in 9/12 NotoSerif
by Cheshire Typesetting Ltd, Cuddington, Cheshire

A CIP record for this book is available from the British Library

ISBN 978-1-3995-2322-6 (hardback)
ISBN 978-1-3995-2323-3 (paperback)
ISBN 978-1-3995-2324-0 (webready PDF)
ISBN 978-1-3995-2325-7 (epub)

The right of Juliane House and Dániel Z. Kádár to be identified as the authors of this work has been asserted in accordance with the Copyright, Designs and Patents Act 1988, and the Copyright and Related Rights Regulations 2003 (SI No. 2498).

Cross-Cultural Pragmatics
and Foreign Language Learning

To the memory of Willis J. Edmondson, 1940–2009

Contents

List of figures and tables	viii
About the authors	xi
Acknowledgements	xiii
Series introduction	xiv

1	Introduction	1
	1.1 Background	1
	1.2 Conventions	2
	1.3 Contents	7
	1.4 Recommended reading	9
2	The foundations of cross-cultural pragmatics	12
	2.1 Introduction	12
	2.2 The development of cross-cultural pragmatics	12
	2.2.1 The birth of cross-cultural pragmatics	14
	2.2.2 The CCSARP project	15
	2.3 The basics of cross-cultural pragmatics	18
	2.4 What makes pragmatic contrasting possible?	20
	2.5 Conclusion	23
	2.6 Recommended reading	23
3	Our contrastive pragmatic framework and its use in L2 pragmatics	26
	3.1 Introduction	26
	3.2 Our framework	26
	3.3 Pitfalls in previous L2 pragmatic research	27
	3.4 Our interactional typology of speech acts	30
	3.5 Research procedure	34
	3.6 Conclusion	37
	3.7 Recommended reading	37

4 Exploring speech acts through expressions in L2 pragmatics — 40
4.1 Introduction — 40
4.2 Selected previous studies — 41
4.3 Analytic procedure — 41
4.3.1 The corpus-based study of RFIEs — 42
4.3.2 The L2 pragmatic study of RFIEs — 58
4.4 Conclusion — 69
4.5 Recommended reading — 69

5 On the problem of altered speech act indication in L2 pragmatics — 73
5.1 Introduction — 73
5.2 The first phase of our research — 73
5.3 The second phase of our research — 77
5.3.1 Analysis and results — 79
5.4 Conclusion — 87
5.5 Recommended reading — 88

6 Speech acts and interactional acts 1: the case of criticising — 90
6.1 Introduction — 90
6.2 Selected previous studies — 91
6.3 Methodology and data — 92
6.3.1 Part 1 — 92
6.3.2 Part 2 — 93
6.4 Analysis — 93
6.4.1 Part 1 — 93
6.4.2 Part 2 — 99
6.5 Conclusion — 105
6.6 Recommended reading — 106

7 Speech acts and interactional acts 2: the case of ritual congratulating — 108
7.1 Introduction — 108
7.2 Selected previous studies — 109
7.3 Methodology and data — 110
7.4 Analysis — 113
7.4.1 Results of the Chinese DCTs — 114
7.4.2 Results of the learner DCTs — 120
7.5 Conclusion — 124
7.6 Recommended reading — 125

8 Types of Talk in L2 pragmatics 1: greeting in English as a foreign language — 127
8.1 Introduction — 127
8.2 Selected previous research — 127

	8.3	Methodology and data	129
		8.3.1 Step 1	132
		8.3.2 Step 2	133
	8.4	Analysis	133
		8.4.1 Step 1	133
		8.4.2 Step 2	142
	8.5	Conclusion	150
	8.6	Recommended reading	150
9	Types of Talk in L2 pragmatics 2: the case of extracting		152
	9.1	Introduction	152
	9.2	Case study	152
		9.2.1 Contrastive research	154
		9.2.2 Discussion	162
	9.3	Conclusion	163
	9.4	Recommended reading	163
10	Types of Talk in L2 pragmatics 3: the case of phatic Opening versus Business Talk		165
	10.1	Introduction	165
	10.2	Case study	165
		10.2.1 Experiment	165
		10.2.2 Outcome	167
	10.3	Conclusion	170
	10.4	Recommended reading	170
11	Conclusion		172
	11.1	Retrospect	172
	11.2	Prospect	173

Glossary	176
References	180
Index	190

List of figures and tables

Figures

1.1	Units of analysis	3
1.2	Types of talk	4
2.1	The focus of cross-cultural pragmatics (adapted from House, 2005)	20
3.1	Our radically minimal, finite and interactional typology of speech acts	30
3.2	Display of our research procedure	34
4.1	Our procedure of studying RFIEs in corpora in a contrastive way	42
5.1	Types of relationship between expressions and speech acts	76
6.1	(In)directness of various addressing solutions in our DCT corpus	98
7.1	Our typology of speech acts (displayed again)	112
8.1	Our typology of speech acts, with focal points added	131
8.2	Outcome of our twofold analysis – English	148
8.3	Outcome of our twofold analysis – Chinese	149
11.1	The typological distance-based contrastive approach	174

Tables

4.1	Allocation of the RFIE *please* in the corpus	45
4.2	Allocation of the RFIE *could you please* in the corpus	46
4.3	Allocation of the RFIE *if you please* in the corpus	48
4.4	Allocation of the RFIE *qing* in the corpus	49
4.5	Allocation of the RFIE *fanqing* in the corpus	50
4.6	Allocation of the RFIE *jingqing* in the corpus	51
4.7	Allocation of the RFIE *sorry* in the corpus	53
4.8	Allocation of the RFIE *I am sorry* in the corpus	54
4.9	Allocation of the RFIE *duibuqi* in the corpus	56
4.10	Allocation of the RFIE *duibuqi + object* in the corpus	56
4.11	Allocation of the RFIE *upgrader + duibuqi + object* in the corpus	57

Figures and tables ix

4.12	Contrastively salient uses of the RFIEs studied	58
4.13	The response rate of the British English respondents	63
4.14	The response rate of the Chinese respondents	63
5.1	Quantitative results of the task sheet responses (+ indicates appropriate responses, – indicates inappropriate responses)	80
6.1	The frequency of the RFIEs *qing, buyao* and *zhuyi* in our DCT corpus	94
6.2	Formulae of addressing in our first corpus in decreasing frequency	97
6.3	Speech act categories and their frequency in our DCT corpus	98
6.4	Chinese and foreign respondents' evaluations of the RFIE-utterances presented in Task 1	101
6.5	Chinese and foreign respondents' evaluations of address realisations in Task 2	103
6.6	Chinese and foreign respondents' evaluations of the speech acts presented in Task 3	104
7.1	The results of the DCTs featuring the interaction ritual act of congratulating for the birth of a child	114
7.2	The results of DCTs featuring the interaction ritual act of congratulating for an eighteenth birthday	116
7.3	The results of DCTs featuring the interaction ritual act of congratulating for an eightieth birthday	117
7.4	The results of DCTs featuring the interaction ritual act of congratulating for a wedding	118
8.1	The Greet expressions compared	132
8.2	Stand-alone uses of *Hi*	134
8.3	Uses of *Hi* in Greet→Speech act	134
8.4	Stand-alone uses of *Hello*	135
8.5	Uses of *Hello* in Greet→Speech act	136
8.6	Stand-alone uses of *Good morning/afternoon/evening*	137
8.7	Uses of *Good morning/afternoon/evening* in Greet→Speech act	137
8.8	Stand-alone uses of *Ni-hao*	138
8.9	Uses of *Ni-hao* in Greet→Speech act	138
8.10	Stand-alone uses of *Nin-hao*	140
8.11	Uses of *Nin-hao* in Greet→Speech act	140
8.12	Stand-alone uses of *Zaoshang/Xiawu/Wanshang-hao*	141
8.13	Uses of *Zaoshang/Xiawu/Wanshang-hao* in Greet→Speech act	141
8.14	British responses to the first [Priv] question	143
8.15	British responses to the first [Pub] question	143
8.16	British responses to the second [Priv] question	143
8.17	British responses to the second [Pub] question	144
8.18	Chinese responses to the first [Priv] question	144
8.19	Chinese responses to the first [Pub] question	145
8.20	Chinese responses to the second [Priv] question	145
8.21	Chinese responses to the second [Pub] question	146

9.1	Frequency of Extractor and other speech acts in the Closing phase in our Chinese DCT corpus	155
9.2	Frequency of Extractor-indicating honorifics in our Chinese DCT corpus	156
9.3	Frequency of deferential and quasi-familial forms of address in our Chinese DCT corpus	157
9.4	Frequency of speech act types in the Closing phase in our English DCT corpus	158
9.5	Frequency of Extractor-indicating routine formulae in our English DCT corpus	159
10.1	Choices of our British respondents	167
10.2	Choices of our Chinese respondents	168

About the authors

Juliane House received her PhD in applied linguistics from the University of Toronto, Canada, and honorary doctorates from the Universities of Jyväskylä, Finland, and Jaume I, Castellon, Spain. She is Professor Emerita at the University of Hamburg, Germany, where she was a founding member of the Research Centre on Multilingualism. She is currently a Professor at the HUN-REN Hungarian Research Centre for Linguistics. She is also Distinguished University Professor and Director of the Doctoral Program of Language and Communication at Hellenic American University, Nashua, USA, and Athens, Greece. She is Visiting Professor at Dalian University of Foreign Languages and Beijing University of Science and Technology, China. Juliane is Past President of the International Association for Translation and Intercultural Studies. Her research interests include cross-cultural and intercultural pragmatics, discourse analysis, (im)politeness, L2 pragmatics, language and politics, translation theory, and English as a global lingua franca. She has published widely in all these areas. She was co-editor of the ground-breaking volume *Cross-Cultural Pragmatics: Requests and Apologies* (Ablex, 1989). Some of her recent books include *Translation Quality Assessment: Past and Present* (Routledge, 2015), *Translation as Communication across Languages and Cultures* (Routledge, 2016), *Translation: The Basics* (Routledge, 2018), *Cross-Cultural Pragmatics* (with Dániel Z. Kádár, Cambridge University Press, 2021), and *Expressions, Speech Acts and Discourse – A Pedagogic Interactional Grammar of English* (with Willis Edmondson and Dániel Z. Kádár, Cambridge University Press, 2023). She is co-editor of *Cross-cultural Pragmatics – A Cross-Disciplinary Journal* (Brill).

Dániel Z. Kádár is Qihang Chair Professor and Director of the Center for Pragmatic Research at Dalian University of Foreign Languages, China. He is also Research Professor at the HUN-REN Hungarian Research Centre for Linguistics, Hungary, and Professor of English Linguistics at the University of Maribor Slovenia. He is an ordinary member of Academia Europaea (MAE), and he also has a higher doctorate (DLitt) in pragmatics (2015) and PhD in linguistics (2006). His areas of research involve cross-cultural, intercultural and L2 pragmatics, linguistic (im)politeness and interactional ritual, language and politics, and historical and modern Chinese language. He has published many books with internationally leading publishers, and research papers in high-impact journals. He is author of *Relational Rituals and Communication: Ritual Interaction in Groups* (Palgrave Macmillan, 2013), *Politeness, Impoliteness and Ritual – Maintaining the Moral Order in Interpersonal Interaction* (Cambridge University Press, 2017), and co-author of *Understanding Politeness* (with Michael Haugh, Cambridge University Press, 2013) and *Intercultural Politeness – Managing Relationships across Cultures* (with Helen Spencer-Oatey, Cambridge University Press, 2020). His most recent books are *Cross-Cultural Pragmatics* (with Juliane House, Cambridge University Press, 2021), and *Expressions, Speech Acts and Discourse – A Pedagogic Interactional Grammar of English* (with Willis Edmondson and Juliane House, Cambridge University Press, 2023). He is co-editor of *Cross-cultural Pragmatics – A Cross-Disciplinary Journal* (Brill).

Acknowledgements

First of all, we are indebted to the four reviewers and the two clearance readers who helped us enormously to improve the quality of the present manuscript. We are also grateful to Laura Quinn and Helena Heald at Edinburgh University Press both for supporting our work with this book and for helping us to establish the *Edinburgh Studies in Pragmatics* series, which is opened by this monograph. We would also like to say thank you to all those colleagues who contributed to the birth of this book. In particular, we would like to say thank you to Emily Fengguang Liu, who contributed to various case studies involving Chinese learners of English that we present in this book, and all those who agreed to join our case studies as subjects, as well as various colleagues – including Shiyu Liu, Wenrui Shi and many research students at Dalian University of Foreign Languages – who contributed to our research and graciously agreed to give us their precious time.

On an institutional level, we would like to acknowledge the funding of the National Excellence Programme of the National Research, Development and Innovation Office of Hungary (grant number: TKP2021-NKTA-02). This grant, which is the continuation of another one (Momentum Grant of the Hungarian Academy of Sciences, grant number LP2017/5) allowed us to collaborate. We would also like to acknowledge the funding of the National Research Development and Innovation Office of Hungary (grant number: 132969). All the above grants have been hosted by the HUN-REN Hungarian Research Centre for Linguistics. Dániel Kádár is also grateful to Dalian University of Foreign Languages for all the institutional support he received.

On a personal note, this book could have never been completed without the many fascinating and original ideas of Willis Edmondson, who unfortunately passed away some years ago. We dedicate this book to Willis. As well as to Willis, we are indebted to our families for all their loving support. Juliane would like to say thank you to Patrick, Miriam, Tessa, Wissem, Mailin, Lucia and Emilia, as well as Bobby. Dániel would like to say thank you to Keiko, Naoka, Zita, András and Eszter, as well as Koma. Thank you all for bearing with us while we spent very long hours in front of our computers.

Series introduction

The *Edinburgh Studies in Pragmatics* series represents a comprehensive new endeavour to cover all the main areas of pragmatics, offering a systematic mosaic of pragmatics by including studies of individual areas that together create a panoramic overview of the field. The series covers the core topics but also ventures beyond this to examine language use across social, institutional, interpersonal and political contexts and to cover areas such as sociopragmatics, corpus pragmatics and pragmalinguistics and the interface between pragmatics and other disciplines. By publishing innovative and leading work, the series aims to capture the diversity of pragmatics as a field of research, and individual volumes contribute to key critical debates in pragmatics.

The series editors

Juliane House is Professor Emerita at the University of Hamburg, Germany, where she was a founding member of the Research Centre on Multilingualism. She is currently a Professor at the HUN-REN Hungarian Research Centre for Linguistics. She is also Distinguished University Professor and Director of the Doctoral Program of Language and Communication at Hellenic American University, Nashua, USA, and Athens, Greece.

Dániel Z. Kádár is Qihang Chair Professor and Director of the Center for Pragmatic Research at Dalian University of Foreign Languages, China. He is also Research Professor at the HUN-REN Hungarian Research Centre for Linguistics, Hungary, and Professor of English Linguistics at the University of Maribor. He is also an ordinary member of Academia Europaea (MAE).

Find out more about the series at edinburghuniversitypress.com/series-edinburgh-studies-in-pragmatics.

CHAPTER 1

Introduction

1.1 Background

In this book, we invite the reader to follow us on a journey into the realm of foreign language learning approached through the lens of cross-cultural pragmatics. Foreign language learning is a field which encompasses applied linguistic research on how foreign learners acquire their target language. We focus on one major area in foreign language learning – second language pragmatics (henceforth **L2 pragmatics**) – which deals with the pragmatic aspects of foreign language learning. **Cross-cultural pragmatics**, which is also often referred to as **contrastive pragmatics**, involves research through which scholars systematically compare language use across different languages and language varieties, in order to understand a particular phenomenon. While 'contrastive' and 'cross-cultural' pragmatics are often used as synonyms, 'contrastive' is more often used to describe a pragmatic methodology, and the expression 'cross-cultural' refers to a broader field in which the researcher engages in both basic contrastive research and other non-contrastive methodologies, such as interviews and surveys. In other words, 'cross-cultural' is a more comprehensive expression than 'contrastive'. Cross-cultural pragmatics has appeared in applied linguistics mainly in the framework of interlanguage pragmatics, focusing on phenomena such as pragmatic transfer from the learner's first language (henceforth L1) into his or her target language (henceforth L2). However, cross-cultural and interlanguage pragmatics do not cover exactly the same terrain: the interlanguage pragmatician normally studies a whole set of issues surrounding foreign language acquisition, while the cross-cultural pragmatician normally approaches foreign language learning from a comparative angle, as the name suggests. In this book, we aim to bring together cross-cultural pragmatics and L2 pragmatics, by proposing a **bottom-up** and **replicable** contrastive pragmatic framework, which we have developed over the past years, and which will be presented in detail in Chapter 3 of this book and used consistently in all the following chapters.

The authors of this book, together with Willis Edmondson, have developed a system which allows us to engage in cross-cultural pragmatic research – including the study of foreign language learning – in a bottom–up, **corpus-based** and strictly language-anchored way (see House and Kádár, 2021a; Edmondson et al., 2023; House and Kádár, 2024). The present book builds on this system, by incorporating it into applied linguistics. A key element of this system is that we only study conventionalised – i.e. non-idiosyncratic – aspects of language use in order to keep our research replicable. A fundamental aspect of this pursuit of **conventionalisation** is that we never try to look at seemingly interesting but essentially non-replicable data, such as a one-off interaction between two L2 learners, however interesting it may look. We use both large and small corpora, including pre-compiled corpora such as the British National Corpus, and smaller corpora compiled by ourselves, such as corpora of **Discourse Completion Tests** (henceforth DCTs) and other production tasks. Here it is worth noting that 'corpus' involves machine-readable texts of any size.

Along with the above-outlined focus on conventionalisation, our system is essentially **interactional**, i.e. we are interested in how foreign language learning occurs in interaction. For instance, various chapters of this book will show that it is of little use to study a particular phenomenon, such as greeting, on its own. Instead, it is much more productive to interpret any phenomenon as an integral part of interaction, all the more so because L2 learners themselves may ultimately have to learn how to use the phenomena they study in interaction. As part of our pursuit of interaction, we also prefer studying multiple units of language use, including expressions, speech acts, and so on (see more below). This view provides a comprehensive explanatory system. On the level of methodology, we suggest relying on **mixed method approaches**.

The operation of the above-outlined framework will be discussed in detail later on in this book. The reason why we think this comprehensive cross-cultural L2 pragmatic approach is necessary today is the following: applied linguistics is a very broad field, which includes both (a) language-anchored and (b) more culturally and psychologically focused research on foreign language learning. In this book, we are only concerned with the former area and take a relatively critical view on cultural and psychological takes on L2 learning (see Chapter 3). We believe our contribution to the first area mentioned above is that by combining L2 pragmatics with cross-cultural pragmatics we are able to propose a replicable and language-anchored interactional framework of foreign language learning.

1.2 Conventions

In this book, we rely on a number of concepts, which we define here.

We use the term **'linguaculture'** to describe culture manifested through patterns of language use (see House, 2003a; House and Kádár, 2021a).

Introduction

This particular term also relates to how we see culture itself – an issue which we will outline in more detail in Chapter 2.

In our analytic framework – to be outlined in Chapter 3 – we rely on the following four units of analysis, as provided in Figure 1.1.

1. *Expressions*
2. *Speech acts (finite)*
3. *Interactional acts*
4. *Type of Talks (finite)*

⇓ Increasing size

Figure 1.1 Units of analysis

Expression, representing the lowest level of analysis, includes both routine formulae (see Coulmas, 1979) and other pragmatically relevant words. We prefer '**expression**' over 'word' because what we are talking about here is a pragmatic unit, which may include forms of varying size. For example, *Thank you* is a typical pragmatically relevant expression, which is made up of two words.

We will introduce the concept of **speech act** in more detail later in the book but let us provide a brief definition here. A speech act is an utterance considered as an action. Typical speech acts are Request and Apologise, although as we will show in Chapter 3 speech acts have many other types. The reason why we do not provide a figure representing our typology of speech acts here is that speech acts are the core of our framework, and the typology through which we approach and categorise them requires a more detailed and in-depth discussion.

We interpret the notion **interactional act** in a specific way in this book, in order to contextualise speech acts in interaction (for other definitions of the notion of 'interactional act' see e.g. Steuten, 1997; Brown, 2017). As we will explain later in this book, the number of speech acts as we understand them is finite, while the number of interactional acts in which these speech acts occur is infinite. This infiniteness accords with the fact that language users across linguacultures always create new contexts and media of communication, as well as new interactional acts in these contexts and media. This is why we distinguish the units of interactional acts and speech acts. For example, complaining is an interactional act, which can be realised through many different speech acts, such as Complain itself, as well as Request, Remark, and so on. Some other interactional acts, such as online shaming, may sound more 'distinct' from speech acts than complaining, but just like complaining they are also conventionally realised by various speech acts such as Opine. The reason why many interactional acts tend to be conventionally realised through many different speech acts is the following: in real life, language users do not always communicate in the most direct way. For example, to refer to the above-mentioned case of the interactional act of complaining, language users do not always realise this interactional act by the speech act Complain but often choose complex interactional solutions. The same applies to the above case of shaming: while Opine is the most straightforward speech act through which this interactional act can be realised, it can also be realised, for instance, by Request (for information) (e.g. "Is he not a loser?"). Such solutions can vary across linguacultures, and if we intend to examine why their acquisition can cause puzzlement, irritation and difficulties for L2 learners, it is important to be able to break down L2 pragmatics-relevant interactional acts into a finite set of speech acts which exist in any linguaculture. In order to distinguish speech acts and interactional acts in a consistent way, in this book we capitalise speech acts – interactional acts conversely are not capitalised and are always indicated in an -ing form (see e.g. 'Complain' versus 'complaining').[1]

The concept of **Type of Talk** refers to the building blocks of an interaction, which include conventionalised sequences of speech acts. As such, the concept of Type of Talk represents the highest level of discourse in our analytic system. As we argued elsewhere (see Edmondson et al., 2023), Types of Talk make up the structure of an encounter, and they allow us to study speech acts and interactional acts by considering their interactional place. In the cross-cultural L2 pragmatic framework proposed in this book, Types of Talk play an important role because they allow us to contrastively consider which speech acts are frequented in a particular interactional phase in the learner's L1 and L2. The number of Types of Talk is finite in our system. The following Figure 1.2 illustrates how various Types of Talk relate to one another.

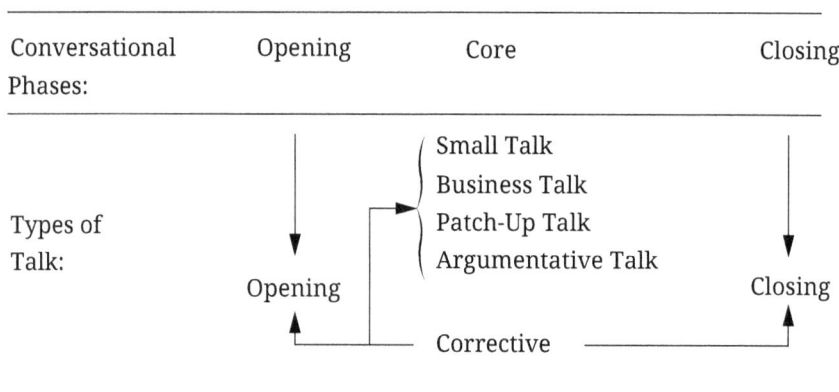

Figure 1.2 Types of Talk

The Type of Talk which occurs in interactional Openings, and in interactional Closings are peculiar to these phases of interaction. The 'Core' of an interaction consists of one or more Types of Talk, distinguishable as either Small Talk, Business Talk, Patch-Up Talk, or Argumentative Talk. Additionally, we have as a distinct Type of Talk the case in which *Corrective* or *Repair* work is carried out in the middle of some other ongoing talk. By Business Talk we mean talk which is oriented towards a goal, plan or decision concerning a future course of action. By Patch-Up Talk we mean talk consequent to an offence. Small Talk is largely phatic and casual, while Argumentative Talk concerns the truth of an issue of substance. The goals of Small Talk are therefore social: showing oneself as agreeable, and basking in the agreeableness of one's interlocutor. The goal of Argumentative Talk is ultimately agreement on a matter of some importance, but each participant seeks that agreement through promulgating his own view. As we already noted, and as will transpire from various chapters, all Types of Talk are conventionally manifested through certain speech acts. As a simple example, we should refer here to Opening Talk which tends to be realised by speech acts such as Greet and How-are-you. In the present book, we denote Types of Talk in capital. Types of Talk of course make up 'discourse' in a broader sense. Discourse includes broader and vaguer categories, such as genres (see e.g. 'classroom talk'), but we do not use such categories in our system.

As in any pragmatic research, context plays a paramount role in the current framework. We often study corpora of language use (see above), and we annotate such corpora by using the following pairs of variables representing contextual variation:

1. The standard sociolinguistic parameters **Social Distance and Power** [+–SD, +/–P].
2. The **Private versus Public** ([Priv/Pub]) nature of an encounter.

In pragmatics, it was the Cross-Cultural Speech Act Realization Project (CCSARP) (Blum-Kulka et al., 1989; see Chapter 2) which first used the variables of [+/–SD, +/–P] on a large scale. Later on, scholars such as Cohen (2008) and McConarchy (2019) introduced other variables, and recently Nilsson et al. (2020: 2) argued that "age, gender, participant roles, medium and venue affect speakers' choice of greeting form". Notwithstanding the importance of such additional variables, in our framework we rely on the basic [+/–SD, +/–P] variables, combined with the variables [Priv/Pub] because in our view these variables are best compatible with contrastive corpus analysis. An interaction is defined as [Priv] when there are clearly no bystanders/overhearers around and when it is uttered for the hearer only. An interaction qualifies as [Pub] when bystanders/overhearers are present either physically or symbolically (see Goffman, 1971).

In this book, the expression '**native speaker**' will often be used. We are fully aware of the large and justified body of criticism of native speakerism, and we agree with Cook (1999), Davies (2004), Kubota (2016) and many others who have pointed out that foreign speakers of English should not be expected to imitate 'native speaker' practices. We ourselves are non-native speakers of English, but we do consider ourselves as expert speakers of English, especially because both of us not only used to live in English-speaking countries for a long time, but also because we have published our research in English. According to this stance, while we will not shy away from using the expression 'native speaker', considering that it is a useful concept in cross-cultural pragmatic research in particular, we refrain from suggesting that speakers of other languages who learn English as an L2 should be 'expected' to ape Anglophone pragmatics conventions (and the same applies to any L2!). This is particularly the case because practically all our case studies involve Chinese–English contrastive research and in many cases our subjects include Chinese learners of English. Considering that the United Kingdom tried (and, to some degree, succeeded in) colonising China in the nineteenth century, we would find it distasteful, for instance, to present a 'role model of English speaker' for Chinese learners of English.

As we are cross-cultural pragmaticians, in this book we use the expressions 'contrasting' and 'contrastive' practically all the time. However, a warning is due about the way in which we use these expressions. Like most applied linguists today, we distance ourselves from the strong contrastive hypothesis that linguacultural differences automatically trigger L2 difficulties (see Fries, 1945; Lado, 1957). Still, we believe that contrastive pragmatic differences between English and Chinese and other linguacultures should not be neglected if one wishes to understand the understudied issue of why and how pragmatics conventions in Anglophone linguacultures may confuse L2 learners of English. For example, in Chapter 8 we will discuss L2 issues triggered by the pragmatic conventions of the interactional act of greeting in English for foreign learners. If one expects the other to utter a greeting and the greeting fails to come, or one is greeted when no such greeting is expected, gut feelings of irritation may emerge. Kádár (2017) explained such irritations through the concept of the 'moral order' of interaction. The moral order is particularly important in interaction **rituals** such as greeting, which are such fundamental parts of our daily encounters that language users are unlikely to devote much attention to them until an interactional breach occurs. Cross-cultural pragmatic analysis may help us understand contrastive differences of greeting conventions which may trigger foreign speaker puzzlement in such a case. In summary, 'contrasting' and 'contrastive' will be used throughout this book, with the above qualification in mind.

Another convention includes the words 'irritation' and 'puzzlement'. As part of our framework to be outlined in Chapter 3, in many contrastive L2 pragmatic investigations we critically consider why and how the realisation of certain speech acts and other units in our system triggers irritations and puzzlement for L2 learners. As part of our investigation into such instances of irritation and puzzlement, we always attempt to avoid relying on sweeping overgeneralisations, often centring on the so-called '**East–West divide**' (see e.g. Simpson, 2008; Kobayashi, 2011, among many others). As soon as one starts to rely on such overgeneralisations, e.g. by talking about 'East–West classroom culture conflicts', one unavoidably follows a top-down logic where one sets out to prove the validity of an assumption one holds at the very outset of our research. Such an approach seems to us to be essentially misguided, and we are certainly not alone with this view (see Leech's 2007 seminal study). We therefore follow a strictly bottom-up view on irritations and puzzlement, in the spirit of Karl Popper (see Edmondson and House, 2011). According to Popper's classic research paradigm, one should never set out to prove one's assumption but rather attempt to falsify it and then, if necessary, propose a revised assumption, and so on.

Our ethical conventions are the following: in each example and other data featured in this book, we anonymise the participants. As part of collecting data, we followed the standard ethical procedure of requesting the consent of the participants and storing data safely. This is a normal procedure in pragmatics, so here we do not waste more words on it. In the spirit of gender equality, we use both the feminine and the masculine pronouns in the subsequent chapters.

We add one or more recommended readings to each chapter to help early career readers. Also, we provide the reader with a glossary of what we believe are the most important technical terms in this book. We mark these terms in bold type when they first occur in the text.

1.3 Contents

In Chapter 2, we introduce the reader to the field of cross-cultural pragmatics. This will help us to position cross-cultural pragmatics and our framework in L2 pragmatics research. Chapter 2 first gives a general overview of how cross-cultural pragmatics has developed, and it also introduces certain important concepts in the field. We will also discuss how it is possible to contrastively examine two comparable units of language use.

In Chapter 3 we introduce our framework. Since this framework pays specific attention to speech acts as the central part of L2 pragmatic research, the chapter devotes special attention to speech act phenomena. As part of introducing our framework, we will present our typology of speech acts, and we outline our methodology through which this typology will be put to use in all the subsequent chapters of this book.

In Chapter 4, we investigate how expressions, as the smallest pragmatic unit of analysis, can indicate speech acts, and the L2 pragmatic issues arising from this assignation. Here we focus on two Attitudinal speech acts, Request and Apologise, indicated by pragmatically important expressions in the learners' L1 and L2.

In Chapter 5 we continue to discuss the relationship between expressions and speech acts in L2 pragmatics by moving on to a more complex phenomenon, namely altered speech act indication. We examine how L2 learners evaluate cases when a particular expression indicates another speech act than what it is conventionally associated with.

In Chapter 6 we discuss a higher level of our analytic system, by bringing together the units of speech acts and interactional acts. Here we investigate how Chinese native speakers and foreign learners of Chinese evaluate instances of the interactional act of criticising in the classroom. As a conventionalised interactional act, criticising is realised by a cluster of expressions and speech acts. We examine such realisation patterns to find out exactly which aspects of criticising may trigger L2 learning difficulties.

In Chapter 7, we again look at the relationship between speech acts and interactional acts in L2 pragmatics by also interconnecting our inquiry with the applied linguistic field of study abroad, as well as interaction ritual theory. Here we examine how and why the realisation of a non-quotidian ritual interactional act – congratulating – triggers realisation difficulties for foreign learners of Chinese in study abroad programmes in China. The rationale behind examining such a non-quotidian and essentially ritual interactional act like congratulating is as follows: due to the notorious absence of complex ritual behaviour in teaching materials, students may never become familiar with the realisation patterns of such interactional acts when they learn Chinese in their home country. Similar to Chapter 8, we approach congratulating as an interactional act by breaking it down into the realisation of different conventional speech acts.

In Chapter 8, we move towards the largest unit in our system, namely Types of Talk (see above). We investigate the interactional act of greeting in English, which can be surprisingly challenging for speakers of other languages. We look at the challenges which greeting in English can pose for speakers of Chinese, by exploring deep-seated differences between English and Chinese greeting conventions. By 'greeting' we mean the seemingly 'simple' interactional act of choosing conventionalised expressions and related speech acts at the Opening Talk of an encounter.

In Chapter 9, we present yet another case study where we use our framework to examine an L2 pragmatic issue through the unit of Types of Talk. Here we focus on the interactional act of extracting, which describes the behaviour of a speaker who wants to end the conversation, while the other goes on relentlessly talking. Similar to the interactional act of greeting which occurs in the Opening phase, extracting is an act that occurs in the Closing phase of an interaction, and it tends to be conventionally realised by various speech acts across linguacultures.

In Chapter 10, which again deals with Types of Talk, we present a case study featuring an experiment we conducted to find out whether Chinese learners of English are able to recognise cases when the speech act Complain is realised in a context where Opening Talk may conventionally be expected. In other words, we investigated whether L2 learners can cope with a situation when one Type of Talk – Opening – transforms into another Type of Talk, i.e. Business Talk. Such transformations often occur in real life, and, as our case study will show, they can be challenging for L2 learners.

Introduction

Finally, in Chapter 11 we conclude the book. First, we present a brief reflective overview of the contents of the book and then we discuss some areas for future research.

As the above summary illustrates, we organised Chapters 4–10 according to the units of analysis we presented in Figure 1.1, hence providing a synopsis of the whole spectrum of L2 pragmatics as it is seen through our framework. All these chapters feature case studies, and all follow a relatively similar organisation.

1.4 Recommended reading

Taguchi, Naoko and Shuai Li. (2021). Cross-cultural pragmatics and second language (L2) pragmatics: Approaches to assessing L2 speech act production. *Contrastive Pragmatics* 2(1), 1–23.

Naoko Taguchi is one of the leading experts of L2 pragmatics. Readers with an interest in the relationship between L2 pragmatics and cross-cultural pragmatics may want to consult the above paper written by Taguchi and her colleague. The following excerpt presents a general overview of this theme:

> Second language (L2) pragmatics is a subfield of second language acquisition (SLA) that investigates L2 learners' ability to perform communicative functions in a social context, how such ability develops over time, and what factors affect the process of development (Taguchi and Roever, 2017; Taguchi, 2019). The primary practice of the field has been to collect data on L2 learners' pragmatic performance and to evaluate their performance so we can understand their current stage of development.
>
> When evaluating pragmatic performance, or more narrowly speech act performance, two approaches have dominated the field's practice. One approach (contrastive linguistics approach), rooted in the tradition of cross-cultural pragmatics, involves identifying learners' linguistic strategies in speech acts and comparing them with those of native speakers to see how their linguistic forms approximate native speakers' forms. Within this approach, similarities to native speaker forms are considered as a sign of learners' development, while differences are considered to indicate their underdevelopment.
>
> Another approach, rating scale approach, comes from the tradition of performance-based language assessment. This approach involves evaluating learners' speech acts by using a rating scale (holistic or analytic) that includes a series of predetermined score bands. The most typical implementation of this approach in the field has been to recruit native speaker raters to assign scores on learners' speech acts based on a set of preconstructed rating criterion, and interrater agreement is sought to confirm the reliability of their scoring. Criteria in rating scales used

in this approach often focus on pragmatics concerns, such as degree of politeness, directness, and formality of speech acts, as well as other dimensions (e.g., grammatical accuracy and aspects of interaction). While a holistic rating scale is used to assign one score to a pragmatic utterance based on an overall evaluation of all dimensions under consideration, an analytic rating scale is used to assign multiple scores to a pragmatic utterance based on multiple dimensions under investigation. These two common approaches, both prominent in the field, have both advantages and disadvantages. (Taguchi and Li, 2021: 1–2)

Jucker, Andreas. (2012). Pragmatics in the history of linguistic thought. In Keith Allan and Kasia M. Jaszczolt (eds), *The Cambridge Handbook of Pragmatics*. **Cambridge: Cambridge University Press, pp. 495–512.**
The above-cited chapter written by the pragmatician Andreas Jucker is relevant to readers who wish to learn more about the history of pragmatics. The following section overviews the development of the field:

> It is the American mathematician and philosopher Charles S. Peirce (1839–1914) who is generally credited with the coining of the term "pragmatism." ... however, ... it was the psychologist William James (1842–1910) who introduced it as the "principle of Peirce" into philosophical discourse. But Peirce is the father of pragmatism, a theory of meaning that is based on a theory of signs and the effects which they have on our conduct ... The theory also focuses on the connection between thought and action. Later, Peirce changed the term "pragmatism" to "pragmaticism" in order to differentiate it from James's use of the term, taking "pragmaticism" to be a term "so ugly that ... no one would dare steal it" ...
>
> The American philosopher Charles Morris (1901–1979) integrated ideas from Peirce's pragmatism or pragmaticism into his own theory of signs, which he called "semiotic," using a term coined by John Locke (1632–1704). Today the field is commonly known as "semiotics." Morris distinguished three types of semiotics: syntactics, semantics and pragmatics, which are devoted to the syntactical, semantical, and pragmatical aspects of signs. Syntactics deals with signs and their relationship towards each other. Semantics deals with the signs and their meanings. And pragmatics deals with the signs in relation to their users ...
>
> Rudolf Carnap (1891–1970), on the other hand, was influential in narrowing down the scope of pragmatics. He conceptualized Morris's semiotic triangle in the following way. If in an investigation explicit reference is made to the speaker, or to put in more general terms, to the user of the language, then we assign it [the investigation] to the field of pragmatics ... If we abstract from the user of the language and analyze only the expressions and their designata, we are in the field of semantics. And, finally, if we abstract from the designata also and analyze only

the relations between the expressions, we are in syntax. (Carnap 1938; quoted by Levinson 1983: 2–3.)

This definition of pragmatics focuses on the user of the language. It does not invoke the effects on the audience or the larger social and cultural context in which language is used. (Jucker, 2012: 497–498)

Note

1. For us, interactional act is a unit of analysis which belongs to the level of speech act. Because of this, in this book we distinguish 4 units of analysis but 3 levels of analysis.

CHAPTER 2

The foundations of cross-cultural pragmatics

2.1 Introduction

In this chapter, we introduce the foundations of cross-cultural pragmatics as we understand the field. This introduction will help us to position cross-cultural pragmatics in general and our framework in particular in L2 pragmatic research in Chapter 3. The present chapter will first provide a general overview of the development of the field of cross-cultural pragmatics, as well as various of its key concepts such as speech acts, which play a major role in our approach. Following this, we will cover what we believe are the main pillars of present-day contrastive pragmatic research. Finally, we will discuss the procedure of contrasting two entities of language use.

2.2 The development of cross-cultural pragmatics

Pragmatics started to develop in the mid-twentieth century when the philosopher Ludwig Wittgenstein proposed to study "meaning in use" (Wittgenstein, 1958: paragraph 43), proposing that utterances should be explained in relation to the activities (or 'language games') in which they occur. Later, the language philosophers John Austin and John Searle proposed to look at language as a means to get things done. At that time, linguistics was still dominated by the study of how sentences are formed, including the truth conditions of the meanings of sentences, hence ignoring the way in which sentences are put to use by human beings. This view was challenged by Austin (1962) and Searle (1969, 1979) who came up with the concept of the speech act. Austin (1962: 20) suggested the following:

> The more we consider a statement not as a sentence (or proposition) but as an act of speech ... the more we are studying the whole thing as an act.

The foundations of cross-cultural pragmatics

Austin's disciple Searle later defined the speech act as a unit of communication:

> The unit of linguistic communication is not, as has generally been supposed, the symbol, word or sentence, or even the token of the symbol, word or sentence, but rather the production or issuance of the symbol or word or sentence in the performance of the speech act. (Searle, 1969: 16)

Austin and Searle suggested a number of categories for speech acts in the form of typologies. Austin's (1962: 151) original typology was revised by Searle (1969, 1979) as follows:

1. Representatives (Assertives): This speech act category consists of speech acts committing the speaker to the truth of his proposition. Example: "This is a huge museum."
2. Directives: This speech act category consists of speech acts which are attempts by the speaker to get the addressee to do something. Example: "Can you open the window?"
3. Commissives: This speech act category consists of speech acts which commit the speaker to some future course of action. Example: "I promise that I will be there."
4. Expressives: Expressives include speech acts expressing cognitive states. Example: "I apologise."
5. Declarations: Declarations influence the institutional state of affairs. Example: "I name this ship Queen Elizabeth the First."

In our approach, to be outlined in Chapter 3, we build on a speech act typology from Edmondson and House (1981) and Edmondson et al. (2023). A key advantage of this typology is that it is based on real-life multilingual data, and it is interactional in scope, which makes it particularly amenable for contrastive research.

Since pragmatics focuses on language in use, the pragmatician normally considers utterances rather than sentences. According to Searle (1969), a speech act is an utterance that has a particular function in communication. Further, pragmatics devotes attention to the relationship between language use and the context in which language use is embedded. This view reflects Austin's (1962) distinction between a locutionary act, i.e. the words uttered, an illocutionary act, i.e. the pragmatic meaning of these words, and a perlocutionary act, i.e. the illocutionary act's effect on the recipient. In pragmatic research, locution is less important than illocution.

Another key contribution to the development of pragmatics was made by H. Paul Grice, who described several overarching assumptions that guide the use of language. Grice (1969, 1975) argued that interactants tend to engage in 'cooperation', assuming that what their interactants say is meant to make sense in the given context, and also that other interactants will follow the same assumption of cooperation. Grice subsumed cooperation in meaning making – which is not cooperation in an interpersonal sense – under what he called the **Cooperative Principle**. The Cooperative Principle consists of four basic Maxims, which are guidelines for language use. These Maxims are based on the idea that if language users want to express what they mean most effectively, they must always provide enough information (Maxim of Quantity), which is true (Maxim of Quality), is relevant to the topic of a conversation (Maxim of Relevance) and is expressed in an appropriate manner (Maxim of Manner). In real language use interactants often 'flout' these Maxims. For instance, upon realising a speech act Request – which is essentially an imposition on the hearer – the speaker often says more than what is strictly necessary, hence flouting the Maxim of Quantity. The speaker can assume that the hearer will understand his reason for this flouting because usually flouts follow conventional patterns and, as far as the interactants cooperate in meaning making, the recipient will 'decode' the conventionalised flout.

As this brief overview has illustrated, the emergence of pragmatics triggered an interest in language in context. This interest in context, in turn, led to the birth of cross-cultural pragmatics. In the following we discuss areas of research through which cross-cultural pragmatics came into existence in the 1980s.

2.2.1 The birth of cross-cultural pragmatics

A key contribution to the nascent field of cross-cultural pragmatics was made by John Gumperz (1978). He coined the term '**contextualisation cue**', by which he meant forms which direct the hearer's attention to contextually important information, such as who the speaker is, where she came from, her social class, age, and so on, as well as the contextual meaning of the utterance as a whole, such as whether a particular utterance is meant to be constructive or destructive. Gumperz argued that one can only study speech acts and other pragmatic phenomena legitimately if one relies on real-life data. According to Gumperz (1978), contextualisation cues in spoken language include paralinguistic and prosodic features, e.g. rhythm, pitch register, loudness and many other micro-level aspects of language use. As Gumperz notes, such "contextualization phenomena tend to go unnoticed in everyday situations although their effect is constantly felt" (Gumperz, 1978: 23–24). Gumperz's studies were very important for the development of cross-cultural pragmatics, particularly because his idea of 'contextualisation cues' alerted researchers to consider particular phenomena that offer themselves to be contrastively investigated across various linguacultures.

Another important researcher whose work influenced cross-cultural pragmatics is Dell Hymes (1962, 1964). Hymes examined socially and culturally embedded communicative practices, pointing out that any investigation of communicative interactions should start from linguaculturally embedded real-life data:

The foundations of cross-cultural pragmatics

the starting point [for any research on language use] is the ethnographic analysis of the communicative habits of a community in their totality, determining what count as communicative events, and as their components, and conceiving no communicative behavior as independent of the set framed by some setting or implicit questions. (Hymes, 1962: 13)

Hymes proposed what he defined as a 'speaking model', which consisted of eight contextual parameters. Hymes (1971) proposed another concept with a high impact on cross-cultural pragmatics, as well as applied linguistic research in general, namely, communicative competence. Hymes argued that in the study of language use one needs to focus on communicative competence, i.e. whether a speaker can use language according to certain contextual criteria. This concept has also influenced the development of cross-cultural pragmatics, given that language learning and teaching, and applied linguistics in general, have been key areas in the field (see Edmondson et al., 1982, 1984).

Another important area for the development of cross-cultural pragmatics was research into the role of cognitive factors in situated language use. An early representative of this body of enquiries is the cognitive research of Hoppe-Graff et al. (1985) who proposed a distinction between 'standard' and 'non-standard' situations in the realisation of speech acts. According to Hoppe-Graff et al. (1985: 90), a situation qualifies as 'standard' for language users if "the speaker assumes with a fair amount of certainty that the partner is able and willing to perform act A", while in 'non-standard situations' the speaker needs to engage in an active search for, and use of, information from the environment. The experiments of Hoppe-Graff et al. showed that in standard situations participants tend to use different ways to realise speech acts than in non-standard situations. As House (1989) argued, the notion of **standard situation** – which will also be used in this book – is essential for any research that pursues replicability. This is because language use can be reliably contrasted across linguacultures if we focus on the relationship between linguistic forms/forms of behaviour and the situations they normally indicate.

2.2.2 The CCSARP project

Cross-cultural pragmatics came formally into existence with the launch of the **Cross-Cultural Speech Act Realisation Project (CCSARP)**. It is worth noting here that 'cross-cultural' and 'contrastive' can be used synonymously in the field – readers with more interest in this terminological issue are advised to consult House and Kádár (2021a). CCSARP was led by the first author of this book and her colleagues Shoshana Blum-Kulka and Gabriele Kasper. The results of this project were presented in the edited volume *Cross-Cultural Pragmatics: Requests and Apologies* (Blum-Kulka et al., 1989), which continues to be heavily cited and applied to this day in both pragmatics and language learning and teaching. The work of the CCSARP team focused on two speech acts: Request and Apology. These speech acts were found to be particularly relevant for setting up a framework for contrasting linguacultural data because they are often realised according to significantly different conventions across linguacultures. Blum-Kulka et al. (1989: 12–13) summarised the goals of CCSARP as follows:

> The general goal of the CCSARP investigation is to establish patterns of request and apology realisations under different social constraints, across a number of languages and cultures, including both native and non-native varieties ... The goals of the projects are: 1) To investigate the similarities and differences in the realisation patterns of given speech acts across different languages, relative to the same social constraints (cross-cultural variation). 2) To investigate the effect of social variables on the realisation patterns of given speech acts within speech communities (sociopragmatic variation). 3) To investigate the similarities and differences in the realisation patterns of given speech acts between native and non-native speakers of a given language, relative to the same social constraints (interlanguage variation). The study was designed to allow for a reliable comparability both along the situational (sociopragmatic), cultural, and native/non-native axes.

The CCSARP team studied data drawn from the following linguacultures: British, American and Australian English, Canadian French, Danish, German and Hebrew.

On the methodological level, the CCSARP team conducted discourse completion tests (DCTs) in order to elicit realisations of the two speech acts Request and Apologise. DCTs consist of scripted dialogues that represent socially differentiated situations in particular linguacultures. Each dialogue is preceded by a short description of the situation, specifying the setting and the social distance between the participants and their status relative to each other. The dialogue following this introduction is deliberately incomplete, and it was the participant's task to complete it, thereby providing the speech act aimed at. A typical DCT looks like the following:

(2.1) In the following examples of test items, (a) is constructed to elicit a request and (b) to elicit an apology.

(a) At the university. Ann missed a lecture yesterday and would like to borrow Judith's notes.
Ann: _____
Judith: Sure, but let me have them back before the next week.

(b) The college teacher's office. A student has borrowed a book from her teacher, which she promised to return today. When meeting her teacher, however, she realises that she forgot to bring it along.
Teacher: Miriam, I hope you brought the book I lent you.

Miriam: _____
Teacher: Okay, but please remember it next week.
(Blum-Kulka et al., 1989: 14)

The original CCSARP questionnaire included eight situations in which Requests were elicited and eight situations in which Apologies were elicited. In order to enable a replicable contrastive analysis of the linguaculturally embedded data, the sixteen situations provided in the CCSARP questionnaire systemically varied according to the sociolinguistic parameters of social distance and 'dominance' (power). These parameters – which will occur in many subsequent chapters of this book – were provided in a binary choice; that is, a relationship in a situation was defined as either socially distant or not, and either dominant or not. The situations presented in the dialogues reflected everyday occurrences of language use in the linguacultures under investigation. The participants filling out the DCT forms consisted of roughly 200 speakers of each language studied, including both 'native' and 'non-native' speakers.

The data collected using the above-discussed methodology were analysed by the CCSARP researchers who were native speakers of the languages involved. The unit of analysis was the 'discourse filler', i.e. the utterances provided by the respondents who filled in the 'blank lines' in the DCTs. During the analysis, each of the DCT responses was categorised into pragmatic components affording contrastive pragmatic analysis. The following analysis of the filled-in utterance in example (a) in (2.1) above may illustrate how a particular utterance can be broken down to different components:

(2.2)   Judith, I missed class yesterday, do you think I could borrow your notes? I promise to return them by tomorrow.

The request sequence in this example includes the following categories:

1. 'Alerter': "Judith"
2. 'Preposed Supportive Move': "I missed class yesterday"
3. 'Head Act': "Could I borrow your notes"
4. 'Downgrader': "Do you think?"
5. 'Postposed Supportive Move': "I promise to return them by tomorrow"

These categories will also be used in the analyses presented in this book. The number of such components in the project was finite and anchored in the pragmatic theory of Edmondson and House (1981) and Edmondson (1981). The framework could be used to comparatively study various linguacultures in a replicable way due to this linguistic anchor.

CCSARP was recently given new life by the authors of this book (see House and Kádár, 2021a), who believe that it is important to keep the replicable and rigorous elements of the project in cross-cultural pragmatics. The present book is also heavily influenced by the CCSARP investigation, although it is definitely not an updated 'replica' of the CCSARP analysis because the framework tackles many issues which at the time were not considered, such as using larger corpora, incorporating interaction and real-life language use in one's analysis, studying the interactional embeddedness of speech acts, and so on.

2.3 The basics of cross-cultural pragmatics

Having outlined the formation of the field, in the following we discuss what we believe are the distinctive features and basics of cross-cultural pragmatics.

As the name suggests, cross-cultural pragmatics always includes an element of contrasting. However, we advise contrastive pragmatic research not only to rely on a single contrastive study but rather to include various methodologies, often featuring ancillary research by means of which one establishes what is worth comparing in the contrastive research (see e.g. Chapter 4), or to follow the contrastive research by testing its validity (see e.g. Chapter 5). In research on L2 pragmatics, for example, it is worth conducting pilot studies to identify learner irritations, which in turn can be investigated through contrastive research.

In House and Kádár (2021a: 4–5), we suggested the following key criteria for contrastive pragmatic analysis. Some of these criteria will also be highlighted when we discuss the framework used in this book:

1. *Corpora:* Contrastive pragmatic research needs to be based on corpora. As already noted, the expression 'corpus' refers to a searchable collection of machine-readable texts of any size. For example, in research on language learning, a collection of DCTs typically represents what we call a 'DCT corpus'.
2. **Qualitative and quantitative research methods**: Contrastive pragmatic research can be – and, ideally, is – both quantitative and qualitative. In quantitative research, one examines and compares data by looking into the frequency of occurrence of a pragmatic phenomenon: such research involves measuring, counting and analysing statistical data. In qualitative research, one engages in a detailed comparative examination of individual interactions, in order to gain a deeper understanding of the phenomenon under investigation.
3. *More than one language:* Contrastive pragmaticians may pursue interest in intracultural and intralinguistic variation of languages, including social and regional dialects, style levels, variation of language according to gender and age, and so on. However, contrastive pragmatic research ideally includes various languages. The more typologically distant these languages are, the more rewarding it may be to contrastively examine them.

The foundations of cross-cultural pragmatics 19

4. **Emic and etic perspectives**: The anthropologist Kenneth Pike (1967) defined the language and culture insider's view on certain phenomena as 'emic', and he defined the language and culture outsider's perspective on the same phenomena as 'etic'. Considering that the researcher's view of contrastive pragmatic data is very often etic because various language are involved in contrastive analysis, it is important to balance etic and emic views. Such balancing can be done by involving experts who are lingua cultural insiders of the languages studied as informants. For example, in most case studies presented in this book we involved Chinese colleagues and students, in order to obtain their emic views on the data.
5. *Linguistically based terminology:* Cross-cultural pragmatics use a strictly linguistically based terminology, reflecting an endeavour to shy away from using cultural and psychology concepts such as 'ideology', 'values' and 'identity'.
6. *Comparability:* An important issue in contrastive pragmatic research is how we conduct the comparison itself. This is something which we will outline in more detail in section 2.4 in this chapter, because it is the heart and soul of the field.

As part of discussing the basics of cross-cultural pragmatics, it is worth touching on how this strictly language-anchored field conceptualises culture. The concept of 'culture' has been discussed in many different disciplines, such as philosophy, sociology, anthropology, literature and cultural studies. The definitions offered in these fields vary according to the particular frame of reference invoked. In 1952, Kroeber and Kluckhohn had collected as many as 156 definitions of culture. In all academic attempts at coming to grips with the notion of 'culture', two basic views have emerged: the humanistic concept of culture, and its anthropological counterpart. The humanistic concept centres on the 'cultural heritage' as a model of refining the concept of culture. Culture here refers to an exclusive collection of a community's masterpieces in literature, fine arts, music etc. The anthropological concept of culture refers to the overall way of life of a community or society, i.e. all those traditional, explicit and implicit designs for living which act as potential guides for the behaviour of members of a culture (see Geertz, 1973). Culture in the anthropological sense captures a group's dominant and learned set of habits, conventions and traditions – all of which are, of course, neither easily accessible nor verifiable. Contrastive pragmatic research is based on this anthropological sense of culture.

House (2005) distinguished four analytical levels on which culture can be characterised (see also Figure 2.1 below). The first one is the general human level, at which human beings differ from animals. Human beings, unlike animals, are capable of reflection, and they are able to creatively shape and change their environment. The second level is the societal, national level, culture being the unifying, binding force that enables human beings to position themselves vis-à-vis systems of government, domains of activities, religious beliefs and values in which human thinking expresses itself. The third level corresponds to the second level but captures various societal and national subgroups according to geographical region, social class, age, sex, professional activity, and topic.

Cross-cultural pragmatics clearly pursues interest in the second and, to a more limited degree, the third layers of the interface between language and culture. The first general human level is hardly relevant for our concern in this book, considering that cultural variation does not include distinctions between humans and animals. Equally irrelevant to our concern in this book is the fourth level, because cross-cultural pragmatics needs to draw abstractions from individual behaviour and cognition in order to arrive at replicable patterns of the use of languages. Idiosyncrasy is explicitly excluded from contrastive pragmatic analysis. The most important two levels are thus the second and third ones. The natural 'partner' of contrastive pragmatic research is the second level; that is, language use across distinctively different linguacultures. Along with this level, contrastive pragmaticians also pursue interest in the third level, which encompasses instances of variation. Figure 2.1 summarises the various levels of the language and culture interface, and the related focus of contrastive pragmatic research.

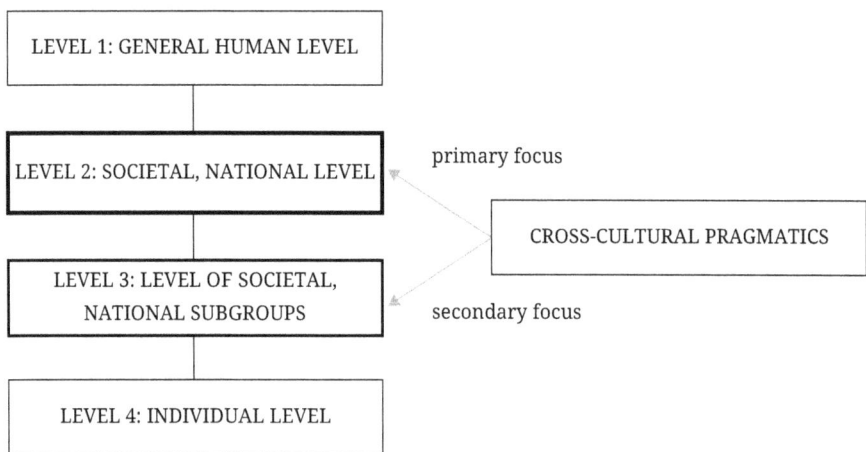

Figure 2.1 The focus of cross-cultural pragmatics (adapted from House, 2005)

2.4 What makes pragmatic contrasting possible?

Any rigorous contrastive pragmatic study needs to work exclusively with contrastable data. A key problem for the contrastive pragmatician is that not everything can be contrastively examined. Most typically, idiosyncratic behaviour – i.e. individual pragmatic behaviour which does not follow recurrent linguacultural patterns – cannot be contrasted across various linguacultures. This is why it is fundamental for the contrastive pragmatician to consider whether the phenomena compared are sufficiently *conventionalised* in the respective linguacultures. Conventionalisation describes the degree of recurrence of a particular pragmatic phenomenon in how members of a social group or a broader linguaculture use and evaluate language.

The idea that the use of language follows conventions has been present in modern linguistics ever since the field was founded by Ferdinand de Saussure (1916). Saussure distinguished the concepts of 'langue' and 'parole': the former refers to language as an abstract system, whereas the latter refers to language in use. Saussure argued that while 'langue' is characterised by an arbitrary nature, 'parole' operates according to conventionalised language use. Harris (1988: 48–49) summarised this thought as follows:

> Although the use of the term is perhaps not entirely consistent throughout the *Cours* [i.e. de Saussure's work], it is evident that Saussure is reluctant to concede that the institution of *la langue* is merely or entirely conventional. This is because for Saussure the notion of convention, unless further qualified, generally implies a practice which people are free to adopt, adapt, flout, or change by mutual agreement; furthermore, a practice in which there is an element of the rational and the non-arbitrary. Conventions can be decided on in order to suit the interests of the parties concerned: but this is never, for Saussure, characteristic of the establishment of a linguistic sign. And although it is perfectly possible to set up whole communication systems by convention, this is not in fact the case with *la langue*.

According to what Saussure argued, our day-to-day language use is very often heavily conventionalised; that is, while language users may have the illusion that they are somehow 'original', in fact, they very often follow pre-existing pragmatic patterns (see Sinclair, 1991). From a pragmatic point of view, an essential function of conventions is that they facilitate meaning making in interaction.

While conventionalisation assumes shared pragmatic knowledge, in contrastive comparisons it is a grave error to assume the existence of this sharedness. There are various reasons why the concept of conventionalisation needs always to be carefully considered in contrastive pragmatic analysis. This is because there is always a sense of potential variation in the degree of conventionalisation of language use across linguacultures. This is why it is important to define – often with the aid of non-speech-act-anchored research – whether the phenomenon that one intends to compare is equally conventionalised in the linguacultural settings contrasted. Without considering whether what we intend to compare is equally conventionalised in a particular standard situation we may not have a proper *tertium comparationis*.

The notion of conventionalisation is also of particular relevance for the field of language learning. As previous research has shown (see House, 2003a; Kasper and Rose, 1999), it is not self-evident that learners of a language are aware of what counts, and what does not count, as conventionalised in a particular context. Both foreign and second language learners are often unfamiliar with the conventionalised load of certain phenomena in their target language, even though this load may be 'self-evident' for native speakers. A prime example of the conventionalisation-related difficulties foreign or second language learners may face is provided in the study of Bardovi-Harlig and Vellenga (2012) who found that, in second language learning settings, even basic conventionalised expressions may lead to pragmatic failures. As an example, Bardovi-Harlig and Vellenga refer to the following case in which various learners of English chose an inappropriate response (2.3b) to a conventionalised expression (2.3a) instead of its mimetically expected and preferred counterpart (2.3c):

(2.3) a. Thanks for coming
b. You are welcome*
c. Thanks for inviting me
(Bardovi-Harlig and Vellenga, 2012: 85)

It is only (2.3c) which is acceptable as a conventionalised response for (2.3a). Conventionalisation becomes more complex when we venture beyond the realm of routine formulae (see Coulmas, 1979, 1981) such as *Thanks for coming* and *Thanks for inviting me* studied in Bardovi-Harlig and Vellenga (2012). For instance, language learners may face significant difficulties in realising speech acts such as a Request because they may not be familiar with the conventional realisation patterns of such speech acts. The following example from Taguchi (2006) illustrates this point:

(2.4) Native Speaker (NS) data. A native speaker of English is asking a lecturer to reschedule an upcoming exam [wording slightly changed by us]:
NS: I, look, I have a big favor to ask you. I know our exam is this week on Friday, but my friend is getting married that day. Is there any chance, like, maybe I can take it earlier or later or some other time?

Language learner data. An advanced learner of English is asking a lecturer to reschedule an upcoming exam ("L" refers to "learner" and "I" refers to "interlocutor"):
1 L: Ah, so I'm here to ah, can you do me a favor? Because I heard there is gonna be test next Friday, but I do need to go to my friend's wedding. ((gap))
2 I: OK, ah, yeah, ah ((pause)) what kind of favor do you want me to do?
3 L: Ah, I hope I can do, I can shift the test date.
(Cited from Taguchi, 2006: 525–526)

The advanced learner featured in example (2.4) is apparently fluent in English. However, when it comes to the conventionalised use of the speech act Request, his behaviour may frustrate 'native speaker' instructors. He may be perceived as 'verbose' because he provides 'irrelevant' details for the Request on hand, at least from a US American linguacultural perspective. From the instructor's point of view, the topic introducer *"I heard there is gonna be* [sic.] *test next Friday"* causing the delay is unnecessary because the lecturer obviously knows about the test that he himself will organise.

Language acquisition and the related acquisition of conventionalised language use obviously do not always take place in classrooms and in clear 'native' *versus* 'non-native' settings. For example, Hyland (2002) provides a noteworthy case study of instances where different conventionalised practices of 'sounding academic' in English academic writing cause frustration for learners of English. Hyland (2002: 1105) refers to the case of Chinese students who, in the course of learning academic English, indirectly expressed disagreement with the overemphasis of an impersonal style in research essays, which was at that time deemed necessary by textbook writers.

2.5 Conclusion

In this chapter, we have outlined the foundations of cross-cultural pragmatics, which paves the way for the remainder of this book. Many of the notions and procedures discussed here will recur in various chapters of this book because cross-cultural pragmatics is a field in which researchers are advised to conduct rigorous and replicable empirical research. In the following Chapter 3, we will discuss how our framework, including our contrastive view, can be brought together with L2 pragmatics.

2.6 Recommended reading

Juliane House and Dániel Z. Kádár. (2021a). *Cross-Cultural Pragmatics.* **Cambridge: Cambridge University Press.**
The authors of this book previously published a monograph dedicated to cross-cultural pragmatics, which is a synonym for contrastive pragmatics as we interpret these terms. In the following section, we discussed the foundations of cross-cultural pragmatics:

> Cross-cultural pragmatics encompasses the comparative study of the use of language by human beings in different languages and cultures. The present book examines this field. The following is a simple example of what we examine in cross-cultural pragmatic analysis:

(1.1) *Can you open the window?* (English)
   Bang wo dakai chuanghu. (Chinese)
   帮我打开窗户。
   Help me open the window.

From the cross-cultural pragmatician's point of view, comparing even seemingly simple conventionalised utterances like the ones featured in example (1.1) is full of hidden intricacies. For instance, we may note the following key pragmatic difference between the English and Chinese requests in example (1.1): English prefers the modal verb can, while in Chinese the corresponding request may be formulated as an imperative. Of course, to make such a comparative claim we also need to make sure that our two utterances are actually comparable.

The expression 'cross-cultural' conventionally describes the comparison of behavioural patterns in two or more cultures. A notion closely related to the concept of 'cross-cultural' is 'intercultural', which usually refers to the study of encounters between members of two or more cultures. In pragmatics, 'crosscultural' investigations focus on similarities and differences between patterns of the use and interpretation of language across cultures. Such a cross-cultural line of inquiry differs from intercultural pragmatics, as the latter generally studies interaction between language users with different cultural backgrounds. The term 'cross-cultural' emerged first in the social sciences in the 1930s, largely as a result of a cross-cultural survey provided by the anthropologist George Murdock in 1969. Murdock studied the statistical compilations of anthropological data drawn from various cultures. Although Murdock was not a linguist, his work remains relevant to cross-cultural pragmatics, largely because he pointed out that any rigorous cross-cultural comparison of cultural patterns can only be done in a strictly data-based way. As the present chapter will illustrate, having a reasonably large collection of data is perhaps the most important distinctive feature of the field of cross-cultural pragmatics. Until the 1970s, the notion 'cross-cultural' had not been frequented in linguistics; it had mostly been associated with other fields such as cross-cultural psychology. In linguistic pragmatics, interest in cross-cultural research had started to grow from the late 1970s (see e.g. Coulmas, 1978; House, 1979). The year 1989 marked a turning point in the development of the field: in this year, a group of scholars, including the first author of this book, published the results of a research project called the 'Cross-Cultural Speech Act Realization Project' (CCSARP) (Blum-Kulka et al., 1989). This project provided, for the first time, a systematic way of comparing realisations of pragmatic phenomena across different languages and language varieties. Following the global success of the CCSARP project, cross-cultural pragmatics became a household term and one of the most influential areas within pragmatics. The CCSARP Project provided the field with various basic criteria for conducting rigorous cross-cultural pragmatic analysis, such as how one can systematically compare levels of directness in comparable language use across various languages. Unfortunately, in later years, cross-cultural pragmatics seems to have lost much of its original focus and rigour, in that various well-known studies such as Wierzbicka (1991) and Goddard and Wierzbicka (2004) all but abandoned the strictly linguistics-anchored approach of the field. Such studies not only proposed universalist concepts for cross-cultural pragmatics research but also deployed psychological and sociological analytic categories – very different from Blum-Kulka et al. (1989) who argued that crosscultural pragmatics needs to rely on an essentially linguistically anchored pragmatic analytic inventory.

CHAPTER 3

Our contrastive pragmatic framework and its use in L2 pragmatics

3.1 Introduction

In this chapter we introduce our framework, which gives specific attention to speech acts as the central part of contrastive L2 pragmatic research. We will first introduce our framework, by devoting special attention to how it views speech acts and how this view relates to previous L2 pragmatic research. We will then introduce our typology of speech acts, and also our view that in the use of this typology one should always study speech acts in relation to the other pragmatic units of expressions and discourse. Finally, we will outline our methodology through which this typology will be put to use in the remainder of this book.

3.2 Our framework

Let us start by positioning our framework in L2 pragmatics. The very first thing to note here is that our framework is based on a radically minimal, finite and interactional typology of speech acts. By using such a speech act typology, it becomes possible to integrate speech acts and interaction. The following argument helps us to summarise the central issue in our framework:

> When we describe language behaviour, we sometimes use terms such as 'suggest', 'request' and so on, which roughly indicate illocutionary values, and sometimes terms such as 'agree', 'accept', 'contradict', 'turn down', 'refuse', which are more indicative of the significance of the utterance relative to a preceding one. What we need to do is to distinguish between these two aspects of a communicative act – the illocutionary and the interactional. (See Edmondson et al., 2023: 25–26)

The reason why we believe the typology proposed in this book is key for L2 pragmatic research is the following: while many scholars in L2 pragmatics now certainly view speech acts in an interactional way, to date little attempt has been made to apply a rigorous and finite interactional system of speech acts through a clearly defined procedure. For example, while with the surge of discursive pragmatics (Kasper, 2006) and research on interactional competence (Young, 2011) various L2 pragmaticians have adopted an interactional view on speech acts (e.g. Al-Gahtani and Roever, 2015; Youn, 2020), such research essentially focused on how speech acts get co-constructed in longer stretches of interaction. We are certainly in agreement with this body of research, and we believe that the interactional typology of speech acts we are proposing in this book neatly complements such research due to two interrelated reasons. Firstly, our system was designed to capture speech acts on the level of utterance, and by so doing we are able to quantify and contrast our data, i.e. this typology is essential for bringing together L2 pragmatics and cross-cultural pragmatics. Secondly, previous research has been interactional in a somewhat different way from what we are proposing here: while the above-cited scholars definitely studied speech acts in interaction, they did not rely on an interactionally situated typology *per se*. Thus, the model we present is not at all in contradiction with previous research but rather complements it. The finite and interactional typology we are suggesting can also help us to bring together the unit of speech acts with the other key units of discourse and expressions.

3.3 Pitfalls in previous L2 pragmatic research

Here we critically discuss three procedures in traditional L2 pragmatic research involving speech acts:

1. Inventing new speech acts *ad libitum*.
2. Conflating illocution and interaction.
3. Studying speech acts in isolation.

Why are procedures 1–3 problematic? As regards the case of freely inventing new speech acts, *ad hoc* categories such as 'threatening', 'refusing', 'confessing' and 'admonishing' – which in our view represent interactional acts – are unhelpful if our goal is to undertake replicable research based on speech acts with relevance to L2 pragmatics. If one wants to understand speech act-related puzzlement experienced by L2 learners, it is highly advisable to systematically investigate contrastive pragmatic differences and similarities between the learners' L1 and L2, without however falling into the trap of the strong contrastive hypothesis. Yet, it is only possible to contrastively examine pragmatic phenomena that are conventionalised to a comparable degree in both the L1 and L2 of the learner (see House and Kádár, 2021a). The idea of only working with comparable and conventionalised units of analysis clearly precludes proliferating speech acts *ad libitum*. Here we refer to the invention of new speech acts whenever it suits the researcher's agenda. This has been such a common practice that we are unable to provide a comprehensive overview of so-called 'speech acts' invented for L2 pragmatic purposes. While we find it difficult to pin down exactly where the idea of freely invented speech act categories originates, we believe that it appeared in the pragmatic literature at least as early as Wierzbicka's (1985) study, which triggered a wealth of 'innovative' speech act categories, such as that of 'self-sacrifice' (for a most recent example see Allami and Eslamizadeh, 2022). Proliferating speech acts *ad libitum* precludes the desired replicability of any research because, when it comes to 'exotic' speech acts, there is unavoidably a strong variation across linguacultures in terms of their conventionalised existence and realisation (see House and Kádár, 2021a). This variation is particularly problematic in the global classroom where students come from many different linguacultural backgrounds, which means that the researcher is often unable to conveniently refer to culturally homogenous learner groups – which is a key problem to consider from a contrastive pragmatic point of view.

Regarding the second case of conflating illocution with interaction, e.g. defining interactional categories such as 'refusing' and 'agreeing' as speech acts, this procedure compromises the very concept of speech act which allows us to differentiate between illocution and interaction. Edmondson and House (1981), Edmondson (1981) and Edmondson et al. (2023) argue that a systematic use of speech acts in the study of discourse and interaction can be achieved if we rely on a finite number of speech act categories and various interactional acts through which these speech acts are conventionally interconnected in interaction. For example, the speech act Invite may be 'refused' in interaction through the realisation of many different speech acts, such as Opine, Request (not-to-do-x), Disclose, and so on (see Figure 3.1 below). Technically speaking, all such speech acts function as responses to an invitation, i.e. all of them are 'refusals' from an interactional point of view. Precisely because of this, they do not represent the speech act *of* refusal, but rather they are speech acts *through which* the interactional act of refusing can be realised. It seems to us that many L2 pragmaticians have tended to conflate the illocutionary and interactional values of a communicative act. For example, many scholars have often taken for granted that 'refusal' is an illocutionary category (see e.g. Cohen, 2005; Félix-Brasdefer, 2008; Eslami, 2010), some others have claimed the same about 'agreeing' (see e.g. LoCastro, 2000; Holtgraves, 2007), and still some others have argued the same about 'compliment response' (see e.g. Golato, 2003; Yu, 2004; Sharifian, 2008; Ishihara, 2010; Zhang, 2021; Culpeper and Pat, 2021). To illustrate why such a conflation is in our view problematic, let us refer here to the case of compliment response. Responding to a compliment is an interactional act and this act can be realised by different speech acts. If one does not systematise such responses as different speech acts, one unavoidably fails to capture linguaculturally situated conventions of speech act realisation in this particular interactional slot because one lumps together such conventions under the umbrella of one single 'grand' speech act.

Regarding the third practice of studying speech act in isolation, it has also been criticised by various interactional L2 pragmaticians we align ourselves with. Such a narrow focus does not trigger a speech act theoretical problem, unlike the other two procedures criticised above. However, this isolationist view of speech acts ignores the fact that speech acts are inseparable parts of interaction and should only be analysed from the departure point of interaction. Regarding this third pitfall of studying speech acts in isolation, we believe that it may have its roots in the 1980s. L2 pragmatic research involving speech acts can be said to have started in that period (see an early overview in Blum-Kulka and Olshtain, 1984), with the Cross-Cultural Speech Act Realisation Project (CCSARP; Blum-Kulka et al., 1989). Although the CCSARP was conducted more than three decades ago, its methodology continues to be used worldwide up to the present day (see e.g. Kasper and Blum-Kulka, 1993; Rose and Ono, 1995; Cohen, 2005; Cunningham, 2017; Vacas Matos and Cohen, 2022). A key strength of CCSARP-based studies is that they operate with strictly defined pragmatic categories, enabling researchers to annotate and compare L2 speech act performance in a rigorous way. However, just like CCSARP itself, this body of research has zeroed in on preset speech act categories, such as Apologise and Request. This pre-determination of the object of analysis unavoidably led to a top-down take on speech acts in a body of L2 pragmatic research based on the CCSARP methodology. While this approach allows the scholar to examine speech act performance, it cannot capture more complex speech act-related problems, which only emerge when one views speech acts embedded in interaction in their whole complexity. For example, some scholars have studied the speech act Greet in isolation to examine realisations of greeting (see e.g. Shleykina, 2016). Such a focus distracts the researcher from studying the inherently important interactional embeddedness of the speech act Greet. In our view, it is far more realistic and thus fruitful in terms of L2 pragmatics and cross-cultural pragmatics to examine linguaculturally embedded L1 and L2 conventions of speech act realisation in the larger Opening phase of an interaction where Greet may (or may not) occur, instead of studying Greet in isolation. Accordingly, we believe it is essential to consider whether the Opening phase of an interaction tends to be realised by a Greet or another speech act in the learner's L2 linguaculture, and how this compares with the pragmatic conventions of Opening in the L1 linguaculture. Such differences (and similarities in other cases) can in turn help us also to better understand the irritations and puzzlement expressed by foreign language learners.

3.4 Our interactional typology of speech acts

In the following, we present our finite and interactional speech act typology, which we recently published in Edmondson et al. (2023), where we revised and updated an original model of Edmondson and House (1981), by relating it to present-day discourse analysis and interaction ritual theory. We then discuss why this typology – which we define as '**radically minimal**' – may be beneficial for interactional L2 pragmatic research and cross-cultural pragmatics.

Figure 3.1 displays our typology.

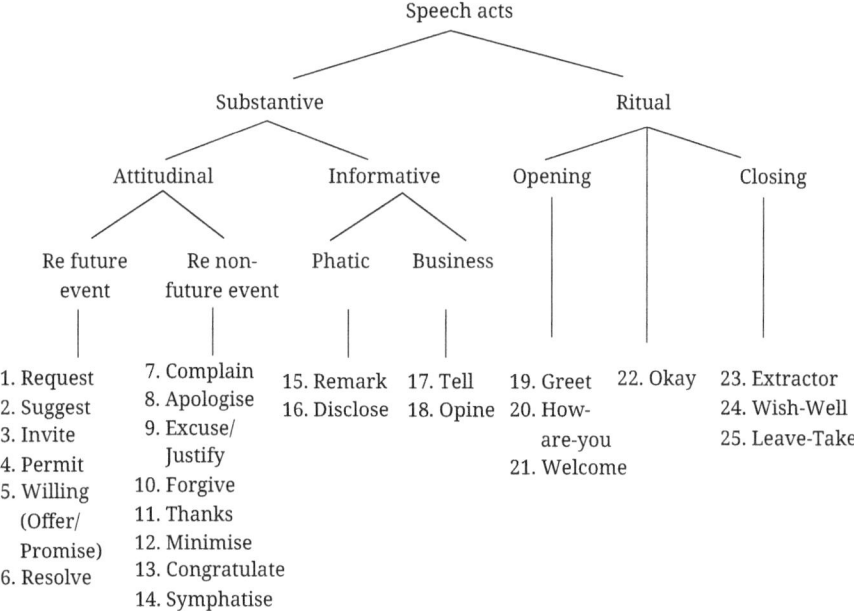

Figure 3.1 Our radically minimal, finite and interactional typology of speech acts

This typology includes twenty-five basic speech acts derived from the basis of the interactional analysis of multilingual corpus data drawn from a variety of languages, such as English, German, Chinese, Japanese and Hungarian. Originally, Edmondson and House set up this typology in 1981 on the basis of relatively small English and German corpora. In Edmondson et al. (2023) we tested the applicability of this typology by examining whether it can be replicably used for data analysis with the aid of large corpora, drawn from a variety of typologically distant languages, such as Chinese, Japanese and Hungarian.

The typology is divided into two main types: 'Substantive' and 'Ritual'. The 'Substantive' group includes speech act types which are generally considered to be 'meaningful', while 'Ritual' speech acts tend to occur in specific parts of an interaction and are, therefore, highly predictable, and have a social meaning, such that the literal meaning of the utterance – if any – is almost incidental to the significance of the utterance for the interactants. As House and Kádár (2021b), and Edmondson et al. (2023) argued, this typology represents the default function of speech acts, and any speech act can 'migrate' into other slots included in the typology. For example, in certain contexts, a Substantive Attitudinal speech act can take on a conventionalised Ritual function. When one encounters a speech act-related problem in L2 pragmatics, the above interactional typology prompts one to consider which speech acts are frequented in a given interactional phase in the L1 and L2 of the foreign language learner.

To give an example of the above notion of **'migration' of speech acts** and the general use of this typology in the study of interaction, let us refer to Chapter 8, dedicated to the L2 pragmatic investigation of the interactional act of greeting. This research began as Dániel Kádár – who is a foreign learner of Chinese – mentioned the problem that it is the absence of the realisation of the speech act Greet in certain contexts in Chinese, rather than certain 'alien' forms of Greet, which puzzles him. In studying this puzzlement, we did not immediately zero in on the speech act Greet, but rather contrastively studied the interactional phase of Opening Talk to investigate which speech acts tend to be conventionally realised in the L1 and L2 of various foreign learners of Chinese. In other words, in interpreting our L1 and L2 data we ventured beyond the assumption that Greet is a universally inherent part of Opening Talk, and also designed our methodological approach accordingly. The results of this study were different from what some other researchers argued before, namely that the Chinese 'do not greet one another'. For example, we learnt that, in Chinese Opening Talk, the phatic speech act Remark is frequented while Greet is non-ubiquitous, which in turn helped us to explain L2 learner irritations and puzzlement.

Let us now discuss why we believe that this typology is beneficial for L2 pragmatics, in particular to those L2 pragmatic studies which like our own take an interactional view on speech acts. Here we depart from the admittedly radical statement that speech act-related L2 pragmatic research needs to be based on a finite – and thus replicable – interactional typology of speech acts. We will start this discussion with the notion of finiteness. Ever since Austin and Searle, the idea that speech act categories need somehow to be finite has been present in the field of pragmatics (see e.g. Habermas, 1979; Vanderveken, 1990; Croft, 1994; Kasper, 2006; Kissine, 2013), with Levinson (2017) revisiting this issue recently. As various scholars have noted, the reason why finiteness is potentially controversial is that with the passing of time one may 'identify' new speech acts. To provide a few examples, Nelson (1991) distinguished 'new speech acts' in world Englishes, and Kogan (2008) identified speech acts coming into existence owing to technological advancement. While such approaches surely have their own rationale, we ourselves adopt a different position: as we argued in our recent book (Edmondson et al., 2023), we take the aforementioned explicitly radical stance on speech acts by proposing a finite set of replicable and interactionally defined speech act categories and arguing that they *should not be* complemented with other new speech act categories. The question may rightly emerge: Is a particular set of interactionally embedded speech acts 'sufficient' and can others not rightly identify new speech acts? Also, can we somehow 'reserve the right' of insisting that only our speech act categories legitimately exist? These would be fair questions to ask, and our response would be that the speech acts we propose are 'minimal' in the Chomskyan sense, i.e. they are designed to represent the basic pragmatic unit of a speech act which is meant to be smaller than units of interaction. This is also why such speech act categories are not 'ours', in that a radical finite typology of speech acts needs to include only those speech acts which are such simple and basic constituents of language use that they can easily be replicated in the contrastive pragmatic study of interaction across language and data types.

Along with finiteness, let us also explain what we mean by interactionality. When one uses a typology of speech acts such as the one we are suggesting in our book, one may want to break down interaction into moves, and as part of this to examine how moves relate to one another, as 'initiating', 'satisfying', 'countering' and 'contraing' moves (see Edmondson et al., 2023). Initiating refers to speech acts through which an exchange is started, satisfying includes speech acts through which an initiating speech act is satisfied, countering points to speech acts through which an initiation is countered but not entirely rejected, whereas if it is turned down it would be contraed in our terminology. This view is compatible with conversation analysis (CA), in that we interpret all basic speech acts as interactionally interrelated phenomena through which more complex interactional phenomena can come into existence. The reason why we do not use the CA notions of 'adjacency pair' and 'preference organisation' is as follows: as Paul Drew and his colleagues explained (Drew and Walker, 2010; Drew, 2013), convincingly in our view,[1] conversation analysts use speech act theory to interpret particular conversationally relevant turns-at-talk in their data. They also study how speech acts are co-constructed in interaction, hence taking a relatively 'broad' view on speech acts. We definitely believe that this view is valid and important. However, in our approach we use speech act categories to interpret *every* turn in any data as a speech act or cluster of speech acts, and also unlike conversation analysts we do not operate with the notion of extended speech act. Because of this, we also interpret the turn-by-turn relationship between speech acts and attempt to capture and quantify pragmatic conventions of this relationship by using the above-outlined non-CA terminology. Such a quantification is key in particular if our goal is to bring together L2 pragmatics with cross-cultural pragmatics, considering that pragmatic contrasting assumes some form of quantification. Let us briefly illustrate how our terminology can be operationalised in L2 pragmatic research with a simple example. A structurally 'initiating' speech act Invite ("Would you like to come to my party tonight?") may, in our terms, either be 'satisfied' ("Would love to thanks"), 'countered' ("I have to ask my wife"), or 'contra-ed' ("Can't, I am afraid"). We may use these terms in an L2 pragmatic study of English by arguing that they show that an Invite in English can be 'accepted' in popular terms with the speech act Thank – instead of the 'responsive speech act' 'invitation-thanking' – it can be kept in abeyance with the speech act Tell, and it can also be conventionally 'turned down' with the speech act Resolve, instead of 'refusal' which is an umbrella term.

As this description illustrates, finiteness and replicability as we interpret these notions provide a very different insight into speech acts from a body of research dedicated to so-called 'responding speech acts'. We believe that our approach has both academic and pedagogic advantages. Take the case of 'compliment response' mentioned above as an example. We do not deny the easy applicability of this category in teaching. However, there may be students who would like to know exactly what the broad phenomenon of 'response' actually includes in their L1 and L2. For example, US American students of Chinese may wonder why native speakers of Chinese do not utter the speech act Thank at all when they receive a compliment, which would be the convention in American English. Instead, speakers of Chinese either tend to realise the speech act Minimise when they respond to compliments, for instance saying *Buhui* ('I can't') when they are complimented as being skilful in something, or other speech acts such as a self-denigrating Opine (e.g. *Wo yifu bu zenme piaoling* 'My cloth is not beautiful at all'). Our typology therefore allows one to teach compliment responses to L2 learners in a *differentiated* way, by drawing learners' attention to the linguaculturally diverse realisation patterns of the phenomenon on hand. We believe that the approach we are proposing here not only has a definite learning and teaching advantage, but also it does not actually run counter to the findings of previous response-oriented research and learning and teaching practices. That is, instead of denying the validity of such research, we simply reinterpret speech act-responding phenomena at a different level of analysis, i.e. as interactional acts rather than speech acts.

Another advantage of our interactional typology of speech acts is that it enables systematic comparison of speech act-related phenomena in both the learner's L1 and L2. While using a contrastive methodology can have its own pitfall (see an overview in House and Kádár, 2021a), we would like to emphasise the important conceptual and methodological advantage of incorporating a contrastive comparative approach to speech act analysis. Let us provide an example: in the study of speech act realisation patterns in the Closing phase of an interaction, we cannot assume that it is inherently the speech act Leave-Take which is realised in both the learner's L1 and L2, even though it may appear to be ritually 'normal' from a 'Western' point of view to expect the speech act Leave-Take to be realised in this interactional slot by default. However, in many interpersonal scenarios speakers of languages such as Chinese clearly disprefer using the speech act Leave-Take in Closing.

Rather, speakers of Chinese tend to close an interaction with the speech act Remark in various interpersonal relationships. Failing to consider comparability can therefore lead to *a priori* assumptions that do not pass the test of language use in real life.

Having discussed the benefits of the typology of speech acts proposed here, let us now discuss a replicable procedure through which this typology can be applied in empirical research.

3.5 Research procedure

Figure 3.2 illustrates our research procedure:

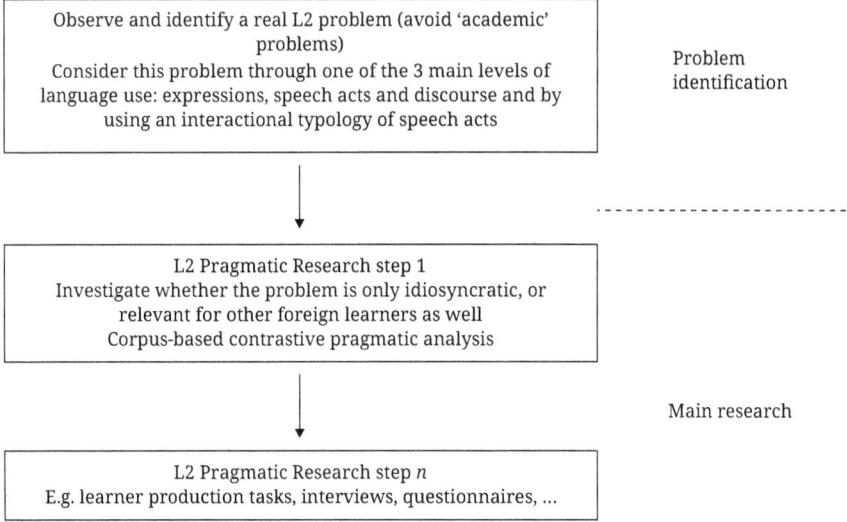

Figure 3.2 Display of our research procedure

Regarding the first phase of problem identification illustrated by the upper part of Figure 3.2, in our view L2 pragmatic research needs to start with the observation of a real problem. In the investigation of speech acts, we interpret this problem through the lens of our finite and interactional speech act typology. We find it problematic to study predominantly academic research questions (see also above), such as which forms of Greet should be taught to a certain learner group, without having proof of an actual learner problem relating to the use of the speech act Greet. This is why we propose focusing on instances of learner irritation and puzzlement. The departure point of learner irritation and puzzlement also allows us to interconnect our speech act research with a large body of L2 pragmatic studies starting with such issues (see e.g. Jaworski, 1994; Schauer, 2022).

As Figure 3.2 shows, we use our typology of speech acts in the stage of identifying a problem of language use faced by L2 learners. For example, in Chapter 8 we report on a study where we examined instances of puzzlement experienced by foreign learners of Chinese who do not know what to say when congratulations are due in certain ritual occasions in their L2 linguaculture. In interpreting such cases of puzzlement, we analysed what these learners preferred to say in relevant situations, and also what was pragmatically expected from them in their target linguaculture in such situations. This problem is more important than meets the eye because L2 learners may not only need to be able to realise congratulations on those few occasions (if ever) when they participate in a liminal ritual event (Turner, 1969) in their L2, but also on much more mundane occasions such as workplace meetings when a colleague casually tells them about a related family event, such as the eightieth birthday of a family member. This investigation led to the finding that many foreign learners of Chinese preferred to realise the speech act Wish-Well in ritual congratulations, instead of the speech act Congratulate, and this pragmatic transfer was one of the reasons that triggered their puzzlement when they faced real instances of congratulation in the Chinese linguaculture.

As both the cases of greeting and congratulating above show, the interactional and finite nature of our typology is fundamental when it comes to problem identification. In both cases we did not depart from focusing on a single speech act but rather we investigated phases of interaction in which certain speech acts conventionally occur and relate to one another.

As Figure 3.2 shows, the second major phase in our procedure includes the main (L2 pragmatic) research. This phase has as at least two steps, including separating idiosyncratic behaviour from conventionalised pragmatic behaviour, and the follow-up L2 pragmatic investigation. The latter may include various steps, e.g. one may include here DCTs, questionnaires, interviews and other productions in one's analysis.

Regarding the first step in this second phase: once we identify an L2 learning problem relating to pragmatics and consider it through our interactional typology of speech acts, the next step is to investigate whether this problem is only idiosyncratic and thus trivial or is contrastively relevant for other L2 learners as well. Here we are not arguing against including individual learner considerations in one's research (see Takahashi's 2019 recent authoritative discussion on this topic), but rather we wish to point out that in the course of doing rigorous and replicable contrastive research in L2 pragmatics involving issues of speech act realisation, it is essential to identify interactional conventions of language use, including those that trigger learner puzzlement. As soon as we know that a problem is worth investigating, corpus-based research can be particularly useful to get to the heart of the cross-cultural pragmatic reasons for learner puzzlement. That is, through a corpus-based and language-anchored study, the researcher may be able to unearth deep-rooted reasons underlying L2 puzzlement – particularly if such investigations involve a contrastive scope – and consider such reasons through the lens of the proposed typology of speech acts. Let us provide an example here. In Chapter 5, we report on a study where we investigated the following language learning-related problem: Chinese learners of English often find 'altered' uses of expressions associated with certain speech acts in English, such as complaining uses of *thank you very much*, difficult to interpret. Here *thank you very much* may not indicate the speech act Thank, but rather the very different speech act Complain, as the speaker comments on something that annoys her or him. In other words, a 'migration' of speech acts can be observed here (see our discussion below Figure 3.1). To understand what causes learner irritation and puzzlement in this case, we conducted a contrastive pragmatic investigation of two groups of comparable 'Thank expressions' in the British National Corpus and the Balanced Chinese Corpus. Expressions such as *Thank you very much* were found to operate in a pragmatically much more diverse way than their Chinese counterparts such as *Ganxie*, which in turn provided a gateway to understand and explain the problem mentioned by the L2 learners involved in our study.

In this step, it is important to make sure that the analyst interprets the eventual outcomes of such corpus analysis in a language-anchored way, i.e. without overinterpreting the results by attributing them to cultural values and other grandiose non-linguistic notions. By so doing, one can avoid relying on notions such as 'cultural values', 'cultural ethos', 'individualism', 'collectivity', face-sensitivity' and the infamous 'East–West divide'. Why do we argue against a non-language-anchored cultural view? Unfortunately, various scholars such as Byon (2002), Meier (2010), Maíz-Arévalo (2017) and Hosni (2020) discussed speech act performance in L2 pragmatics through cultural notions such as 'collectivism' and 'individualism' and related deep East–West contrasts, arguing that such assumed cultural characteristics determine language learners' behaviour. By following such an essentialist approach, the researcher unavoidably makes *a priori* assumptions, implying that any pragmatic difference they identify between the L1 and L2 of the learner is unavoidably influenced by innate cultural ascriptions. By degrading learners to the level of cultural robots, the researcher precludes unearthing fine-tuned pragmatic conventions which – unlike 'collectivism' or its lack – may trigger *real* L2 learning difficulties. For instance, it may be tempting to **exoticise** corpus results relating to Chinese when it comes to the above-mentioned instances of the speech acts Greet and Thank, falling into the trap of presenting L2 learners as people with essentially predictable behaviour. While phenomena such as 'face-sensitivity', 'collectivity', 'Confucian ideology', and so on could be interesting for some, we believe that they should be avoided because they preclude looking at speech act realisation in interaction with the cold eye of the researcher. Also, there is no way to reliably interpret corpus-based results by using such cultural notions, if for no other reason than because no corpus is perfect nor representative (see Sharoff et al., 2013).

We believe that corpus-based research as described above might be ideally complemented by L2 production tasks assigned to learners, or interviews conducted with learners. Methodologically, such tasks should again rely on an interactional typology of speech acts such as ours, and also they might ideally be multimethod in nature. Let us here refer to Chapter 9. In this study, we examined the L2 pragmatic features of a particular type of Closing phase in which one interactant intends to leave the scene while the other relentlessly goes on talking – a phenomenon we define as 'extracting' oneself from an interaction. English-speaking conventions of extracting were found to be challenging for Chinese learners of English because extracting oneself from an interaction often triggers significant face-threat to one's interlocutor.[2] We first administered DCTs to these learners and compared them with DCTs administered to 'native' speakers of English,[3] both featuring the interactional situation of extracting oneself from an interaction rather than a particular speech act (like Extractor itself). Following the DCTs, we conducted interviews with the same L2 learners and native speakers of English in order to tease out their metapragmatic interpretations of the phenomenon studied.

3.6 Conclusion

In this chapter, we have introduced the framework for our research in this book. This framework is centred on speech acts, which we approach in an interactional way. This interactional view in turn implies that we always study the unit of speech act in relation to the other pragmatic units we presented in Chapter 1. In the rest of this book, we will first discuss contrastive L2 pragmatic issues relating to the learning of expressions through which speech acts tend to be indicated. We will then discuss the relationship between speech acts and interactional acts, such as congratulating and criticising from a contrastive L2 pragmatic of view. Finally, we will bring together phases of interaction, or Types of Talk as we call them, such as Opening Talk, with speech acts.

3.7 Recommended reading

Edmondson, Willis, Juliane House and Dániel Z. Kádár (2023). *Expressions, Speech Acts and Discourse: A Pedagogic Interactional Grammar of English.* **Cambridge: Cambridge University Press.**
Various ideas in our framework have their roots in our previous collaboration, perhaps most importantly in the above-mentioned book. The following section discusses in detail why there is a need for a finite and replicable system in pragmatics:

> The central claim in this grammar is that, in contributing to an interaction, a speaker produces an utterance, i.e. an instance of language use,

which has a dual function: in the first place it reveals the speaker's beliefs, attitudes, desires and so on about some state of affairs; and secondly, it plays a part in building up the ongoing conversation, being significant both with respect to what has already been said, and with respect to what may follow. These two aspects of utterance meaning in discourse we may call the illocutionary value (relating to the speaker), and the interactional value (relating that illocutionary value to a possible outcome of the interaction).

Consider, for example, a simple bit of dialogue as follows:

(1)	Speaker	Utterance	Illocution
	A:	Can you wash up now Mandy?	Request
	B:	Okay	Willing

In saying "Okay" the second speaker, Mandy, expresses an attitude of willingness towards the idea that she should wash up. This we may call the illocutionary significance of what she says. At the same time, through this utterance Mandy clearly agrees to A's Request. An outcome has been arrived at in (1) such that A assumes that Mandy will now wash up and Mandy herself may be assumed to intend to do so. Because of the placing of the utterance, we might wish to call it a 'promise', in fact.

Consider further:

(2)	Speaker	Utterance	Illocution
	A:	Hey – you've not washed up yet	Complain
	B:	Yeah – I've been doing my homework all this time	Excuse
	A:	Okay then –	Forgive
		but do the washing up now please	Request
	B:	Yeah – okay	Willing

In common sense terms, A makes a complaint and B gives an excuse. The interactional function of the excuse is to counter the complaint, i.e. cause A to withdraw it. It follows then that the utterance "Okay then" counts as an acceptance of the excuse, i.e. shows that A 'forgives' B and the complaint is thus annulled.

Note that when we describe language behaviour, we sometimes use terms such as 'suggest', 'request', and so on, which roughly indicate illocutionary values, and sometimes terms such as 'agree', 'accept', 'contradict', 'turn down', 'refuse', which are more indicative of the significance of the utterance relative to a preceding one. *What we need to do is to distinguish between these two aspects of a communicative act – the illocutionary and the interactional.* This is the most important distinguishing mark of the current book because unlike many other speech act typologies we make this crucial distinction, allowing us to limit our typology of speech acts to a finite number of categories. (Edmondson et al., 2023: 24–26)

Notes

1. See also relevant research on speech actions in Sbisà and Turner (2013).
2. Here we use the term 'face' in the sense of Goffman (1955).
3. Here we put the expression 'native' into inverted commas because native speakerism has been found very problematic – and rightly so! – in L2 pragmatics.

CHAPTER 4

Exploring speech acts through expressions in L2 pragmatics

4.1 Introduction

In this chapter, we will use our framework by focusing on a seemingly simple question, namely how expressions – representing the lowest pragmatic unit of analysis – can indicate speech acts, and what kind of L2 pragmatic issues arise from this assignation. At this stage, we will make only a simple use of our speech act typology, in order to gradually introduce the reader into the system proposed in Chapter 3. That is, here we study how two particular Attitudinal speech acts – Request and Apologise – are indicated by certain expressions in the learners' L1 and L2. However, even at this stage we will make use of certain elements of the research procedure outlined in Figure 3.2, in that we will rely on multiple research methods, including a corpus-based contrastive analysis and the contrastive use of DCTs.

Before venturing into the case study featured in this chapter, let us define expressions through which speech acts tend to be indicated across linguacultures. In our framework, we call such expressions '**ritual frame indicating expressions**' (henceforth RFIEs). This designation refers to the following: in every language, certain expressions are popularly associated with speech acts. These expressions are also normally associated with 'politeness', although this latter association often fails to hold the test of real life, in that there are no inherently polite or impolite speech acts. Also, the popular association between expressions and speech acts tends to be subject to linguacultural and contextual variation, as this chapter will show. Thus, in order to avoid claiming a direct link between these expressions and speech acts, we define them as expressions that indicate rights and obligations in standard situations which can be recognised by everyone (see House and Kádár, 2021a). In interactional ritual theory, such standard situations with clear rights and obligations are ritual, hence the name RFIE.

RFIEs have a strong pragmatic load, and because of this even advanced L2 learners tend to face significant difficulties when they try to contextually interpret them. Since RFIEs are pragmatic tools through which language users maintain rights and obligations and the related ritual frame in standard situations, pragmatic failures in the use of RFIEs can lead to intercultural difficulties.

The structure of this chapter is as follows. In section 4.2, we look at previous studies and point out why the study of RFIEs is relevant to pragmatics in general and L2 pragmatics and applied linguistics in particular. In section 4.3, we introduce a research design through which RFIEs can be studied in a simple way, with the aid of contrastive corpus research and follow-up L2 pragmatic research. We call this procedure 'simple' because here we still do not use our framework in its whole complexity, i.e. we do not consider issues such as the 'migration' of speech acts in our typology (see Chapter 3) – a topic which we will discuss in Chapter 5. Finally, in section 4.4 we will provide our case study analysis.

4.2 Selected previous studies

In interlanguage pragmatics (e.g. Kasper and Blum-Kulka, 1993), metapragmatics and L2 research (House, 1996), pragmatic competence (e.g. Taguchi, 2009), cross-cultural and intercultural misunderstanding studies (e.g. House, 2003b), language socialisation (e.g. Burdelski, 2010), pragmatic awareness and second language acquisition (e.g. Alcón and Safont Jordà, 2008; Barron, 2003) and pragmatic assessment (see e.g. Kramsch, 1993; House, 1996; Rose and Kasper, 2001; Safont Jordà, 2003; Brown, 2018), the expressions that we define as RFIEs have been somewhat neglected. However, pragmatically relevant expressions have not been entirely ignored in pragmatics and applied linguistics. For instance, in foreign language learning and assessment, 'politeness expressions' have received significant attention, as a body of research such as Davies (1987), Meier (1997), Bou-Franch and Garces-Conejos Blitvich (2003), Byon (2004) and Bardovi-Harlig (2012) illustrates. Yet, little academic work has been undertaken on the contrastive examination of how groups of learners of two different linguacultures acquire and evaluate expressions that are generally considered to be linguacultural 'equivalents'.

4.3 Analytic procedure

In the following, we outline an analytic procedure through which one can study RFIEs in L2 pragmatics in a contrastive way. This procedure already reflects the mode of operation outlined in Figure 3.2, i.e. it combines a corpus-based study of a contrastive pragmatic problem and a follow-up L2 pragmatic research. In section 4.3.1, we present a detailed description of how one can study RFIEs in large corpora in general. Next, in section 4.3.2 we show how the outcomes of such corpus research can be put to use in L2 pragmatic inquiries.

4.3.1 The corpus-based study of RFIEs

Following the general language choice of this book, here we study RFIEs in English and Chinese. These RFIEs are most commonly associated with the speech acts Request and Apologise. Our contrastive pragmatic analytic procedure allows one to analyse RFIEs and the resulting standard situational spread of the conventionalised use of expressions in a bottom-up fashion. Figure 4.1 illustrates the replicable model which forms the basis of our methodology:

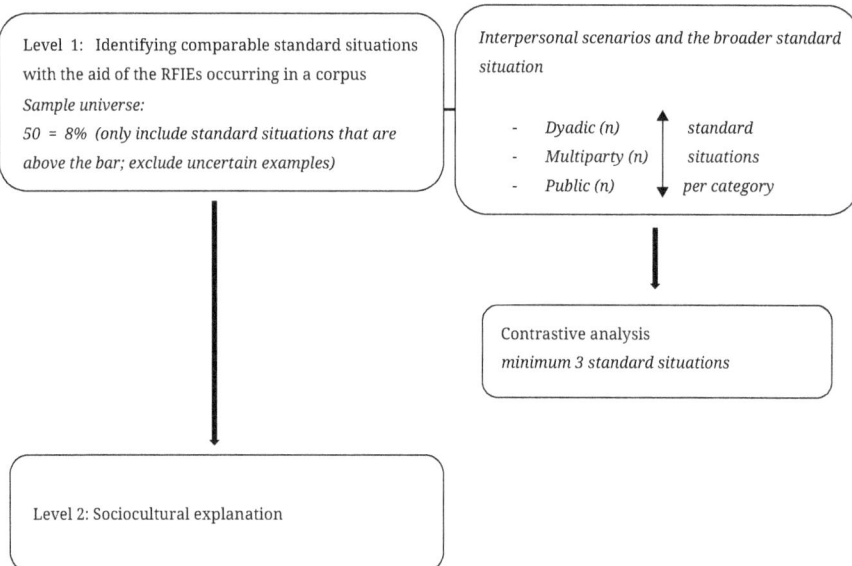

Figure 4.1 Our procedure of studying RFIEs in corpora in a contrastive way

The procedure depicted in Figure 4.1 consists of two levels. On the first level, the initial task is to identify the RFIEs in the data that one intends to compare. Various criteria may be used to identify comparable RFIEs. We suggest frequency as the basic criterion. As an L2 pragmatics-related methodology, we suggest involving panels of native speakers of the languages involved in our L2 pragmatic project in order to confirm whether the RFIEs we intend to contrastively examine are comparatively frequent. For instance, in the case study we are discussing in this chapter, we have involved five native speakers of similar sociocultural, educational and gender-related backgrounds per linguaculture in the identification of comparable RFIEs. The selected speakers provided the following lists which in their view best represented the respective RFIEs in their native languages. Each RFIE group includes three expressions (in decreasing frequency), and includes a 'simple' one-word RFIE (most frequent) and two multi-word RFIEs:

Exploring speech acts through expressions in L2 pragmatics 43

1. English 'please'-group: *please; would/could you please; if you please*
2. Chinese 'qing'-group: *qing* 请; *fanqing* 烦请 (lit. 'trouble you by requesting'); *jingqing* 敬请 (lit. 'respectfully ask')[1]
3. English 'sorry'-group: *sorry; I am/I'm sorry; I am very/so sorry*
4. Chinese 'duibuqi'-group: *duibuqi* 对不起; *duibuqi + object; upgrader + duibuqi + object*

These RFIE groups represent English and Chinese expressions that are commonly associated with the speech acts Request and Apologise. Note that there is a certain sense of discrepancy between the Chinese and English RFIE groups, in that more complex RFIE groups are frequented in formal written rather than spoken interaction, whereas their English counterparts seem to be more equally spread between spoken and written types of interaction.

After the RFIE groups to contrastively investigate have been chosen, a sample universe needs to be collected. In the case study we are discussing here, a key practical issue to consider was the following: multi-word RFIEs appeared much less frequently than their one-word counterparts in our corpora. Because of this, we decided to collect a minimum of fifty examples which featured a particular RFIE in each group.

The next criterion in the first level of RFIE analysis is to identify the standard situations which are conventionally indicated by a particular RFIE. Any contrastive pragmatic research on RFIEs needs to ensure that a manageable number of such standard situations is obtained. In our case, we applied a threshold of three for our dataset of fifty examples. In other words, we proposed implementing a minimum 8 per cent rate of occurrence threshold to ensure that a particular standard situation was indicated by an RFIE in a sufficiently recurrent and as such conventionalised way. While in applying the notion of standard situation in RFIE analysis we need to make sure that our subject of analysis is as replicable as possible, and the current chapter will show certain standard situation categories interconnect our analysis of various expressions, standard situations are subject to variation both across linguacultures and across data types. Because of this, the idea in deploying the notion of standard situation is not to create grand categories applicable to any analysis, but rather to deploy categories which – on the basis of our empirical observations – can used to contrastively examine RFIEs across different corpora. Thus, we may even afford having some overlap between certain categories, and some standard situations may be of narrower in scope that others.

There are various ways in which one can collect a sample dataset of fifty examples. For instance, we collected fifty hits by randomly sampling batches of five examples in our corpora. We excluded examples that we classified as being invalid, such as metareferences to an RFIE. Our data sampling took place in two stages, firstly by collecting an initial dataset, and then by replacing the invalid examples with valid ones that occurred before the batches of five examples in the corpus.

We identified two commonly occurring standard situations, namely 'institutional with power-salience' and 'institutional without power-salience'. These standard situations frequently occur in our data because (a) they represent interactional scenes in which conventions and/or ritual become relevant (Kádár, 2013), and (b) they are recurrently indicated by the RFIEs studied in this chapter. We have chosen other standard situations by empirically observing their degree of conventionalisedness.

So far, we have provided an overview of the first (top left-hand) box in Figure 4.1. We now turn our attention to the top right-hand box, which illustrates the application of the variables of the participatory framework that are used to analyse each RFIE, before a contrastive pragmatic analysis is conducted. A standard situation indicated by an RFIE very often comes on a par with conventionalised '**interpersonal scenarios**' frequented in a particular standard situation. A contrastive analysis needs to examine the relationship between a particular RFIE and the standard situation(s) in which it is frequented. In our model, we define three types of interpersonal scenarios, namely (1) 'dyadic', (2) 'multiparty' and (3) 'public', as in the following:

- Dyadic: Interactions in private where there are no overhearers.
- Multiparty: Any interaction involving two participants with either overhearers or situated in a scenario in which dyads are part of a broader relational network. Multiparty interactions tend to feature complex participatory frameworks.
- Public: Interactions which are designed to be accessible to unratified participants (see also Goffman, 1981).

In order to ensure that the dataset of one RFIE is comparable with another one, we suggest creating a cluster of interpersonal scenarios and broader standard situations by breaking down the occurrences of each standard situation that a particular RFIE indicates across the interpersonal scenarios.

The next step is to engage in contrastive pragmatic analysis, as per the bottom right-hand box of Figure 4.1. As part of this process, we contrastively study the pragmatic scope of parallel RFIE groups, each consisting of three expressions. Considering that our L2 pragmatic framework is centred on speech acts, the focus of the investigation here is the relationship between the RFIE groups and 'speech act-anchor' (see also Chapter 5). Due to our focus on the relationship between RFIEs and speech acts, in our analysis we devote attention to the frequency of 'speech act-anchored' versus 'non-speech-act-anchored' functions of the RFIEs being studied. The number of non-speech-act-anchored occurrences of an expression will be indicated in the following tables by underlining and bracketing the figures.

Our data is based on Mandarin Chinese and English corpora of comparable size and comprehensiveness. We opted to use two Chinese corpora because each one is smaller in size than the English corpus. Therefore, to ensure comparability, we extended our Chinese corpus as far as possible. The Chinese

Exploring speech acts through expressions in L2 pragmatics 45

corpora have similar generic features and timespans and include the Modern Chinese General Balanced Corpus (MCGBC; http://corpus.zhonghuayuwen.org/) and the Balance Chinese Corpus (BCC; http://corpus.zhonghuayuwen.org/CnCindex.aspx). The English corpus is the British National Corpus (BNC).

Analysis
Here we analyse the aforementioned Request and Apologise RFIEs in English and Chinese in corresponding groups of three. Following the analysis of the pragmatic features of each group-pair of three RFIEs, we examine the results from a contrastive pragmatic angle, in order to provide a replicable pattern for cross-cultural pragmatic research on expressions.

'Requestive' RFIEs (please-variants) in English
Please
As the pragmatic use of the RFIE *please* is relatively simple, we will only provide a brief overview of how this RFIE is used. Table 4.1 shows the standard situations in this RFIE that is used in our dataset of fifty examples.

Table 4.1 *Allocation of the RFIE* please *in the corpus*

Standard situation	Number of examples	Dyadic (D) Multiparty (M) Public (P)
Institutional with power-salience	17	D6; M7; P4
Institutional without power-salience	15	D4; M7; P4
Service encounters	18	D18

As Table 4.1 illustrates, the occurrence of *please* is spread more or less equally across standard situations. From a contrastive pragmatic angle, an important characteristic of this English RFIE is that it is used in the standard situation 'service encounters', while its single-word Chinese counterpart is not (see below). The English RFIE *please* is allocated relatively evenly across the interpersonal scenarios, with the exception of the standard situation 'service encounters', which is dyadic in nature.

Would/could you please
We initially analysed the RFIEs *would you please* and *could you please* as a pair. However, on closer examination, our research has revealed that their pragmatic scopes are different and, in certain respects, the RFIE *would you please* is somewhat similar to the requestive RFIE *if you please*. As our research involves groups of three RFIEs, we decided to omit the quantitative analysis of *would you please* from the case study presented here. However, to illustrate that, pragmatically, this RFIE represents a 'midpoint' between the other two multi-word RFIEs, we include a number of examples in this section that feature *would you please*, before then moving on to the analysis of the RFIE *could you please*.

The RFIE *would you please* is frequently used in a sarcastic manner (see also Busse, 2002; Oraby et al., 2017), as the following examples illustrate:

(4.1) Would you please fetch me a towel and my cloak before I turn into an iceberg?

(4.2) 'Would you please get on with your work, Sandra?' said Edward with unusual severity.

Would you please can also indicate a Request which is made in a rather deferential manner, as the following examples demonstrate:

(4.3) Would you please come in earlier?

(4.4) With reference to our telephone conversation the other day, would you please sign the enclosed document and return it to me, retaining the attached copy for your files?

As examples (4.1)–(4.4) illustrate, *would you please* has a dual function, i.e. it can be used to indicate sarcasm and also to make a straightforward request, often with a deferential overtone.

Among the English Request RFIEs studied, *could you please* is the most deferential one (see also House and Kasper, 1981; Tatton, 2008). Table 4.2 summarises the spread of this RFIE across the standard situations.

Table 4.2 *Allocation of the RFIE* could you please *in the corpus*

Standard situation	Number of examples	Dyadic (D) Multiparty (M) Public (P)
Institutional with power-salience	7	D3; M4
Institutional without power-salience	12	D5; M4; P3
Strangership in request	31	D31

Table 4.2 reveals a fundamental pragmatic property of the RFIE *could you please*, namely that it is always used in a speech act-anchored manner. As the examples below will illustrate, while the other RFIEs in this English group have both proper Requestive and non-speech-act-anchored functions, *could you please* can only be Requestive because it has a preparatory function one (see House and Kasper, 1981). As Table 4.2 also illustrates, this RFIE is frequently used in dyadic interpersonal scenarios, a fact which we will revisit later.

In terms of standard situations, the RFIE *could you please* indicates both the standard situations 'institutional with power-salience' and 'institutional without power-salience':

Exploring speech acts through expressions in L2 pragmatics 47

(4.5) <u>Could you please</u> identify and date the object?

(4.6) To complete our user records, which the EC Directive also obliges us to keep and update, <u>could you please</u>, as Horticultural representative on the Computing Sub-Group, coordinate a response from AD, GD and HD as to the names of all operators who are estimated to spend at least one hour per day working at a multi-user PC as part of their normal duties (I've already got user names for single-user machines)?

(4.7) <u>Could you please</u> let me know where you would like the cheque sent, and to whom we should make it out?

(4.8) <u>Could you please</u> tell me how to practise levels two and three on Back To The Future 3, as I have tried everything?

Example (4.5) represents the standard situation 'institutional with power-salience': here the utterance is an order veiled as a Request. In example (4.6), the power relationship between the parties involved is less salient but the standard situation is clearly institutional and power is important, in that the RFIE is deployed in an official context in which the recipient must comply with the Request. Examples (4.7) and (4.8) represent the standard situation 'institutional without power-salience', in which the relationship between the participants is relatively insignificant, and the RFIE simply facilitates a Request.

By far the most significant standard situation in which the RFIE *could you please* is deployed in our corpus is what we define as 'strangership in request': in many interactions, the RFIE indicates that the person using it is making a Request to someone whom (s)he does not know. In a sense, this standard situation cuts across both 'institutional with power-salience' and 'institutional without power-salience'. However, we have categorised it as an independent standard situation, not only because of its high frequency of occurrence in our data, but also because when realising Requestive behaviour, a lack of familiarity obviously has a major impact on facework. The following examples illustrate the use of the RFIE *could you please* in this standard situation:

(4.9) '<u>Could you please</u> tell me how to get to Lei-cee-ter Square, please?' I asked wide-eyed, eager and hopeful.

(4.10) <u>Could you please</u> help me?

(4.11) <u>Could you please</u> advise me on a point regarding my Range Rover Turbo D, which was new in August of last year?

As Table 4.2 above illustrates, the RFIE *could you please* is more frequently used in dyadic and multiparty interpersonal scenarios, although it can be used as a formal request in public interactions.

If you please

Table 4.3 indicates how the RFIE *if you please* is used in our sample of fifty examples.

Table 4.3 *Allocation of the RFIE* if you please *in the corpus*

Standard situation	Number of examples (underlined cases indicate non-speech act active uses)	Dyadic (D) Multiparty (M) Public (P)
Institutional with power-salience	17	D8; M9
Institutional without power-salience	19 (3)	D9; M10
Criticism in private	14 (14)	D14

When *if you please* indicates the standard situation 'institutional with power-salience', it is always used in a Requestive manner, as the following examples illustrate:

(4.12) 'Now, now, gentlemen', Regan said gently, 'no acrimony, if you please'.

(4.13) Well just stop talking about it, if you please!

In the 'institutional with power-salience' standard situation, the RFIE *if you please* makes the Request pragmatically stronger, moves it in the direction of an order and provides other non-speech-act-anchored connotations.

If you please also often indicates the standard situation 'institutional without power-salience'. The following examples illustrate this use:

(4.14) 'Three bottles of cider to take away, if you please', he boomed.

(4.15) Speak plainly if you please.

(4.16) And — close the door, if you please.

As these extracts illustrate, the RFIE *if you please* gives the impression that the Request is actually an order. According to Table 4.3 above, when the RFIE is deployed in the 'institutional without power-salience' standard situation, in a small number of cases (3) it operates as an attention-getter (see Edmondson and House, 1981):

(4.17) 'If you please', she said, 'I've come to ask you something'.

Finally, the RFIE *if you please* is frequently used in a sarcastic manner in what we have defined as 'criticism in private', i.e. when the participants perform a speech act Complaining without the complainee being present. In this situation, it indicates a strong sense of annoyance (see Wichmann, 2004: 1524)

Exploring speech acts through expressions in L2 pragmatics 49

and is never used to perform a requestive function (see Table 4.3 above), as the following examples illustrate:

(4.18) 'She wants me to make a thousand currant buns, five hundred sausage rolls and fifty chocolate sponge sandwiches, if you please, in time for the jubilee', Mrs Cartwright exploded as she juggled with dishes and tins and bowls and ladles.

(4.19) I am frozen half to death — and all for a servant, if you please!

According to Table 4.3, *if you please* is frequently used in both dyadic and multiparty interpersonal scenarios, but not in public scenarios.

'Requestive' RFIEs (qing-variants) in Chinese
The 'Requestive' RFIEs studied in this section are the following:

- *qing* 请
- *fanqing* 烦请 lit. 'may I bother you by asking'
- *jingqing* 敬请 lit. 'respectfully ask'

Our panel of native speakers explained that both *fanqing* and *jingqing* are more widely used in written than in spoken interactions, due to their formal style. *Qing* is significantly more widespread in colloquial Chinese than the other two RFIEs. This in itself is an interesting fact, as it reveals that while in English language users are relatively free to choose between the variants of *please*, depending on the pragmatic message that they want to convey, in Chinese the default 'requestive' RFIE is *qing* and variants of this RFIE are non-spoken. In addition, as the analysis of *qing* below will illustrate, even this simplest RFIE is often deployed in ceremonies because it is formal in style. These facts show that the Chinese group of 'Requestive' RFIEs is somewhat more formal and ceremonial than their English counterparts. This has direct consequences for the 'speech act-anchor' of these RFIEs.

Qing
As the RFIE *qing* – just like *please* – is a relatively simple form, we will only briefly discuss its use here. Table 4.4 below illustrates the spread of this RFIE across the standard situations in our corpus.

Table 4.4 *Allocation of the RFIE* qing *in the corpus*

Standard situation	Number of examples	Dyadic (D) Multiparty (M) Public (P)
Institutional with power-salience	27	D5; M12; P10
Institutional without power-salience	15	D2; M6; P7
Ceremonial/Family	17	D3; M5; P9

As Table 4.4 shows, unlike the RFIE *please*, *qing* is used in the standard situation 'ceremonial' but – as far as our corpus is concerned – is not deployed in the standard situation 'service encounters', where *please* is the preferred option. Ceremonies often take place in family settings (Johnson, 2009), and hence our designation 'ceremonial/family'. This difference demonstrates a point which the analysis of the other Chinese 'Requestive' RFIEs will also confirm, namely that the use of these RFIEs is very formal in nature. It is also worth noting that the RFIE *qing* and its variants are always used in a speech act-anchored manner; that is, unlike *please*, for instance, they are not used to gain attention. Table 4.4 also indicates that the use of the RFIE *qing* is spread more equally across the three standard situations than *please*, i.e. its use frequently includes the 'public' interpersonal scenario.

Fanqing

Qing is significantly more ceremonial than its English counterpart *please* because it originated in Classical Chinese where it functioned as an honorific. This honorific feature influences the way in which *fanqing* is used, as Table 4.5 below illustrates.

Table 4.5 *Allocation of the RFIE* fanqing *in the corpus*

Standard situation	Number of examples	Dyadic (D) Multiparty (M) Public (P)
Institutional with power-salience	16	D1; M7; P8
Institutional without power-salience	13	D3; M4; P6
Public announcements and speeches	21	P21

As the table illustrates, due to its honorific character *fanqing* is frequently deployed in the standard situation 'public announcements and speeches', as the following examples demonstrate:

(4.20) 校园博客大赛！烦请投我一票！
It is the Campus Blog Competition! Please (*fanqing*) vote for me!

(4.21) 烦请各位领导闲暇时给予关注
I request (*fanqing*) all leaders to provide attention when they have time.

(4.22) 烦请大家帮忙指正，帮我提高。
I request (*fanqing*) everyone to help me to correct and improve myself.

Example (4.20) is a quasi-formal and (4.21) is a highly formal public announcement, whereas (4.22) is taken from a ceremonial public speech. As these

Exploring speech acts through expressions in L2 pragmatics 51

examples illustrate, the use of the RFIE *fanqing* is explicitly performative and this expression often concurs with honorifics, particularly in written text.

In the 'institutional without power-salience' standard situation, the use of the RFIE *fanqing* in our corpus is limited primarily to workplace settings in which a formal Request takes place, as the following example illustrates:

(4.23) 能不能烦请你转达，告诉她，我曾找过她，如果方便的话，请她回个电话给我
May I request (*fanqing*) you to tell her that I was looking for her? If it is convenient, I would like to ask her to call me.

The use of this RFIE is even more solemn in the standard situation 'institutional with power-salience', as the following example demonstrates:

(4.24) 所以这几天的看书时间 ，他大部分时间都在看那两本书 。烦请您指教下月学习计划，谢谢！
So, for these two days during his reading time he will be reading these two books. I request (*fanqing*) your (*nin*, V pronoun) advice (*zhijiao*, honorific form) on the study plan for next month, with many thanks!

According to Table 4.5, *fanqing* is frequently used in public interpersonal scenarios which indicates that this RFIE, exactly like its simpler counterpart *qing*, is 'speech act-anchored'.

Jingqing
The most deferential Chinese 'requestive' RFIE is *jingqing* 'respectfully ask', which is predominantly a written expression. Table 4.6 illustrates the spread of this RFIE across standard situations.

Table 4.6 *Allocation of the RFIE* jingqing *in the corpus*

Standard situation	Number of examples	Dyadic (D) Multiparty (M) Public (P)
Public announcements	14	P14
Institutional with power[2]	8	M3; P5
Service encounters	28	P28

As indicated in Table 4.6, *jingqing* is used in the standard situation 'public announcements', just like the RFIE *fanqing*. However, unlike the latter, *jingqing* is rarely used in speeches in our corpus because it is primarily a written form of expression. The following examples illustrate the use of this RFIE in public ceremonial announcements:

(4.25) 敬请大家期待偶这里未来一两天的后续报道
I would like to respectfully ask (*jingqing*) everyone to await my further announcement in one or two days

(4.26) 敬请各位把这篇文章贴到你所知道的任何地方。
I would like to respectfully ask (*jingqing*) everyone to stick this notice in every possible place.

Jingqing is also used in institutional settings where power is important (institutional with power), as the following example illustrates:

(4.27) 您是怎样认为呢？敬请发邮件到我信箱。
How do you (formal pronominal form) see this? I respectfully ask you (*jingqing*) to send a mail to my mailbox.

Finally, *jingqing* is used in the standard situation 'service encounters' by companies in the form of written messages and as requests for customers in online and other settings. In such instances, the RFIE indicates the company's awareness of its obligations towards its customers, who should be treated professionally and with respect. In this regard, it indicates a specific business relationship, as the following examples illustrate:

(4.28) 关于会员注册及会员资料等问题敬请来信会员服务信箱 member.service@jimmyspa.com
We respectfully ask you (*jingqing*) to send membership registration and member information and other related information to our service mailbox member.service@jimmyspa.com

(4.29) 车牌号、座位号以及陪同联系方式将在出行前一天以短信形式通知，敬请留意
We respectfully ask you (*jingqing*) to check the SMS that you will receive the day before your journey regarding your train and seat number and contact information

As we discovered in a previous study (see Kádár and House, 2020), the Chinese RFIE *qing* is rarely used in service encounters in our corpus because people do not use *qing* during face-to-face encounters in Chinese services, unlike their English-speaking counterparts. However, this situation would appear to be quite different in written service discourse because it is evident that *jingqing* is frequently used by service providers. As Table 4.6 shows, the RFIE *jingqing* – in a similar way to other 'Requestive' Chinese RFIEs – is most frequently used in public scenarios and, as such, is pragmatically significant and highly deferential.

Contrastive analysis
The analysis of the English and Chinese 'requestive' RFIE groups has illustrated that, in general, the Chinese group is more 'speech act-anchored' than the English group, even though the RFIE *could you please* is also strongly anchored in the speech act Request. This indicates that, while in the English linguaculture a multi-word solution is required to create a firm conventionalised relationship between *please* and the speech act Request, in Chinese *qing* itself is conventionally 'speech act-anchored' due to its historical origin as an honorific. As a consequence of this, the RFIE *please* and its variants are frequently used in non-speech-act-anchored functions, whereas these functions are not readily available in Chinese. In addition, while the Chinese RFIEs are frequently used in public interpersonal scenarios and these scenarios tend to be formal and, as such, trigger deferential language use, this observation is not valid for the English RFIEs, even though *could you please* is occasionally used in public scenarios in our corpus. Ultimately, it is not an overgeneralisation to state that, as far as our case study of RFIEs and their relationship to speech acts is concerned, the Chinese RFIEs tend to be deferential in style but no such generalisation can be made about the English RFIEs.

Apologise RFIEs (sorry-variants) in English
Sorry
Just like *please*, the RFIE *sorry* is of a relatively simple pragmatic use, and here we will only provide a summary of its pragmatic characteristics in terms of our analytic procedure.

Table 4.7 *Allocation of the RFIE* sorry *in the corpus*

Standard situation	Number of examples (underlined cases indicate non-speech-act active uses)	Dyadic (D) Multiparty (M) Public (P)
Institutional with power-salience	19 (<u>11</u>)	D8; M11
Institutional without power-salience	20 (<u>6</u>)	D9; M11
Introductory commenting	11 (<u>11</u>)	D6; M5

As Table 4.7 illustrates, the RFIE *sorry* is frequently used in institutional interactions, both with and without salient power relationships. As the underlined parenthetical figures in the table illustrate, *sorry* often operates as a 'giveaway' expression in English and, as such, is not deferential. This finding is confirmed by the fact that *sorry* is frequented in the function what we defined as 'introductory commenting', i.e. cases when the speaker uses the RFIE *sorry* to indicate that in the particular context he has right to make a (usually critical or sarcastic) comment regarding the other or a state of affairs. It is also worth noting that this RFIE is not used in public interpersonal scenarios in our dataset, a fact which is again related to its lack of speech act-anchor.

I am/I'm sorry

The examination of the RFIE *I am sorry* (and its variant *I'm sorry*) reveals that this RFIE is rather similar to the single-word *sorry* in that it can perform non-speech-act-anchored pragmatic functions which differ from an Apologise, such as indignation, gaining attention and suchlike. Table 4.8 illustrates the spread of this RFIE across standard situations.

Table 4.8 *Allocation of the RFIE* I am sorry *in the corpus*

Standard situation	Number of examples (underlined cases indicate non-speech-act active uses)	Dyadic (D) Multiparty (M) Public (P)
Institutional with power-salience	21 (15)	D7; M14
Institutional without power-salience	12 (8)	D5; M7
Introductory commenting	17 (17)	D13; P4

As Table 4.8 shows, the multi-word *I am sorry*, like its single-word counterpart, is often used in a non-apologetic manner. However, when this RFIE is deployed as a real Apologise, it portrays a sense of seriousness (see Edmondson, 1981), as the following examples illustrate:

(4.30) No – I am sorry, that was a bit provocative.

(4.31) I am sorry to hear about the lavatories.

This expression is not frequently used in the public interpersonal scenarios of our dataset. However, whenever it is deployed in this scenario it indicates irony and the standard situation of what we define as 'Introductory commenting'. This standard situation encompasses contexts in which the speaker has the right (and maybe perceived obligation) to be ironic in introducing particular complaining comments. The following examples illustrate this function:

(4.32) I am sorry if it means opposing the official candidate, but I would vote for Frank Field.

(4.33) I am sorry, Mr Speaker, but I could not hear as an honourable Friend was standing up.

(4.34) I am sorry that the Prime Minister is continuing to run away from the electorate.

As Bull et al. (2020) argue, interactions between politicians and the Speaker of the House in the British Parliament often take the form of commenting. Therefore, it is no coincidence that, in our dataset, the standard situation

Exploring speech acts through expressions in L2 pragmatics   55

'Introductory commenting' consists of political interactions like the above examples, and as such somewhat overlaps with 'Institutional with power salience'.

Even when this RFIE is not used ironically, it often performs a non-apologetic function, as the following examples illustrate:

(4.35) No, I am sorry, but I must conclude.

(4.36) It's nice to get back to Bishop's Castle Railway tickets, but I am sorry to say these are the last you will see as I have no more suitable for reproduction in the journal.

As examples (4.35) and (4.36) demonstrate, the RFIE *I am sorry* is often used as a Disarmer (Edmondson and House, 1981) rather than expressing an Apologise. When this RFIE is accompanied by *well*, it is used to refer to a mistake that the recipient has made (Edmondson and House, 1981), as the following example shows:

(4.37) The crowd was full of pickpockets, as I pointed out to him, and I could have easily said, well, I am sorry Oscar, but you know it is one of the risks here.

I am very/so sorry
We have not categorised the RFIE *I am very/so sorry* into various standard situations and interpersonal scenarios because eleven of its fifty-five occurrences in the BNC do not provide information about pragmatic context. Apart from the assessment provided by our native speakers that this is a frequently used variant of *sorry*, the RFIE *I am very/so sorry* is important to the present investigation because our analysis has shown that it always operates as a real Apologise, as the following example illustrate:

(4.38) I am very sorry to inform you that your appeal was unsuccessful.

(4.39) 'I am so sorry', the woman began without a trace of sorrow in her eyes.

These examples indicate that a direct relationship exists in English between this RFIE form and the speech act Apologise.

Apologise RFIEs (duibuqi-variants) in Chinese
Duibuqi
As the RFIE *duibuqi*, just like the English *sorry*, has a relatively simple conventionalised usage, here we only provide an overview of how it has been used in the various standard situations.

Table 4.9 *Allocation of the RFIE* duibuqi *in the corpus*

Standard situation	Number of examples	Dyadic (D) Multiparty (M) Public (P)
Institutional with power-salience	13	D2; M7; P4
Institutional without power-salience	8	D1; M7
Ceremonial/Family	29	D4; M16; P9

Table 4.9 shows two key interrelated features of this RFIE:

1. Its use is preferred in the standard situation 'ceremonial' (often in family ceremonies).
2. It is often performed in front of various people (multiparty interpersonal settings) or even the public. This is in accordance with the fact that ritual public Apologise is highly desirable in the Chinese linguaculture (see Kádár et al., 2018).

These features all indicate that *duibuqi* is strongly anchored in the speech act Apologise. This is also illustrated by the fact that *duibuqi* – and its multi-word variants studied below – *never* fulfils a non-speech-act-anchored function.

Duibuqi + object

The RFIE *duibuqi* is frequently modified by an object and, in this form, it performs a more deferential function than *duibuqi* alone, as our panel of Chinese native speakers confirmed. Yet, in terms of pragmatic use, this RFIE is rather similar to its single-word counterpart *duibuqi*, as Table 4.10 below illustrates.

Table 4.10 *Allocation of the RFIE* duibuqi + object *in the corpus*

Standard situation	Number of examples	Dyadic (D) Multiparty (M) Public (P)
Institutional with power-salience	13	D3; M4; P6
Institutional without power-salience	6	D3; M3
Ceremonial/Family	31	D3; M9; P19

As Table 4.10 shows, perhaps the most important difference between *duibuqi + object* and *duibuqi* is that the former RFIE is most frequently used in public interpersonal scenarios. It is worth noting that the object element of this RFIE can include the informal second person Chinese pronoun *ni* 你 or its formal counterpart *nin* 您, but it is frequently preceded by a noun that indicates the recipient's interactional identity and/or status, hence making the RFIE even more deferential in nature. The following examples illustrate this use:

Exploring speech acts through expressions in L2 pragmatics 57

(4.40) 锦华，<u>对不起</u>你，我要巡逻去了。
Jinhua, I <u>apologise to</u> (lit. offended) you (T form), I am going on patrol.

(4.41) 老师<u>对不起</u>你。道歉的话不能带到中学去。请你原谅我。
Teacher (respectful reference) I <u>apologise to</u> (lit. offended) you (T form; here indicates emotional proximity). I cannot express this apology at the secondary school. Please forgive me.

Interestingly, the different levels of deference which are conveyed by these two examples do not fundamentally influence the pragmatic weight of the RFIE cluster: both examples are drawn from the standard situation 'institutional without power-salience' and they occur in dyadic interpersonal scenarios. This demonstrates that while the style of the RFIE *duibuqi + object* can vary, this variation does not, in essence, influence its pragmatic power.

Upgrader + duibuqi + object
The speech act-anchor of the RFIE *duibuqi* can be increased if an Upgrader such as *shizai* 实在 ('genuinely') or *zhen* 真 ('really') modifies it. This speech act-anchor does not saliently change the operation of this RFIE compared to its counterparts *duibuqi* and *duibuqi + object*, as Table 4.11 illustrates.

Table 4.11 *Allocation of the RFIE* upgrader + duibuqi + object *in the corpus*

Standard situation	Number of examples	Dyadic (D) Multiparty (M) Public (P)
Institutional with power-salience	16	D4; M9; P3
Institutional without power-salience	8	D2; M2; P4
Ceremonial/Family	26	D1; M11; P14

As Table 4.11 indicates, the RFIE *upgrader + duibuqi + object* is anchored in the speech act Apologise, in keeping with the other *duibuqi*-variants. The following example illustrates the use of this RFIE in a ceremonial public Apologise:

(4.42) 这事我全忘啦，<u>真对不起老人家</u>
I absolutely forgot this matter, and <u>seriously offended the elderly people</u> (*zhen[upgrader]-duibuqi-object*)

Contrastive analysis
From a contrastive pragmatic point of view, the analysis of the English and Chinese groups of Apologise expressions shows a remarkable similarity with that of the Requestive RFIE groups. In the case of Apologise expressions, it is evident that the Chinese RFIE forms are 'speech act-anchored' because of

their honorific origin, unlike their English counterparts. In Chinese, even the single-word RFIE *duibuqi* practically always performs an Apologetic function, and the same is valid for its multi-word counterparts. In English, only one specific multi-word RFIE – *I am very/so sorry* – is Apologetic, while the other expressions are found to have an ambiguous relationship with the speech act Apologise. This difference is manifested in the interpersonal use of the RFIEs we have here examined. The English RFIE *sorry* and its variants are used infrequently in public interpersonal scenarios, whereas *duibuqi* and its variants conventionally occur in solemn public Apologies. This confirms the previous contrastive finding, i.e. the Chinese RFIE forms studied here are deferential by default and have a conventionalised speech act-anchored relationship with speech acts, whereas it is difficult, if not impossible, to argue the same about their English counterparts.

4.3.2 The L2 pragmatic study of RFIEs

The L2 pragmatic part of the case study reported here consists of a questionnaire study, by means of which we aim to obtain L2 learners' evaluations of the RFIEs contrasted. Following this, we conducted interviews with those learners, asking them about their reasons for evaluating the RFIEs under investigation in particular ways.

In preparing a questionnaire for our L2 learners, we decided to simplify the results of our previous corpus-based research. For instance, we ignored the standard situation 'Introductory commenting' because in our view this is not a standard situation an average learner frequently encounters. In addition, we attempted to come up with clear contrasts between the use of the RFIE pairs studied, by approaching them according to what appears to be the contrastively most salient differences between their uses. Table 4.12 summarises the contrastively salient uses of the RFIEs, according to which we built up our questionnaire presented to our students.

Table 4.12 *Contrastively salient uses of the RFIEs studied*

Chinese RFIEs	English RFIEs
qing – contrastively salient context: Family/Ceremonial	*please* – contrastively salient context: Service Encounter
duibuqi – contrastively salient context: Family/Ceremonial	*sorry* – contrastively salient context: Family/Ceremonial

We distributed two different questionnaires to our Mainland Chinese and British respondents via email and WeChat. Both groups received a set of four examples from their L2, consisting of two times two examples of the 'foreign' RFIEs. Two of the four examples were taken from the naturally occurring corpus we investigated in the previous step of our study, while we constructed the other two examples as 'quasi-back translations' (henceforth

Exploring speech acts through expressions in L2 pragmatics

'quasi-BT') of real examples. By 'quasi-back translation' we mean cases in which we mirrored the linguacultural use of an RFIE in the other language, not necessarily by translating an utterance into the other language, but rather by providing the respondents with a case that pragmatically resembled the use of an RFIE in their L1.[3] For instance, we provided the Chinese learners with a fictive example where the RFIE *please* is used in a similar ceremonial fashion to its Chinese counterpart, hence reflecting the Chinese use of *qing*, even though the English *please* is not normally used to indicate ceremonial standard situations. Ultimately, 50 per cent of the examples in the questionnaire (followed by our actual questions) were set up as 'hidden traps' for the respondents.

The complete list of the eight examples that we deployed in this study is as follows:

(4.43) The following utterance takes place during a public ceremony in China. A younger speaker addresses the head of the family in front of various other family members. The person apologising expresses real regret, conveying the utterance in a highly emotive way and with excessive body language.

对不起，也害了妹 ...
Duibuqi, ye haile mei ...
Sorry, we hurt younger sister ... (Chinese corpus)
Authentic example shown to British English learners of Chinese

This is an authentic Chinese public Apology taken from our corpus, in which the RFIE *duibuqi* is deployed.

(4.44) The following utterance takes place during a public ceremony in England. A younger speaker addresses the head of the family in front of various other family members. The person apologising expresses real regret, conveying the utterance in a highly emotive way and with excessive body language.

Sorry for violating the interest of our family. (fictive example)
Quasi-BT of example (1) shown to Chinese learners of English

This is a constructed example – which we have defined in our study as a 'quasi-BT' example – because it is an adaptation of example (4.33) and uses the RFIE *sorry*. We have constructed this example with the intention of gauging the reaction of the respondents.

(4.45) The following example takes place between a lecturer and a student (the utterance is spoken by the lecturer) in a classroom in England. The lecturer speaks in a regular tone, the student and his peers are attentive and the atmosphere in the class is friendly:

How many tens in one hundred? Oh <u>sorry</u>, ten. (British English corpus)
Authentic example shown to Chinese learners of English

Again, this is an authentic example, this time taken from our British English corpus, in which the RFIE *sorry* is deployed to indicate the standard situation of 'classroom', used by a teacher.

> (4.46) The following example takes place between a lecturer and a student (the utterance is spoken by the lecturer) in a classroom in China. The lecturer speaks in a regular tone, the student and his peers are attentive and the atmosphere in the class is friendly:
>
> 15 加 24，对不起，15 加 20，一共是多少？(fictive example)
> *15 jia 24, <u>duibuqi</u>, 15 jia 20, yigong duoshao?*
> Fifteen plus twenty-four, sorry, fifteen plus twenty, how much is it altogether?
> *Quasi-BT of example (3) shown to British English learners of Chinese*

This is a fictive example of a Chinese mathematics teacher saying the 'same' as her or his English 'colleague' in example (4.45). Unlike in British English, in Chinese the use of the RFIE *duibuqi* would be inappropriate in this setting, primarily because it would be too speech act-anchored for the simple act of self-correction.

> (4.47) The following example takes place during a public ceremony in China. The speaker is talking to a highly ranked person in a particularly emotive manner, and people around them are watching the event with reverence:
>
> 你是咱们家乡的文化人，请你多出主意，帮助我们办好博物馆。(Chinese corpus)
> *Ni shi zanmen jiaxiang de wenhuaren, <u>qing</u> ni duochu zhuyi, bangzhu women banhao bowuguan.*
> You are the most cultured person in our village, <u>please</u> give us attention and help us to establish the museum.
> *Authentic example shown to British English learners of Chinese*

This is an authentic example taken from our Chinese corpus, where the RFIE *qing* indicates the standard situation of a public 'ceremony'.

> (4.48) The following example takes place during a public ceremony in England. The speaker talks to a highly ranked person in a particularly emotive manner, and people around them are watching the event with reverence:

Please, you really have to accept this honour. (fictive example)
Quasi-BT of example (5) shown to Chinese learners of English

This is the quasi-BT which mirrors example (4.47) which we constructed for our investigation.

(4.49) The following example takes place in a British store (and is uttered by the vendor). The interaction is ordinary in style, and both the vendor and customer are satisfied with this instance of language use:

That'll be five pounds, please. (British English corpus)
Authentic example shown to Chinese learners of English

The above is an authentic example taken from our British English corpus, in which the RFIE *please* indicates the standard situation of 'service encounter'.

(4.50) The following example takes place in a Chinese store (and is uttered by the vendor). The interaction is ordinary in style, and both the vendor and customer are satisfied with this instance of language use:

先生，请，这个大衣付149块。(fictive example)
Xiansheng, qing, nin zhege dayi fu 149 kuai.
Mister, please, this is going to be RMB 49.
Quasi-BT of example (4.49) shown to British English learners of Chinese

This example is the quasi-BT version of the above example (4.49).

We distributed our questionnaire to the following two groups of foreign learners:

- Seven British learners of Chinese, and
- Seven Chinese learners of British English.

All the respondents were females under the age of thirty. We recruited this small group of students with the help of personal acquaintances in China and the UK. All respondents were graduate students in the humanities, with no language background other than their native language and their single target language.

We first secured the availability of respondents via email and WeChat (the most influential social media messaging app in China). We sent both groups a set of utterances in which the RFIEs investigated were deployed in their target languages in both appropriate and inappropriate ways. We did not show our respondents the use of the corresponding RFIEs in their L1, nor did we provide any information about the pragmatic appropriacy of the examples.

At this stage, we only asked the respondents to evaluate the examples as either 'appropriate' or 'inappropriate'. For reasons of efficiency, we sent the examples to each respondent at different times, i.e. we did not distribute the questionnaires in one batch. Approximately one hour after the questionnaire had been distributed, we called each respondent to interview them regarding their evaluation of the pragmatic appropriacy of the data that had been sent to them. We conducted interviews with all the respondents to gain an understanding of the motivations that lay behind their evaluations.

On average, each interview lasted approximately 10 to 20 minutes, and we conducted these interviews on video-Skype or WeChat. The interviews were conducted in English for both the British English and Mainland Chinese respondents; English was chosen because only one interviewer was sufficiently fluent in Chinese and all the Chinese respondents were fluent English speakers. We transcribed the interviews by using a simple transcription approach.

Analysis and results
In our questionnaire, the following two instructions were presented to the respondents:

1. Read the four examples on the sheet below. Which of these examples do you find acceptable?
2. Why is a particular example acceptable/unacceptable to you? Please reflect on your evaluations and be prepared to be interviewed about them in an hour.

With regard to the first instruction, the respondents returned a short list detailing which examples were 'acceptable' or 'unacceptable' to them. We measured the overall number of appropriate and inappropriate evaluations per group. Tables 4.13 and 4.14 show the summative results of this experiment. Due to ethical considerations, we used acronyms for our anonymised respondents.

The British respondents were very good at evaluating the appropriate examples (4.43) and (4.47), which they appear to have regarded as being typical 'exotic' forms of Chinese pragmatic behaviour. Regaring this phenomenon of exoticisation, a particularly important publication is Said's (1978) seminal study on Orientalism; another relevant work is Katan's (2009) research on exoticisation in the context of pragmatics. The British respondents performed significantly worse in the two inappropriate cases (examples 4.46 and 4.50), the evaluation of which appears to have been anchored in their native English competence, as the interview extracts analysed below will illustrate. Interestingly, the responses of the Chinese group were not demarcated along the lines of whether the examples were appropriate or inappropriate – as was the case with the British respondents – but rather it was example (4.45) (appropriate) and (4.48) (inappropriate) that appear to

Exploring speech acts through expressions in L2 pragmatics

Table 4.13 *The response rate of the British English respondents*

	Example (1) appropriate	Example (4) inappropriate	Example (5) appropriate	Example (8) inappropriate
Respondent 1 Lucy	✓	✗	✓	✗
Respondent 2 Helen	✓	✗	✓	✓
Respondent 3 Debby	✓	✗	✓	✗
Respondent 4 Lizzie	✓	✓	✓	✗
Respondent 5 Alice	✓	✗	✓	✓
Respondent 6 Linda	✓	✓	✗	✗
Respondent 7 Julie	✓	✗	✓	✓
Rate of appropriate responses	100%	28.6%	85.7%	42.9%

Table 4.14 *The response rate of the Chinese respondents*

	Example (2) inappropriate	Example (3) appropriate	Example (6) inappropriate	Example (7) appropriate
Respondent 1 Meifang	✓	✗	✗	✓
Respondent 2 Na	✗	✓	✓	✓
Respondent 3 Xiaolin	✓	✗	✓	✓
Respondent 4 Wenyi	✓	✓	✗	✓
Respondent 5 Yang	✓	✗	✗	✓
Respondent 6 Guimei	✓	✗	✗	✓
Respondent 7 Wei	✗	✓	✓	✓
Rate of appropriate responses	71.4%	42.9%	42.9%	100%

have caused particular evaluative difficulties for this group of respondents. Their overall appropriate response rate for both examples (4.45) and (4.48) was low. Our interpretation of this discrepancy is that the Chinese group's responses are most likely due to transfer from their native interactional norms, as the interview extracts below also illustrate. However, their inappropriate evaluations had nothing to do with stereotypical perceptions of the target linguaculture, but rather reflected their native perceptions of how language should be used in a certain standard situation or context ('classroom' and 'ceremony') in their L1.

The British respondents
The only British respondent to inappropriately evaluate an appropriate use of a Chinese RFIE was Linda, who evaluated example (4.47) as inappropriate. When asked about her evaluation, she replied with the following:

> Because this is such a pompous and ceremonial example, the use of *qing* is inappropriate in that the example obviously represents a very formal interaction. The difference of power here would make the use of 'please' highly unlikely. Why would anybody say 'please' to their superior in such a situation, particularly in a culture like Chinese?

Obviously, Linda exoticised this appropriate ceremonial use of the RFIE *qing*. For the remaining respondents, this example must have matched their perception of the Chinese linguaculture. The appropriate example (4.43), which is equally as ceremonial as example (4.47), was unanimously evaluated as appropriate. Our interpretation of this evaluative tendency is that the ceremonial use of the RFIE *duibuqi* (sorry) is not alien to British learners of Chinese. Various responses, such as Lucy's, also confirm this point:

> To my knowledge, the Chinese are fond of empty public apologies. I saw this so often in soap operas. This example read a bit alien to me, but I think it is okay.

The British interview data becomes even more intriguing when it comes to the interpretation of the inappropriate use of the RFIEs under investigation. Example (4.46) in our questionnaire is a case of interactional repair, in which we quasi-back translated example (4.45) in British English – where the use of the RFIE *sorry* would be perfectly valid – into Chinese. However, in the equivalent Chinese classroom interaction featured in example (4.47), teachers would rarely use the RFIE *duibuqi* ('sorry'), as we have highlighted earlier. Yet, many of the British respondents who had not grown up in China and had only limited experience of interacting with L1 Chinese speaking lecturers – and such experience might not have included the subject of mathematics featured in this example – interpreted the Chinese utterance inappropriately. Thus, the rate of inappropriate responses was high. Helen's response below illustrates this tendency towards an inappropriate evaluation:

> If somebody makes a mistake, say, at the blackboard, if they do something inappropriate, they should apologise. This obviously includes

Exploring speech acts through expressions in L2 pragmatics 65

teachers as well. If you give wrong information to your students, you are supposed to correct yourself.

Interestingly, Lizzie – who appropriately evaluated the inappropriate example (4.47) – rightly stated that, to her knowledge, the Chinese RFIE *duibuqi* is much more momentous than its English counterpart *sorry*, which is often a rather 'light' or 'give-away' expression. This is in accordance with the findings of our corpus-based investigation reported earlier in this chapter. Let us quote here Lizzie's interpretation of example (4.47):

> I think this Chinese sentence is unlikely to have occurred. Actually, *duibuqi* is only used when people MEAN their apology. This is very different from how people in this country [Britain: our addition] use sorry.

Furthermore, Lizzie also stated during the interview that, as a foreign learner of Chinese, she feels insecure using the RFIE *duibuqi* because she perceives this word to be somewhat 'dangerous' to use:

> Using *duibuqi* makes me feel awkward. You don't hear many people saying it on the street. And because of this you don't really know how to use it.

Not all the respondents provided a well-argued explanation for their (mis) interpretation of this example. For instance, Alice inappropriately interpreted example (4.47), saying that the Chinese are "more polite" than the British:

> I think politeness is fundamental in the Chinese culture. Because of this, it is quite logical for a teacher to apologise. The Chinese are just more polite than the Brits, and I think the Chinese learn to use polite words already in school. The Chinese also love authority, and I think children would be pretty much forced on every occasion to use polite expressions, so for a teacher like the one in this example it is simply normal to use a polite word to provide a good example for her students.

The number of inappropriate responses (4 out of 7) was almost as high for example (4.50) as was the case for example (4.47). Again, we can observe a transfer from the respondents' native British linguaculture – where the use of the RFIE *please* is a matter of convention in service encounters – to the Chinese quasi-BT example. Debby explained her evaluation of example (4.50) as follows:

> The Chinese word *qing* is basically the same as 'please' in English. Many Chinese of my generation are very polite and I think it is perfectly fine to use *qing* to a customer in a shop. Chinese businesses are nowadays

completely Westernised because there are so many Western chains in China, like Starbucks and McDonalds. So, I don't see why *qing* could not be used. Like, this is especially the case if someone's buying a coat rather than some cheap item in a shop. But in your example the coat seems to be sold for a friendly price.

Obviously, Debby's response reflects a major pragmatic transfer from her native tongue to her target language. Various other respondents also misinterpreted example (4.50) as appropriate, but their responses during the interview were more nuanced. For example, Lizzie, who appropriately interpreted the other three examples, explained her inappropriate evaluation as follows:

I wasn't exactly sure whether this example is appropriate or not. However, I had the feeling that it could work because in a shop it may be okay to use *qing*, depending on an individual's style. While I haven't heard this word [i.e. *qing*; our addition] too often in Chinese shops, it could be fine.

To sum up, what the British interviewees and their explanations reveal is that British learners of Chinese are mostly able to appropriately interpret the appropriate uses of the RFIEs in question, primarily because such uses coincided with their stereotypes of the Chinese linguaculture. However, in the case of the invalid use of the RFIEs, inappropriate evaluations and related metapragmatic explanations emerged primarily because the British respondents relied on pragmatic transfer from their native linguaculture, i.e. they reinterpreted non-conventionalised uses of the RFIEs as conventionalised and heavily ritual uses. We found significant variation between the insights provided by the respondents into the pragmatic differences between British and Chinese linguacultures. Such differences could be due to many reasons, including the personal backgrounds of the interviewees, their length and quality of exposure to the Chinese linguaculture, the amount and level of Chinese teaching they had received or simply their lingua cultural sensitivity.

The Chinese respondents

Example (4.49) was interpreted appropriately by all the Chinese respondents. In the interviews, they confirmed that this example was more or less in accordance with what they had learnt from their English language textbooks, which included many examples of business transactions. In other words, the Chinese respondents were pragmatically competent in this particular standard situation and related conventionalised language use. For instance, Wei explained her evaluation as follows:

I know many British students from my university, and I also played role games in class. While I've never been to Britain, this language you can see in all the textbooks. So, it must be appropriate.

Exploring speech acts through expressions in L2 pragmatics 67

Na voiced a much more sophisticated view of what happens in buying–selling ritual scenarios in the two cultures:

> My cousin studied in Sussex and just returned home with a degree in literature. We talked a lot about life in the UK, and she told me that the British people in shops are very robotic and say the same things on many occasions. In China, if you know the people owning the shop, you will have a special and very friendly relationship with them. Nobody will speak like a robot. The English can be both very polite and friendly in their style, but my cousin felt that they don't really mean what they say. It's funny that this topic came up in this interview because my cousin actually mentioned *please*. For a Chinese person, using '*please*' all the time is strange.

We found Na's response insightful, as she provided a very detailed metapragmatic account on the use of the RFIE *please* in the British English standard situation and the related ritual frame under investigation.

Example (4.44) – which represents a quasi-BT of a public Apologise – also triggered many appropriate evaluations. Meifang provided an insightful explanation as to why she thought this example was inappropriate:

> In Chinese culture, apologising in public is needed sometimes. We are a polite nation. The Chinese is an ancient culture where sometimes you need to express your regret for having done something by saying sorry to someone else in front of others. This restores harmony between people. We even apologise to others in our families. Actually, in my family people would definitely apologise to each other in front of other family members if there was a need for this because family matters more than outside people. I have the impression that Westerners don't do this. When I spoke to Western people, I felt that they are less emotional than us Chinese and they don't care about their families as much as we do, and it would be difficult to imagine Westerners apologising in front of others because they mostly think of themselves.

While Meifang's response is, of course, heavily loaded with cultural stereotypes, it clearly illustrates that public apologies are perceived differently in the two linguacultures. Unlike Meifang, both Na and Wei failed to properly evaluate this example, although they evaluated all the other cases appropriately. Na provided the following explanation:

> It doesn't matter where you are, people apologise everywhere. If you offend one of your family members badly, it is natural to apologise.

The appropriate example (4.45) – which features a British classroom scenario – triggered a surprisingly large number of inappropriate evaluations.

Almost all the respondents who provided an inappropriate evaluation voiced their opinion that a lecturer is not supposed to apologise in a classroom, i.e. they misinterpreted the use of the RFIE *sorry* as a real Apologise when it was simply a 'self-correction'. In our view, the reason for this could be that the RFIE *duibuqi* is used to indicate substantial transgressions in the Chinese linguaculture. For instance, Guimei told us the following:

> Why would a teacher ever apologise if he hasn't done anything wrong? He has the authority, and apologising would destroy this authority. If a teacher apologised, it would make the students feel uncertain and nervous, and they would think that the teacher is not a good teacher. This is not good for the students, and also not for the teacher himself.

Yang also appears to have misunderstood the situation. However, her explanation is slightly different from Guimei's, in that she related her misunderstanding of the pragmatic use of the RFIE to her personal life experience, by stating the following:

> I have never heard any teacher in China apologise in front of students. If there was something wrong and a teacher had to apologise, he would do this in private, maybe by involving the parents of the students. In Chinese culture, if an apology was made to a student, it would also concern the student's family because Chinese families are very close, and a school needs to communicate with the parents of a student.

The inappropriate example (4.48) triggered an equal number of inappropriate evaluations as were triggered by example (4.45). Example (4.48) is not 'exotic' from a Chinese point of view. In Chinese it is perfectly acceptable to deploy the RFIE *qing* ('please') when speaking to a highly ranked person in the ritual frame triggered by a public ceremony. The Chinese respondents might have found the similar use of the RFIE *please* to be acceptable in the fictive English example. Wenyi explained this by referring to customs in Chinese ceremonies:

> While the example doesn't tell who the speaker is, he must be lower-ranking than the prince. So yes, using *please* is all right here. Respect is important in ceremonies all over the world, and to be honest we use a lot of such words in Chinese ceremonies. I think this also works in English.

Unlike Wenyi, Na rightly evaluated the example as inappropriate, by saying the following:

> I don't think that the English would say something like this. The sentence sounds like a translation of Chinese because *please* sounds so

strange here. In English, people use please to ask for things, but I am not sure if this man asks for something at all. Is it not that he GIVES something to the prince?

While Na was unable to respond in the way that a pragmatician would, her response is important to us because it coincides exactly with what our corpus-based research on the RFIEs *please* and *qing* has revealed: while *qing* is frequently used in ceremonies, *please* is not an expression that would indicate this standard situation in our British corpus.

To sum up, the above L2 pragmatic study has shown that the evaluative failures of the Chinese respondents were quite different from the evaluative failures of their British counterparts. In the former case, the failures were primarily motivated by pragmatic transfer and the related overinterpretation of the examples that were presented to them. The Chinese respondents appear to be less influenced by stereotypes than their British peers. At the same time, they have been more prompt to apply their own Chinese norms of language use to foreign language data.

4.4 Conclusion

In this chapter we have examined how cross-cultural pragmatics can be brought together with L2 pragmatics in the study of expressions associated with speech acts, i.e. RFIEs. Here we only provided a relatively simple use of our model, in that we only focused on two speech acts, i.e. Request and Apologise, by considering whether RFIEs indicate them in a particular context (speech act-anchored use) or not (non-speech-act-anchored) use. Notwithstanding the simplicity of this question, our analysis has shown that by bringing together contrastive pragmatic corpus analysis and contrastive L2 research, one can tease out complex differences between the linguacultures involved, and these pragmatic differences may trigger L2 learner difficulties and misunderstandings. In Chapter 5, we will present a more complex step in the L2 pragmatic study of the relationship between expressions and speech acts, designed as *altered speech act indication*.

4.5 Recommended reading

Edmondson, Willis. (1981). On saying you're sorry. In Florian Coulmas (ed.), Conversational Routine: Explorations in Standardized Communication Situations and Prepatterned Speech. The Hague: Mouton, pp. 273–287.
Edmondson's study is particularly relevant for readers who are interested in why the use of expressions that we have defined as RFIEs in this chapter is important to indicate standard situations and related rights and obligations. The following is an excerpt from this study:

There is a sense in which most, if not all, of everyday conversational activity can be described as 'routinal' or 'conventionalized'. This follows from the notion of discourse structure, the notion that "the moment of conversation is started whatever is said is a determining factor for what in any reasonable expectation may follow" (Firth, 1964: 94). We may indeed go further and suggest that given a situational context, social members have strong expectations as to what types of conversation may occur in such a context, and how such a conversation may be started. (See here Hasan 1978, as the notions of a 'structural formula' and 'contextual configuration,' specifying the behavioral options for participants in classes of social events.) Thus it is perfectly feasible to chart behavioral possibilities both for the case in which a conversational goal is determined by a specific goal of conversational opening ... and for the case in which a specific situation limits severely the types of transaction that may licitly occur in that situation. For example to join a queue in front of a box office, or to take a seat in a restaurant is to commit oneself in advance to specific types of conversational behavior with the ticket-seller or waitress ... Consider here Halliday's remark that "From a sociological point of view, a text is meaningful not so much because we do not know what the speaker is going to say, as in a mathematical model of communication, as because we do know" (Halliday, 1975: 129).

In order to interpret such remarks, and begin to discuss some different types of routine in discourse, I wish initially to make two central relevant discussions: firstly between what conversationalists may be said to 'know' as opposed to what they actually do, which I shall link with a distinction between communicative and social competence, and secondly, between what is said in an ongoing conversational encounter, and what is done thereby (Labov, 1972). (Edmondson, 1981: 273)

Bardovi-Harlig, Kathleen. (2012). Formulas, routines, and conventional expressions in pragmatics research. *Annual Review of Applied Linguistics* **32, 206–227.**
Kathleen Bardovi-Harlig has done significant work on expressions, which we also studied in this chapter. In the excerpt below, Bardovi-Harlig presents a definition of the term formula:

The use of the term *formula* in contemporary empirical pragmatics refers to recurrent strings or expressions used for specific pragmatic purposes. Formulas often succinctly capture the illocutionary force of a contribution by virtue of the fact that the speech community in which they are used has tacitly agreed on their form, meaning, and use. In contrast to many of the other articles in this volume that represent different perspectives, this article considers formulas primarily for their social and pragmatic value.

Following Crystal (1997), pragmatics is "the study of language from the point of view of users, especially of the choices they make, the constraints they encounter in using language in social interaction and the effects their use of language has on other participants in the act of communication" (p. 301). Outside of pragmatics, authors often cite pragmatics as an area in which formulas are frequent. Granger (1998), for example, attributed the growing research in pragmatics as one impetus to study formulas. Inside pragmatics, researchers are interested in formulas because they are one type of linguistic resource available to speakers to do things with words, and they may be extraordinarily effective at doing those things; they reflect norms of speech communities; and they are targets of learning for both newcomers (or novices) and language learners. Coulmas (1981) described routine formulae as "highly conventionalized prepatterned expressions whose occurrence is tied to more or less standardized communication situations" (pp. 2–3) and emphasised the social aspect of formulas by describing them as "tacit agreements, which the members of a community presume to be shared by every reasonable co-member. In embodying societal knowledge they are essential in the handling of day-to-day situations" (p. 4).

Knowledge of conventional expressions forms part of a speaker's pragmalinguistic competence, and knowledge of their use and the contexts in which they occur is part of sociopragmatic competence. Coulmas (1981) and Edmondson and House (1991) emphasized the social contract to which reasonable comembers of a speech community are party, and Terkourafi (2002) showed that formulas are used to demonstrate membership. In pragmatics, definitions of formulaic language include three parts: the form as a recurrent sequence, its occurrence in specific social contexts, and the idea of the social contract which extends to members of a particular speech community. (Bardovi-Harlig, 2012: 207)

Notes

1. The English RFIEs could, in theory, be 'translated' into Chinese. For instance, the RFIE *could you please* could be 'translated' as *nengfou-qing* 能否请 'may I request you to'. However, as native speakers of Chinese confirmed, this translation sounds rather 'artificial'. In addition, as far as our corpus is concerned, such forms only occur infrequently. Also note that two of our respondents mentioned *kenqing* 恳请 as a possible RFIE candidate to study, but they mentioned that *kenqing* is archaic in style and is less frequent in present-day Chinese (written) interaction than *fanqing* and *jingqing*.

2. Note that this RFIE is also used in the standard situation that we have defined as 'institutional without power'; however, in our sample of fifty utterances which have been selected for this chapter, this standard situation fell below the threshold of 8 per cent.
3. We avoided mirror-translating our examples, otherwise we would have had to compromise on how 'authentic' our examples sounded.

CHAPTER 5

On the problem of altered speech act indication in L2 Pragmatics

5.1 Introduction

In this chapter, we continue discussing the relationship between expressions and speech acts in L2 pragmatics by moving on to a more complex phenomenon than the one we covered in the previous chapter, namely altered speech act indication. More specifically, staying with our interest in Chinese learners of English and foreign learners of Chinese, here we examine how Chinese learners of English evaluate what we call **'altered speech act-indication'** of those expressions that are conventionally associated with one particular speech act. As we pointed out in Chapter 4, in every language there is a strongly conventionalised relationship between expressions – which we defined as RFIEs – and speech acts, even though the type of this relationship is subject to linguacultural variation. The notion of 'altered speech act-indication' has its origin in the fact that many RFIEs can conventionally indicate more than just one speech act, or completely lose their speech act-indicating function.

We explore the phenomenon of 'altered speech act-indication' by focusing on the evaluations of such expressions by Chinese learners of English. In this chapter we proceed as follows. First, we present the results of a contrastive pragmatic corpus-based inquiry to examine an L2 pragmatic issue, similar to how we proceeded in Chapter 4. Following this, we present the results of a DCT. Finally, we conclude the chapter.

5.2 The first phase of our research

Our L2 pragmatic study builds on a previous corpus-based investigation of the use of RFIEs normally associated with the speech acts of Thanks and Greet in Chinese and English (see House and Kádár, 2021a). In that study, we followed Coulmas (1979) who had argued early on that one is advised to use contrastive research to rigorously map the use of routinised expressions across linguacultures.

Our corpus-based study was based on an interview in which two panels of ten native speakers of Chinese and English identified comparable RFIEs in Chinese and English. The native speakers were requested to provide three expressions which in their view are frequently used to realise Thanks and Greet in their native tongues. The respondents were also asked to provide reasons for their choices of expressions. The interviewees were told that practically any expression is acceptable, irrespective of whether the context involves power or social distance. We also informed the interviewees that they were to accept expressions used in both spoken language and other modes of interaction such as phone calls and computer-mediated communication. As an outcome of the interview results, we decided to focus on the following pairs of most frequently mentioned RFIEs:

Thanks

1. *Thank you (English)*
   Xiexie[ni] 谢谢[你] *(Chinese)*
2. *Thank you very much (English)*
   Feichang ganxie[ni] 非常感谢[你] *(Chinese)*

Greet

1. *Hello/Hallo (English)*
   Wei 喂 *(Chinese)*
2. *Good morning/afternoon/evening (English)*
   Ni hao 你好 *(Chinese)*

The interviewees were requested to reflect on the following issues relating to their choices:

1. The difference between the expressions *Thank you* and *Thank you very much*, which seemed to use being essentially variants.
2. The prevalence of the typically phone-call response expression *Wei* ('Hello') which many of the Chinese respondents mentioned.

With regard to point 1, various interviewees stated that they mentioned both *Thank you* and *Thank you very much* because these RFIEs imply different things for them:

> *Respondent 5 (English)*
> *Thank you* and *Thank you very much* are two different RFIEs in British English. Essentially, while *Thank you* is a simple expression, *Thank you very much* can be both very genuine and very sarcastic.

Feedback from the respondents showed that it is important to look at *Thank you* and *Thank you very much* as two different RFIEs associated with the speech act Thanks. As regards point 2, the Chinese respondents confirmed that *Wei* should be discussed separately from *Ni hao* not only because the former is frequented in phone calls but also because it has noteworthy functions in face-to-face interaction. See, for example, the following interview excerpt:

> *Respondent 1 (Chinese)*
> 当然，"喂"在电话通过中更为常见。但同时，"喂"在口语中的使用很频繁。
> Of course, *Wei* occurs frequently in phone conversations. But at the same time *Wei* has complex uses in spoken language as well.

Such feedback revealed that the expression *Wei* should be studied alongside *Ni hao* as a most frequent form of Greet in Chinese.

Our work (House and Kádár, 2021a) has shown that the relationship between RFIEs and speech acts should be approached through the following binary and non-binary pairs of analytic categories:

1. Normal speech act-indicating use of RFIEs versus **transformed speech act-indicating use** of RFIEs (*binary pair*). This pair implies that certain RFIEs such as *Thank you* can either indicate the speech act of Thanks it is normally associated with, or can indicate an entirely different speech act such as Complain.
2. Normal speech act-indicating use of RFIEs versus **non-speech act-anchored use** of RFIEs (*binary pair*). This pair implies that certain RFIEs such as *Hello* in English and *Wei* in Chinese can either be used to indicate the speech act they are normally associated with – in this case Greet – or can lose this function entirely and be used in non-speech act-anchored ways, such as an attention-getting Alerter (see Blum-Kulka et al., 1989: 276).
3. Normal speech act-indicating use of RFIEs plus **modified speech act-indicating use** of RFIEs (*non-binary pair*). This pair implies that a given expression may indicate various speech acts simultaneously. For example, both *Thank you* and *Xiexie* can mutually indicate the speech acts of Thanks and Leave-Take.

Figure 5.1 illustrates this system of analytic pairs:

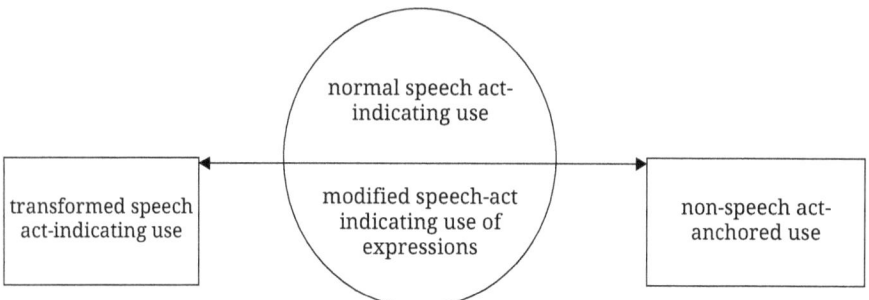

Figure 5.1 Types of relationship between expressions and speech acts

Figure 5.1 shows that the transformed, non-speech act-anchored and modified-speech act-indicating uses all represent parts of a broader category which we defined as *altered* speech act-indication. Clearly, the relationship between RFIEs and speech acts is even more intricate than as we argued in Chapter 4, i.e. in many cases it cannot be pinned down through the concepts of speech act-anchor only.

In terms of L2 pragmatics, a key implication of the system displayed in Figure 5.1 is that Chinese and English RFIEs have different altered speech act-indicating capacities. The first binary pair of 'normal versus transformed' functions can typically be found in the English data but definitely not in the Chinese data: the Chinese Thanks expressions are invariably used to indicate the speech act of Thanks, i.e. they do not permit transformed uses such as Complain as far as our data is concerned. Regarding the second binary pair of 'speech act-anchored use of expressions versus non-speech act-anchored use of expressions', our previous study of Greet expressions has revealed that there is no major difference between such English and Chinese RFIEs. That is, both the English and the Chinese Greet expressions under investigation tend to be used in both speech act-anchored and non-speech act-anchored ways, such as Alerters. As to the third non-binary pair of 'normal speech act-indicating use of expressions plus modified speech act-indicating use of expressions', our analysis has shown that both English and Chinese expressions of Thanks can simultaneously indicate the normal speech act of Thanks and the speech act of Leave-Take.

As part of the framework outlined in Chapter 3, in the present study we rely on radically minimal, finite and interactional speech act typology. As we argued in Chapter 3, the interactional and finite nature of this typology allows us to capture the 'migration' of altered speech acts that we describe in this chapter in a rigorous and replicable way.

The corpus-based contrastive study discussed so far represents the first step of our research. In our follow-up L2 pragmatic inquiry we set out from the following hypothesis: it is only transformed speech act-indicating uses of English RFIEs which cause problems for Chinese learners of English because other altered speech act-indicating functions have Chinese counterparts.

5.3 The second phase of our research

The second phase of our research is based on a DCT distributed to ten Chinese learners of English in a university located in the north-east of China, which was followed up by interviews with these learners, made on the basis of the results of the task sheets. All the respondents were advanced undergraduate students with an English major.

We first secured the availability of the respondents via WeChat. The interviewees were provided with a set of utterances in which the Thanks and Greet expressions investigated were deployed in various functions, involving both normal and altered speech act-indicating uses. All the examples were drawn from the British National Corpus. We did not reveal information to our respondents about the various normal and altered speech act-indicating functions of the RFIEs featured in the examples given in the sheet, and simply requested them to translate all the English examples to Chinese as their main task. For reasons of efficiency, we sent the task sheet to each respondent at different times, i.e. we did not distribute the task sheets in one batch. Approximately two hours after the task sheet had been distributed, we called each respondent to interview them regarding their evaluations of the pragmatic functions of the RFIEs in the utterances, based on the translations they provided. The respondents were given twenty minutes to translate the ten examples, i.e. approximately two minutes per example. The follow-up interviews lasted approximately ten minutes each. In this chapter we only involve the interviews conducted with the students in our detailed qualitative analysis, whereas the results of the task sheets and the related quantitative analysis featured in Table 5.1 below are based on an interpreting procedure of the appropriacy of the translations (for details of this translational evaluation procedure see House, 2015).

Our task sheet consisted of the following utterances:

Examples of 'Thank you': According to our previous research, 'Thank you' fulfils three different functions including (a) the normal speech act-indicating use, (b) the transformed use, and (c) the modified use of simultaneously indicating the speech acts of Thanks and Leave-Take. Accordingly, we presented the following items in the task sheet:

(5.1) Thank you for your support, do come again.
[This example represents a normal speech act-indicating use of the expression *Thank you*, indicating the speech act of Thanks.]

(5.2) Dear Professor, <u>Thank you</u> for your curt note.
[This example represents a transformed speech act-indicating use of the expressions *Thank you*, indicating the speech act of Complain.]

(5.3) Well, I'm afraid we won't be needing you, lovey, <u>thank you</u>. (looks at clipboard) Could we have the next candidate, please?
[This example represents a modified speech act-indicating use of the expression *Thank you*: here *Thank you* simultaneously indicating the speech acts of Thanks and Leave-Take.]

Examples of 'Thank you very much': According to our previous research 'Thank you very much' fulfils three different functions including (a) the normal speech act-indicating use, (b) the transformed speech act-indicating function, indicating a Complain, and (c) the modified use of the simultaneous indication of the speech acts of Thanks and Leave-Take:

(5.4) <u>Thank you very much</u> for sending us the samples of prints from the English In Focus video taken from the Sony UP 5000 video printer.
[This example represents a normal speech act-indicating use of the expression *Thank you very much*, indicating the speech act of Thanks.]

(5.5) <u>That'll be quite enough of that, thank you very much.</u>
[This example represents a transformed speech act-indicating use of the expression *Thank you*, realising the speech act of Complain.]

(5.6) I've nothing further to add, <u>thank you very much</u>.
[This example represents a modified speech act-indicating use the expression *Thank you very much*, simultaneously indicating the speech acts of Thanks and Leave-Take.]

Examples of 'Hello': The expression 'Hello' (and its variant 'Hallo'[1]) can either indicate the speech act of Greet or operate as an attention-getting Alerter. In this latter function 'Hello' loses its function as an indicator of Greet.

(5.7) <u>Hello</u>, Dr Streeter, how was your holiday?
[This example represents a normal speech act-indicating use of the expression *Hello*, indicating the speech act of Greet.]

(5.8) You are facing up to yourself in a very moving and powerful way — <u>hello</u>?
[This example represents the use of *Hello* as an Alerter. Here the speaker alerts the other, basically drawing attention to the fact that he is now talking.]

(5.9) Oh, I wish — <u>hello</u>, what's that?
[This example represents the use of *Hello* as an Alerter. We included both example (8) and (9) in our task sheet because while *hello* in example (8) is other-directed, in example (9) it is self-directed.]

(5.10) <u>Good Morning</u>. You're listening to Dial David Johnston on Max A M.
[This example represents the use of the expression *Good morning*, functioning as a Greet. As opposed to *hello*, the more formal cluster of Greet expressions *Good morning/afternoon/evening* can only be used in its normal function as a Greet according to our previous research, i.e. these expressions never afford altered speech act indication as far as our corpus research was concerned. Because of this lack of altered speech act-indicating capacity, we only included the above example featuring this expression in our task sheet.]

In presenting these examples, we did not provide background information about the context of the utterances, even though the British National Corpus from which we drew these examples in our original research affords retrieving such information. Our reason for omitting background information is as outlined previously in this chapter: all speech act-indicating functions – including normal and altered ones – of an expression tend to be conventionalised, and so interpreting such uses should only necessitate what Terkfourafi (2005) defines as 'minimal context'. As part of presenting the utterances in the task sheet to the respondents, we underlined the RFIEs under investigation and requested our respondents to particularly focus on the appropriacy of these RFIEs in their translations.

Along with the task sheets, our data consists of personal interviews conducted with the respondents of the task sheets about their translations, reflecting their comprehension of instances of altered speech act-indication. The audio-recorded interviews of approximately two hours in length were transcribed by using simple transcription conventions for easy readability. For ethical considerations, we anonymised both the task sheet responses and the interviews, and stored all the data securely, following the standard research ethics procedure in pragmatics.

5.3.1 Analysis and results

In Table 5.1 below we present the analysis and results of the second phase of our research.

The data in Table 5.1 show that the normal speech act-indicating use of the RFIEs under investigation triggers minimal to no difficulties for students: the appropriacy rate of responses to examples (5.1), (5.4), (5.7) and (5.10) featuring such uses ranges between 90 per cent and 100 per cent. There is a much larger

Table 5.1 Quantitative results of the task sheet responses (+ indicates appropriate responses, – indicates inappropriate responses)

Example no.	Student 1	Student 2	Student 3	Student 4	Student 5	Student 6	Student 7	Student 8	Student 9	Student 10	Appropriacy
(5.1)	+	+	+	+	+	+	+	+	+	–	90%
(5.2)	–	–	–	+	–	–	–	–	+	–	20%
(5.3)	–	+	+	–	+	–	–	+	+	+	50%
(5.4)	+	+	+	+	+	+	+	+	+	+	100%
(5.5)	–	–	–	–	–	–	–	–	+	–	10%
(5.6)	–	+	+	–	+	+	+	–	–	+	60%
(5.7)	+	+	+	+	–	+	+	+	–	+	90%
(5.8)	+	+	–	+	+	+	+	–	+	–	70%
(5.9)	+	+	–	+	+	–	+	+	+	–	70%
(5.10)	+	+	+	+	+	+	+	+	+	+	100%

variation between examples featuring altered speech act indication, and here it is worth considering the following quantitative results:

- There is a very low appropriacy rate for examples (5.2) and (5.5): on average the appropriacy rate was only 15 per cent. These examples feature Thanks expressions that fulfil the transformed function of indicating the speech act of Complain. The failure of the respondents to detect this transformed function accords with the fact that comparable Chinese expressions usually do not afford such transformed functions according to our previous research.
- Examples (5.3) and (5.6) feature modified uses of *Thank you* and *Thank you very much*, simultaneously indicating the speech acts of Thanks and Leave-Take in Table 5.1. While the Chinese equivalents of these expressions (*Xiexie [ni]* and *Feichang ganxie [ni]*) can also fulfil this modified function, the appropriacy rate is nevertheless low: the students only captured the situated meaning of these expressions in 55 per cent of the cases on average.
- Examples (5.8) and (5.9) include non-speech act-anchored uses of the expression *hello*. The students' evaluations of this expression had a relatively high appropriacy rate of 70 per cent. Here, along with examining responses in the task sheet, we also investigated a particular issue regarding the translations the respondents provided: many students revealed metapragmatic awareness of the non-speech act-anchored use of the expression *hello*, by translating it in diverse ways, such as using *Wei* and *Hai* 嗨 instead of the more formal expression *Ni hao* (see more in section 5.4 below).

In sum, the quantitative analysis shows that unlike our preliminary hypothesis it is insufficient to confine our investigation to transformed uses of the RFIEs under investigation, but rather we should also qualitatively examine learners' evaluations of all the three above-identified types of altered speech act indication.

Transformed speech act-indicating uses of the expressions Thank you and Thank you very much
As Table 5.1 shows, it is the transformed speech act-indicating use that posed the most difficult problem for the respondents. In the task sheet, we factored in the sociocultural variable of '+/– authority': example (5.2) features an utterance in which a professor is involved, while in example (5.5) there is no such an authority figure. One could hypothesise that inappropriate student evaluations of *thank you* in example (5.2) may have resulted from pragmatic transfer, considering that in East Asian lingua cultures such as the Chinese talking to teachers who are generally figures of authority often triggers the use of honorifics and other forms of respect, as Ide (1989) has famously pointed out. Interestingly, however, the response rate for example (5.5) in which the authority variable is missing had an even lower appropriate response rate than example (5.2). This reveals that it is essentially the transformed speech act-indicating use itself – that is the use of Thanks expressions as indicators of

the speech act of Complain and the related ironic meaning – which is rather 'alien' to the Chinese respondents.

In the following we will present again the original examples in the task sheet, to facilitate easy reading, and then provide selected examples of appropriate and inappropriate student responses.

>Example (5.2)
>Dear Professor, <u>Thank you</u> for your curt note.

Inappropriate responses:

>(Student 1)
>>Interview excerpt: 表示一种感谢，这里应该指老师给学生的作业标记了一些笔记，学生对老师的感谢。
>>[This expression] indicates thanking. Here it must show that the teacher had commented on the student's homework, so the student expresses his thank you to the teacher.

Student 1 clearly misinterpreted *Thank you* in example (5.2) as a 'proper' Thanks expression.

>(Student 3)
>>就像一种敬语，是客气的话，因为这里的说话对象是教授，是对上级。
>>Here [*Thank you*] is an honorific expression and the speaker is only being polite [*keqi* 客气, an expression for 'superficial' politeness in Chinese], because here the person addressed is a teacher who is the student's superior.

A noteworthy feature of Student 3's response is that she – unlike Student 1 and many other students – provides a metapragmatic definition for *Thank you*, by arguing that it is a 'politeness expression' (*jingyu* 敬语), which is a linguistic definition often used in Chinese to describe honorifics both in Chinese and 'honorific-rich' foreign languages such as Japanese. Despite this technical description, the student's evaluation turned out to be as equally inappropriate as that of Student 1.

Appropriate responses:
Only two students evaluated the example appropriately, and in the following we include excerpts from their comments made during the follow-up interviews:

>(Student 4)
>>我觉得是看语义，这里"curt note"是比较指简略的阐述，那就是有点讽刺的意味，因为正常教授会说的比较详细一些，这里却说的比较简略，可能不表示感谢。

I feel one needs to consider the semantics of "curt note", which describes here overtly simplistic feedback, so it has a somewhat ironic meaning. Because normally a professor's feedback is expected to be sufficiently detailed, arguing that it is "curt" reveals that the expression does not realise a thank you.

While Student 4 did not explicitly use our speech act category Complain – and we did not expect students to use the very same definitions as we do – she properly captured the transformed use of *Thank you* by arguing that it does not have a genuine Thanks function in the utterance.

(Student 9)
因为这里出现了"curt note",我觉得就是回答得比较敷衍,有点阴阳怪气的感觉,所以并没有感谢的感觉。
Because here [the expression] "curt note" occurred, so I think that the utterance here is bantering and does not express any thanking.

Again, while Complaining was not mentioned in the interview, Student 9 clearly recognised the transformed use of *Thank you* through its pragmatic effect. Note that while practically all respondents translated *curt note* in the example appropriately, it was only Students 4 and 9 who could properly interpret the irony of *thank you* stemming from *curt note*.

Example (5.5)
That'll be quite enough of that, thank you very much.

Inappropriate responses:

(Student 3)
比如说一个人给了你东西,你要谢谢他的好意,然后接受他的好意。
When someone gives you something, you must say thanks to express your gratitude for this person's goodwill.

This is a straightforward misunderstanding of the use of the expression *Thank you very much*.

(Student 7)
这句话可能出现在餐厅吃饭的场景中,当服务员给你倒酒后,
你会说"够了,不用倒了,谢谢,"That'll be quite enough of that"
是对服务生的一种指令,后面"Thank you"是一种礼貌用语,
可以缓和语气。
This excerpt may be from a restaurant. When a waiter pours you some wine, you may say "That'll be quite enough of that" [which can be translated to Chinese as] *Goule, buyong daole, xiexie* "够了, 不用倒了,谢谢" [Enough, don't pour more, thank you]. I think the

utterance is an order and *Thank you* here is a politeness expression, softening the tone.

Although this student provided a detailed hypothetical scenario of the contextual use of *Thank you very much*, his interpretation is equally inappropriate as that of Student 3 as he failed to recognise the transformed use of *Thank you very much* in this example.

Appropriate response:
Since there was only one appropriate evaluation in our data, in the following we present an excerpt from the follow-up interview conducted with Student 9:

(Student 9)
我觉得这里是说话人比较反感，想让对方别再说了，一种反话。
I feel that the speaker here is irritated and maybe he wants the other to stop talking, so [the expression] fulfils an ironic function.

Modified speech act-indicating uses of the expressions Thank you and Thank you very much, simultaneously involving the speech acts of Thanks and Leave-Take
The general accuracy rate of evaluations of modified speech act indicating uses of *Thank you* and *Thank you very much*, featured in examples (5.3) and (5.6), was much higher than that of the transformed use, averaging 55 per cent. Yet, considering that Chinese Thanks expressions also afford such modified uses indicates that the inappropriacy rate of 55 per cent is remarkable. It is beyond the scope of our bottom-up language-anchored framework to identify sociocultural and educational reasons behind the incorrect evaluation tendency observed here. However, we assume that such errors are teaching-induced: in China, altered speech act-indication is rarely featured in standard textbooks.

Due to space limitation, in the following we will only present a single inappropriate and another appropriate interview interpretation of each example in the task sheet.

Example (5.3)
Well, I'm afraid we won't be needing you, lovey, thank you. (looks at clipboard) Could we have the next candidate, please?

Inappropriate response:

(Student 10)
就是委婉的拒绝，面试官对采访者的表现不太满意，所以委婉拒绝他，也是一个礼貌用语，我觉得现在的 "thank you" 很多时候都不是想表达真正

> 的感谢，就是随口一说，就是一种礼貌的说法，... 其实我觉得不管是国内还是国外，很多人说话并不都是直接的，很多时候都会说一些比较委婉的话，客套话，这是一种社交礼仪。
> Here a job interviewer isn't satisfied with the interviewee's performance, so he uses this expression to euphemistically reject the interviewee. It's a politeness expression. I think nowadays *thank you* doesn't represent a sincere thank you and people who utter it only use it to sound polite in a casual way ... No matter whether we talk about China or abroad, people always use euphemisms like this. It's a typical set phrase, being part of social etiquette.

Despite her detailed explanation, the student seems to have misunderstood the meaning of *Thank you* as an expression of finality. It is exactly this finality that precludes the use of *Thank you* as a 'casual' politeness expression here.

Appropriate response:

> (Student 2)
> 因为这里应该是一个人面试没有成功，然后面试官用一种委婉的方式送他离开，就是感谢你参加我们的面试，但是我们不会录用你。
> In this scenario, the interviewer uses thanking to euphemistically tell the interviewee to leave because the interviewee fails to pass the interview. The sentence also means 'thank you for participating in the interview but we won't hire you'.

Student 2's evaluation and subsequent explanation in the interview is correct because this student grasped the simultaneous realisations of the speech acts of Leave-Take and Thanks, as witnessed by the words *song ta likai* 送他离开 ("dismiss the other", trans. "tell the interview to leave").

Example (5.6)
> I've nothing further to add, <u>thank you very much</u>.

Inappropriate response:

> (Student 8)
> 就是一个客套的回应，让人觉得很有礼貌，是一个礼貌用语。
> The speaker is just being polite. It's polite to say thanks, so here we have a politeness expression.

Student 8 did not grasp the Leave-Take function of *Thank you very much*.

Appropriate response:

(Student 2)
> 比如我们在做小型演讲的时候，PPT最后通常会写"感谢观看"，这里我觉得就是一种礼貌用语。
> For example, when we prepare our presentation for our English class, we may type *Ganxie guankan* "感谢观看" ("Thanks for your watching") in Chinese, marking the end of the PPT. I think it is a type of politeness expression.

While Students 2 and 8 both argued that *Thank you very much* is a 'politeness expression', it is only Student 2 who correctly recognised the symbiosis between Thanks and Leave-Take in the pragmatic use of this expression.

Non-speech act-anchored uses of Hello
As Table 5.1 shows, the non-speech act-anchored uses of the expression *Hello* – featured in examples (5.8) and (5.9) – had a high appropriacy rate, averaging 70 per cent, which accords with the fact that Chinese conventionalised expressions of Greet also often fulfil an Alerting function. The fact that in example (5.8) *Hello* is other-directed and in example (5.9) it is self-directed does not appear to have caused any major discrepancy between the appropriacy of the responses, as Table 5.1 shows. The following are excerpts from inappropriate and appropriate interview feedback:

Example (5.9)
> Oh, I wish — <u>hello</u>, what's that?

Inappropriate response:

(Student 6)
> 这句话我是通过 what's that? 判断的，我觉得这里hello是一个比较试探性的话，比如当你去到一个未知的地方，你会用 hello 来试探性地提问，希望得到一个回答。
> Judging from the utterance "what's that?", I feel that "hello" here has a tentative meaning. For example, when you go somewhere unknown, you may say "hello" to make a tentative greet, in order to solicit a reply.

The student here misinterpreted the Alerting use of the expression *Hello* as a Greet. This is likely to be a teaching-induced error.

Appropriate response:

(Student 4)
>这里在说"我希望 ... 的时候,突然看到了一个东西,被打断了,于是引起另外一个话题,希望让别人注意一下。
>The speaker here said "Oh, I wish" and then something suddenly interrupted his train of thought, so he utters "Hello" to change the topic and attract the listener's attention.

While Student 4's interpretation that there is a topic change here may be inappropriate, she correctly recognised that the expression *Hello* has an attention-getting function.

It is worth noting that in Chinese both the RFIEs *Ni hao* and *Wei* can fulfil an Alerting function, with *Wei* being the stronger Alerter. Many of our respondents demonstrated awareness of this pragmatic feature in the task sheets where they provided their own Chinese translations of the English utterances: six out of ten students translated the expression *Hello* as *Wei*.

5.4 Conclusion

In this chapter, we have further explored the expression–speech act interface in L2 pragmatics through the lens of our framework, by considering a more complex phenomenon than we studied in Chapter 4, namely altered speech act indication. We have examined whether Chinese learners of English are able to appropriately recognise what we have defined as the altered speech act-indicating functions of RFIEs associated with the speech acts of Thanks and Greet. We started from the hypothesis that it is only the transformed speech act-indicating uses of conventionalised English RFIEs which cause problems for Chinese learners of English, considering that other altered speech act-indicating functions have Chinese counterparts. While our findings confirm that transformed speech act-indicating uses indeed trigger a very high rate of inappropriate responses, the hypothesis itself was disconfirmed because the other altered functions of modified and non-speech act-anchored uses also triggered inappropriate responses, albeit to a lesser degree than the transformed uses. It may be safe to assume that the high rate of inappropriate responses in this study stems from the fact that altered speech act-indication is not featured in teaching materials.

In this chapter, we once again relied on the replicable framework we proposed in Chapter 3 to examine an understudied L2 pragmatic area. From now on, we will move beyond the analytic unit of expression and its relationship to speech acts, even though RFIEs of course continue to be relevant for our analysis. That is, we will now move towards the use of our framework in the study of speech acts and interactional acts.

5.5 Recommended reading

Terkourafi, Marina. (2015). Conventionalization: A new agenda for im/politeness research. *Journal of Pragmatics* **86, 1–18.**
Marina Terkourafi conducted intriguing research about the concept of conventionalisation, which also plays a key role in the phenomenon of altered speech act indication studied in this chapter: without having different degrees of conventionalised relationship between expressions and speech acts, language users would have no means to express and interpret the altered speech act indicating function of expressions in certain contexts. In the following excerpt Terkourafi discusses the concept of conventionalisation:

> At this point, it is paramount to clarify what I mean by "conventionalization." I consider an expression to be conventionalized for some use relative to a context for a speaker if it is used frequently enough in that context to achieve a particular illocutionary goal to that speaker's experience. This makes conventionalization a three-way relationship between an expression, a context, and a speaker. I comment separately on each of these below. By "expression" I mean a form of words, including their prosodic contour, that tend to be used together to achieve a particular illocutionary goal. That is, an expression is a specific form/function combination with certain parts being fixed and others being open variables, akin to constructions in Construction Grammar (Goldberg, 2006). Examples include the ubiquitous 'Can you VP?' for requests, but also 'NP is/looks really ADJ' for compliments in AmE, and 'exi NP/exete NP?' for requests in some transactional contexts in Cypriot Greek. "Context" refers to the situational context which, by a process of abstraction over real-world contexts, comes to be stored in memory as a combination of extra-linguistic features that include, but are not limited to, the age, gender, and social class of the interlocutors, the relationship between them, and the setting of the exchange – what Terkourafi (2009) calls a "minimal context." The precise list of extra-linguistic features as well as their relative weights can vary: ethnicity may be important for some expressions but not others. What matters is that certain social features of the situation that are often preemptively fixed from sensory data are recorded together for the purposes of classification and easy retrieval as a whole later on (cf. Minsky, 1975). The combination of an expression with a minimal context thus understood is what I call a "frame" (Terkourafi, 2001, 2009, 2012). The final parameter in the above definition is the speaker. Because conventionalization is a matter of one's experience, the degree to which an expression is conventionalized relative to a context can vary for different speakers, as well as for the same speaker over time. An expression can be conventionalized for two people, for members of a group (e.g., a sports team), for a social category (e.g., men), or for an entire language variety/culture (e.g., American English).

An example will make this clearer. The expression "my bad!" is described as "an American idiom ... made popular by basketball players in playground games in the 1970s and 1980s. It usually means "my fault", "my mistake", "I apologize" or "mea culpa." It gained popularity with urban players of streetball and then spread into mainstream popularity ... once other basketball players started using "my bad!" to apologize, it became less and less necessary to go through the full process of implicature derivation: exposure to repeated uses of it as an apology in that type of context would be enough to ensure prompt identification of its illocutionary force by group members. "My bad!" would then be understood as an apology via an I-type Generalized Conversational Implicature (Levinson, 2000) associated with the minimal context of being basketball players on the court (the stereotypical way of apologizing in that minimal context ... . (Terkourafi, 2015: 15–16)

Note

1. Etymologically *Hello* comes from *Hallo* (see e.g. Lerer, 2003).

CHAPTER 6

Speech acts and interactional acts 1: the case of criticising

6.1 Introduction

In this chapter, we bring the reader into a higher level of our analytic system, namely the study of speech acts and interactional acts. Thus far we have focused on how particular expressions indicate speech acts. However, speech acts themselves do not exist in a vacuum, but rather they tend to realise more complex interactional phenomena, which we define in this book as interactional acts. As we argued in Chapter 3, unlike speech acts, interactional acts are infinite, and their acquisition can trigger noteworthy L2 pragmatic problems.

As a case study, we investigate how Chinese native speakers and foreign learners of Chinese evaluate instances of the interactional act of criticising. By criticising we mean disciplinary acts through which lecturers criticise their students for violating the classroom order. In our view, criticising is not a speech act but rather an interactional act. As a conventionalised interactional act, criticising is realised by a cluster of expressions and speech acts. Following our approach, we examine such realisation patterns in a bottom-up way, in order to find out exactly which aspects of criticising may trigger L2 learning difficulties. In studying such difficulties, we make use of our framework outlined in Chapter 3 already in a fully-fledged way. That is, our analysis departs from an actual L2 pragmatic issue experienced by the second author of this book. We then investigate this issue first by conducting a contrastive pragmatic study of DCT corpora, followed by an L2 pragmatic inquiry involving a rating task. In the analysis we build on what has been presented to the reader thus far, i.e. we involve both RFIEs and speech acts in our inquiry.

Criticising is relevant for L2 pragmatics in general, and the learning and teaching of Chinese as a foreign language in particular because instances of criticism are parts of both classroom and everyday life. Since criticising is notoriously absent from Chinese language teaching, one may rightly ask whether foreign learners of Chinese interpret such criticisms like Chinese

Speech acts and interactional acts 1 91

speakers do? This is an intriguing question because criticising in the classroom occurs in a public ritual space, and as such it inherently threatens the face of the recipient in the conventional Brown and Levinsonian (1987) sense. It is therefore worth investigating how Chinese native speakers realise criticising and compare how foreign and Chinese students interpret this phenomenon. Such a line of inquiry also helps us venture beyond many sweeping overgeneralisations, such as the infamous idea that Chinese is a 'face-sensitive culture' (e.g. Spencer-Oatey, 2005).

The structure of this chapter is as follows. First, we provide selected previous studies to position the research described in the chapter. Second, methodology and data, followed by an analysis and a conclusion.

6.2 Selected previous studies

In their seminal work, Austin (1962) and Searle (1969) defined criticising as a typical 'expressive' speech act. This definition was later taken up by Brown and Levinson (1987: 66), even though they did not pursue much interest in speech act theory. They argued that criticising is a typical face-threatening act. Wierzbicka (1985) in her work on so-called 'cultural speech acts' also defined criticising as a speech act. In our view, this definition is problematic. As we pointed out in Chapter 3, the rationale behind using speech act as an analytic tool is that it provides a replicable minimal category through which discourse phenomena can be systematically broken down into components. If one considers how criticising is normally realised in real-life scenarios, it becomes evident that it often manifests itself through complex interactional behaviour realised through many different contextually embedded speech acts. Consider the following case, representing the L2 pragmatic problem which stimulated the case study:

> On one occasion, our Chinese colleague criticised a Chinese student by uttering the conventionalised phrase *Ni xiuxi-yixia* 你休息一下 ("Have some rest"). In this particular context, Dániel Kádár who works at that university and who was present at the incident, was not sure whether the speech act Request was meant to be criticising the student, or not. However, he did notice that something was wrong because the atmosphere of the classroom changed. Later, the Chinese colleagued explained to Kádár that she had intended to criticise the student.

As this example illustrates, recognising the interactional act of criticising not only represents a noteworth L2 problem, but also the complex interactional phenomenon of criticising was realised here by the speech act Request. So, we believe that a problem of defining criticising as a speech act is that by so doing one conflates illocution and interaction.

It is worth mentioning here that Tracy et al. (1987) defined criticising as a speech act in contrast to the speech act Complain. In our typology Complain is a typical speech act

> whereby a speaker expresses his negative view of a past action by the hearer (i.e. for which he holds the hearer responsible), in view of the negative effects or consequences of that action vis-à-vis himself … It is clear that a Complain flouts the H-supportive maxim. (Edmondson and House, 1981: 144)

While Complain can be described as a speech act consisting of various components or strategies (see Olshtain and Weinbach, 1993), this does not mean that Complain represents an interactional act because different realisation strategies do not compromise its status as one unitary speech act. Consider the following example:

> I think you are simply unreliable.

This utterance is clearly a speech act Complain, initiating an interaction following an offence. It is not an interactional act to be analysed through different speech acts, as is the case with criticising. For instance, it would not be legitimate to argue that the above utterance is a speech act Opine operating as a Complain. Thus, here we have something very different from the above-quoted Request operating as an interactional act of criticising:

> 你休息一下！
> Have some rest!

6.3 Methodology and data

Our research followed the bipartite design of main research outlined in Figure 3.2 in Chapter 3.

6.3.1 Part 1

First, we administered DCTs involving fifty Chinese native speaker university lecturers. We aimed to identify the pragmatic patterns of disciplinary criticising in Chinese university classrooms. We presented the following three different violations of the classroom order – in increasing severity – to examine whether the degree of a student's offence influences realisation patterns of criticising:

1. 课堂上，您正在讲课，发现一名同学在玩手机。您会说：
   While you are teaching in the classroom you see a student playing on his mobile. What would you say?

Speech acts and interactional acts 1   93

2. 课堂上，您正在讲课，发现一名同学在和其他同学小声说笑。您会说：
   While you are teaching in the classroom you see a student murmuring with others. What would you say?
3. 课堂上，您正在讲课，发现一名同学在和其他同学大声说笑。您会说：
   While you are teaching in the classroom a student is talking and laughing aloud with others. What would you say?

We categorised recurrent expression and speech act types in our participants' responses, in order to pin down conventionalised realisation patterns of criticising in Chinese. Focusing on conventionalisation was important because criticising in the classroom usually occurs when the moral order and the ritual flow of teaching get violated, and responses to such violations may trigger idiosyncratic pragmatic solutions (see Kádár, 2017), which however were irrelevant for our inquiry.

The design of our DCTs and our subsequent analysis of expressions and speech acts that our framework of 'ritual frame indicating expressions' (RFIEs) outlined in the previous Chapters 4 and 5, as well as the radically minimal, interactional and finite speech act typology, were introduced in Chapter 3. More specifically, first we considered the pragmatic significance of frequented expressions. Second, we categorised speech acts through which criticising was realised in our DCTs through our typology of speech acts. Following Edmondson et al. (2023), we did not assume that disciplinary criticising is always realised by the speech act Complain or other Attitudinal speech acts. Rather, we considered *all* speech acts through which criticising tends to be realised, including those which typologically do not belong to what Edmondson and House (1981: 98) defined as 'Attitudinal'. In interpreting our results, we considered severity of offence.

6.3.2 Part 2

Part 2 represents our L2 pragmatic inquiry. Here we conducted a rating test, involving a group of ten advanced European undergraduate learners who studied Chinese as part of their university programmes and who had not visited China before, and a group of ten native speaking Chinese undergraduate students. The test was based on the outcomes of Part 1, and its goal was to compare how foreign learners and native speakers of Chinese evaluate conventionalised realisations of criticising. We then interviewed our participants.

6.4 Analysis

6.4.1 Part 1

Recurrent expressions and speech act types in our DCTs include the following:

Expressions
- RFIEs: Chinese lecturers preferred using the following expressions in the interactional act of criticising: *qing* 请 ('please'), *buyao* 不要 ('do/should not') and *zhuyi* 注意 (lit. 'attention', i.e. 'beware'). Since these expressions are pragmatically loaded, their use strongly correlates with rights and obligations, so we categorised them as RFIEs.
- Forms of address: Chinese lecturers also made use of different forms of address, since the strategic use of addressing allowed them to make disciplining more or less direct.

Speech acts
- In our DCT data, criticising was realised through the following speech acts: Request, Tell and Opine.

When we identified different speech acts as Tell and Opine, it would have always been possible to also categorise them as 'indirect Requests', following the Speech Act Realisation Project (see Blum-Kulka et al., 1989). Such a definition would have been equally legitimate because ultimately Tell and Opine both follow the formula *x wants y do p* in the context of classroom criticising. However, we decided to follow Edmondson and House's (1981) proposal of interpreting speech acts at their face value.

RFIEs
In our corpus, we observed the following three RFIEs: *qing* 请 ('please'), *buyao* 不要 ('do/should not') and *zhuyi* 注意 (lit. 'attention', i.e. 'beware'). Table 6.1 displays the frequency of these RFIEs in the three scenarios featured in the DCTs.

Table 6.1 *The frequency of the RFIEs* qing, buyao *and* zhuyi *in our DCT corpus*

	Scenario no. 1	Scenario no. 2	Scenario no. 3
qing ('please')	16/50 (32%)	15/50 (30%)	14/50 (28%)
buyao ('do/should not')	7/50 (14%)	15/50 (30%)	10/50 (20%)
zhuyi ('beware')	7/50 (14%)	3/50 (6%)	9/50 (18%)
Total	30/50 (60%)	33 (66%)	33 (66%)

The frequency of RFIEs is significant. The total frequency of RFIEs does not fully correlate with their frequency in the DCT responses because in some cases *qing* co-occurs with the other RFIEs as *qing ... zhuyi* and *qing ... buyao*, even though such uses are rare (but see examples (6.4) and (6.9) below). The frequent use of RFIEs reflects their authoritative style: RFIEs represent rights

Speech acts and interactional acts 1

and obligations, and in the context of classroom disciplining they animate the institutional right of the lecturer to uphold the order of the classroom.

In the following, we describe the ways in which the above three RFIEs tend to be used in our DCT corpus.

Qing 请 *('please')*
The most frequent RFIE in our DCT corpus is *qing*. *Qing* is normally translated to English as 'please' (see also Chapter 4), although – unlike *please* – *qing* is an expression of honorific origin and it rarely expresses non-requestive interactional meanings such as sarcasm. Further, if uttered from a [+P] position like that of a lecturer in our case, *qing* tends to express a definite sense of authority for speakers of Chinese.

We found it surprising that *qing* frequently occurred in our DCTs because in a previous inquiry we found that this RFIE, unlike the English *please*, is rarely (if at all) used by Chinese lecturers. Apparently, when a social offence occurs, Chinese lecturers frequent this expression to speak in an authoritative way to restore the order of the classroom. The following examples (6.1) and (6.2) illustrate this use of *qing*:

(6.1) 请注意言行举止，尊重课堂上的每一个人。
Qing behave yourself and respect others in the class.[1]

(6.2) 请将手机收起来，下课再玩。
Qing put your mobile phone away – use it after class.

As examples (6.1) and (6.2) show, when uttering RIFEs like *qing*, lecturers rarely use personal pronouns or other individual forms of address. This lack of personal addressing correlates with the authoritative style of *qing*. Thus, in our DCT corpus only communal forms of address occur with *qing*, as illustrated by example (6.3):

(6.3) 请大家认真听课。
Please, everyone, listen carefully.

Here, the lecturer used the collective form of address *dajia* 大家 ('everyone') to formally address the whole of the class, rather than the individual misbehaving student. Some other respondents used *qing + compound address term* forms to address the misbehaving student in the third person, as illustrated by example (6.4):

(6.4) 请说话的同学注意自己的言行，注意公德，影响课堂纪律要受到惩罚。
Qing the students who are talking *zhuyi* their words and actions and *zhuyi* public morality. Disrupting the classroom discipline will be punished.

Buyao 不要 *('do/should not')*
Unlike *qing*, the RFIE *buyao* is not popularly associated with 'politeness' but rather with civil behaviour: this expression is frequently used in public notes displaying norms of 'civility', such as *buyao-jianta-caoping* 不要践踏草坪 ('no walking over the grass') (see House et al., forthcoming). However, in the context of classroom criticising *buyao* and *qing* are used similarly, i.e. both of them are uttered when the lecturer aims to sound authoritative, often without directly addressing the misbehaving student. The following examples illustrate uses of the RFIE *buyao*:

(6.5)　课上不要讲话，打扰其他同学学习。
　　　Buyao talk in the class and disturb the study of other students.

(6.6)　上课时不要说话。
　　　Buyao talk in class.

(6.7)　不要打扰其他同学。
　　　Buyao disturb other students.

Zhuyi 注意 *(lit. 'attention', i.e. 'beware')*
Similar to *buyao*, the RFIE *zhuyi* is frequented in Chinese public signs reminding people about 'civil behaviour', such as *zhuyi-anquan* 注意安全 ('beware of safety'). While this RFIE is less frequently used in our DCT corpus than *qing* and *buyao* (see Table 6.1), similar to the other RFIEs it is also deployed in indirect and authoritative utterances. The following examples illustrates uses of *zhuyi*:

(6.8)　注意课堂纪律！
　　　Zhuyi the classroom discipline.

(6.9)　请注意。
　　　Qing zhuyi.

We found example (6.9) particularly interesting because here the lecturer used a *qing* + *zhuyi* RFIE combination, representing a minimal but pragmatically strong Request.

In summary, we argue that all RFIEs in our DCT corpus represent a strong sense of authority. Although based on its semantic meaning *qing* may seem to be more 'polite' than *buyao* and *zhuyi*, uses of RFIEs in our corpus do not reveal any pragmatic difference between these expressions. This interpretation is also supported by the quantitative features of our DCT corpus: as Table 6.1 above shows, these RFIEs are relatively evenly used to respond to offences with various degrees, i.e. they do not represent more or less 'polite' lexical solutions for restoring the order of the classroom after a violation.

Addressing

Table 6.2 shows the frequency of various forms of addressing in our DCT corpus.

Table 6.2 *Formulae of addressing in our first corpus in decreasing frequency*

	Scenario no. 1	Scenario no. 2	Scenario no. 3
Individual term of address + Second person pronoun / Student's name	7/50 (14%)	10/50 (20%)	15/50 (30%)
Collective term of address	8/50 (16%)	4/50 (8%)	2/50 (4%)
Second person pronoun + Student's name	4/50 (8%)	6/50 (12%)	10/50 (20%)
Total	16/50	17/50	21/50

The use of the second formula of collective terms of address in Table 6.2 was illustrated by examples (6.3) and (6.4) above, so we do not discuss them in detail here. The first formula 'individual term of address + second person pronoun/student name' describes cases when the lecturer uses the formal form of address *tongxue* 同学 (lit. 'fellow student'), together with the second person pronoun *ni* 你 and/or the student's name, as in the following utterance:

(6.10) 李四同学, 你在查哪个单词？查完了就把手机收起来！
Student Li Si, which dictionary are you searching in your mobile? When you're finished, put your phone away!

Example (6.10) is both authoritative and sarcastic in style: the formal form of address *tongxue* counterbalances the strategy of directly pointing to the student. The third formula of 'second person pronoun + student's name' in Table 6.2 is shown in the following example:

(6.11) 张三, 你在说什么？
Zhang San, what on earth are you talking about?

This formula of addressing is typically used in utterances which Edmondson and House (1981) describe through the emotionality marker 'heated'.

The frequency of addressing forms shown by Table 6.2 should be interpreted as follows. First, collective terms of address represent the least frequent category of addressing in our DCT corpus. We interpret this low frequency as follows: while RFIEs may be used together with collective forms of address, they much more frequently occur with no addressing at all. There are also various cases in our corpus when neither an RFIE nor any addressing is used, as illustrated by the following example:

(6.12) 上课得认真听讲!
The class needs to be followed diligently!

Thus, we can argue that there is a 'pragmatic collaboration' between RFIEs and addressing: RFIEs make addressing redundant, and if addressing is used with an RFIE, it is usually collective.

Second, the formula 'individual term of address + second person pronoun/ student name' is more frequent than 'second person pronoun + student's name'. This difference should be interpreted through the above-outlined 'heatedness' of the latter formula. It is worth noting here that the use of both the second person pronoun *ni* and person names is considered 'face-threatening' in public scenarios in the Chinese linguaculture (see Pan and Kádár, 2011).

Referring to the late Geoffrey Leech's (1983) renowned **scalar approach** to language use, it can be argued that the three addressing formule in Table 6.2, as well as their lack, should be envisaged on an indirectness–directness scale. Figure 6.1 illustrates this point:

Lack of RFIE and addressing		Indirect
RFIE + Collective addressing		
Individual term of address + Second person pronoun / student's name		
Second person pronoun + Student's name		Direct

Figure 6.1 (In)directness of various addressing solutions in our DCT corpus

The correlation between the degree of offence involved and the frequency of addressing formulae (see Table 6.2) supports this interpretation.

Speech acts
As Table 6.3 shows, criticising in our DCT corpus is realised through the following three speech act categories:

Table 6.3 *Speech act categories and their frequency in our DCT corpus*

	Scenario no. 1	Scenario no. 2	Scenario no. 3
Request	27/50 (54%)	32/50 (64%)	29/50 (58%)
Tell	13/50 (26%)	15/50 (30%)	14/50 (28%)
Opine	10/50 (20%)	3/50 (6%)	7/50 (14%)

The Attitudinal speech act Request does not need a definition, although it is worth noting that we divide Request to *Request-to-do-x* and *Request-not-to-do-x*, following our typology (Chapter 3). Tell is a typical Informative speech act through which a 'fact' is communicated. Opine is also an Informative speech act, through which a speaker voices an opinion in a subjective way.

Importantly, none of these speech acts is more or less 'direct' or 'indirect' than others because all of them can be modified. In the following, we illustrate how these speech acts tend to be realised in our corpus.

(6.13) 请把手机收起来。
Qing put your phone away.

(6.14) 认真上课，不要搞小动作。
Be more attentive, *buyao* fidget.

In example (6.13), the speaker realises a Request-to-do-x without addressing the student and by using the RFIE *qing*. In example (6.14), a Request-not-do-do-x is realised with the RFIE *buyao*.

(6.15) 上课不要做与课堂无关的事。
In the class disruptive matter *buyao* take place.

(6.16) 上课不许玩手机！
No mobile phones are tolerated in the class.

Example (6.15) represents a Tell, including the RFIE *buyao*: here the lecturer restores the order of the classroom by simply stating what she believes to be a fact. Such Tells are of course not 'innocent': the fact that the lecturer tells the student is supposed to be known by everyone. The same applies to example (6.16). Finally, examples (6.17) and (6.18) represent realisations of the speech act Opine:

(6.17) 有的同学玩起来很专注啊。
Some of the students are apparently having fun.

(6.18) 班级不是你一个人的！
You are not the only one in this class!

6.4.2 Part 2

In the second phase of the main part of our analysis, we first conducted a rating test with a group of ten foreign undergraduate learners who studied Chinese at university programmes, and another group of ten native speaking Chinese undergraduates. Following our framework, the test was designed on the basis of the outcomes of Part 1: we provided various types of RFIEs, address forms and speech acts in examples featuring disciplinary criticising drawn from our DCT corpus. With this rating test we wanted to assess how foreign learners and native speakers of Chinese evaluate conventionalised realisations of criticising. We then interviewed our participants about the reasons for their evaluations.

As part of our testing procedure, we presented various tasks in the test to our students in different phases, in order to prevent them from changing their evaluations of the tasks they had already completed.

The rating test
Our rating test included the following three tasks:

1. Do the following sentences represent request or order?
    (A) '请保持课堂纪律。'   'request'/'order'
        '*Qing* uphold the order of the classroom'
    (B) '注意课堂纪律。'   'request'/'order'
        '*Zhuyi* classroom order'
    (C) '不要违反课堂纪律。'   'request'/'order'
        'One *buyao* violate the classroom order'

The first utterance includes the RFIE *qing*, the second the RFIE *zhuyi* and the third the RFIE *buyao*. Here, we were interested in how foreign learners of Chinese and native speaking students evaluate the pragmatic value of these RFIEs. We used 'request' and 'order' in a popular sense, considering that 'order' (indicating an upgraded Request) is not a speech act in our typology.

2. Rate the following sentences according to their acceptability on a rate of 3 (1 – least acceptable, to 3 – most acceptable)
    (A) '张三/李四，请不要说话。'
        'Zhang San/Li Si, *qing-buyao* talk'
    (B) '请你不要说话。'
        '*Qing* you *bu-yao* talk'
    (C) '请你们不要说话。'
        '*Qing* you [plural] *buyao* talk'
    (D) '请同学们不要说话。'
        '*Qing* students *buyao* talk'

This second task presents different realisations of a Request including the RFIEs *qing* and *buyao*. All the utterances here feature different address forms: the first utterance includes what we defined as an 'individual term of address', the second utterance the second person pronoun *ni*, the third one the plural second person pronoun *nimen* 你们, and the fourth one 'collective addressing'. Here, we wanted to investigate how foreign learners of Chinese and native speakers of Chinese evaluate the pragmatic value of these address forms. We presented the address formulae summarised in Table 6.2 above in a simplified way, e.g. by avoiding formulae like 'Individual term of address + Second person pronoun/student's name', in order to avoid confusing our foreign learners with overly complex formulae.

3. Rate the following sentences according to their acceptability on a scale of 3 (1 – least acceptable, to 3 – most acceptable)
   (A) '好好听课！'
       'Follow the class carefully!'
   (B) '上课不许玩手机！'
       'No mobile phones are tolerated in the class!'
   (C) '这课堂也太欢脱了！'
       'This class is overly happy today!'

This third task presents realisations of the speech acts Request, Tell and Opine. The first utterance is a Request, the second utterance represents a Tell and the third utterance is an Opine. We provided relatively 'minimal' realisations of these speech acts, in order to elicit our respondents' evaluations of the use of the speech acts themselves in the context of classroom criticising. By using exclamation marks, we wanted to prompt our respondents to interpret these utterances as heated.

Outcomes and follow-up interviews
In the following, we discuss the outcomes of our rating test and follow-up interviews together because the interviews reflected on our subjects' solutions of the tasks in the test.

Task 1
Table 6.4 provides a summary of the Chinese and the foreign respondents' evaluations of the RFIE-utterances presented in Task 1.

Table 6.4 *Chinese and foreign respondents' evaluations of the RFIE-utterances presented in Task 1*

	Native speakers of Chinese		Foreign learners of Chinese	
	'request'	'order'	'request'	'order'
(A) 请保持课堂纪律。 '*Qing* uphold the order of the classroom'	3	7	8	2
(B) 注意课堂纪律。 '*Zhuyi* classroom order'	2	8	3	7
(C) 不要违反课堂纪律。 'One *buyao* violate the classroom order'	3	7	0	10

Table 6.4 shows a noteworthy contrastive pragmatic difference between the ways in which the Chinese native speakers and the foreign learners of Chinese interpreted RFIEs in the context of criticising in the classroom. The responses show that native speakers of Chinese evaluated different

RFIE-utterances relatively similarly, mostly as an 'order'. This evaluative tendency shows that native speakers of Chinese were aware of the fact that various RFIEs, including *qing*, do not mark 'politeness'. For example, Respondent 1 argued as follows regarding utterance (A) during the interview:

(6.19) '请保持课堂纪律。' 就像告示牌上 '请勿吸烟' 这种感觉，虽然说请了，但感觉不是一个请求，更感觉是命令 …
'*Qing* uphold the order of the classroom' is like a public note. It is like '*Qing* don't smoke' kind of. Although this sentence includes *qing*, it doesn't sound like a request at all, it's more like an order …

Interestingly, Chinese respondents who interpreted the utterances in this task as a 'request' argued that the Chinese classroom context does not necessitate such 'refined' solutions, i.e. they also did not conflate RFIEs with 'politeness'.

As Table 6.4 indicates, the responses of the foreign learners of Chinese were very different from their native speaking peers: while the former in general realised that the RFIEs *buyao* and *zhuyi* represent authority, eight out of the ten participants evaluated the utterance realised with *qing* as a 'request'. Further, five out of these eight respondents argued in the interviews that the 'request' presented to them was realised *at the beginning* of the class. For example, Respondent 7 stated the following:

(6.20) I think the lecturer asks foreign students to follow local regulations during class. Maybe these foreign students are unfamiliar with Chinese teaching customs, or there is another problem that makes it necessary for the teacher to tell them what to expect.

Many of the respondents similarly misunderstood the *in-situ* nature of the Request presented to them as *pre-situ*. For native speakers of Chinese, the utterance presented in the task could simply not be *pre-situ*, most likely because the authority animated by this RFIE implies that the order of the classroom has already been breached. A related problem type in the evaluations of foreign learners was the following: while certain participants – like Respondent 3 quoted below – realised that the RFIE *qing* occurs in criticising, they argued that the utterance is very 'gentle' in nature. Example (6.21) illustrates this point:

(6.21) This sentence is a very polite way of reminding students to behave. The teacher may not single out a specific student, and I feel he or she may simply want to tell the students to lower their tone of voice or have something like this.

In summary, Task 1 has shown that the RFIE *qing* triggers a major interpretational difficulty for foreign learners of Chinese when it comes to recognising critical disciplinary moves in Chinese classrooms. Considering the relative frequency of *qing* in such settings (Table 6.1), it is safe to argue that this is a

Speech acts and interactional acts 1

significant problem source. In line with our previous research (Chapter 4), we believe that this problem is due to pragmatic transfer: in many 'Western' linguacultures, 'requestive' expressions like *please* are popularly associated with 'politeness'.

Task 2

Table 6.5 shows our two groups' evaluations of the address realisations presented to them.

Table 6.5 *Chinese and foreign respondents' evaluations of address realisations in Task 2*

		Native speakers of Chinese			Foreign learners of Chinese		
		Most acceptable	Acceptable	Least acceptable	Most acceptable	Acceptable	Least acceptable
(A)	张三/李四，请不要说话。 'Zhang San/Li Si, *qing-buyao* talk'	0	3	7	7	3	0
(B)	请你不要说话。 '*Qing* you *buyao* talk'	0	5	5	1	9	0
(C)	请你们不要说话。 '*Qing* you [plural] *buyao* talk'	3	7	0	3	7	0
(D)	请同学们不要说话。 '*Qing* students *buyao* talk'	8	2	0	6	4	0

As Table 6.5 illustrates, there are significant differences between how native speakers and learners of Chinese evaluate utterances (A) and (B), featuring individual addressing: native speakers tended to disprefer these realisations, while foreign learners tended to evaluate them positively. There was no such a divide between the evaluations of utterances (C) and (D), which included communal addressing. During the interviews, the responses of our Chinese participants coincided with what we found in our DCTs, i.e. that individual addressing is considered to be highly face-threatening in the Chinese linguaculture. For example, Respondent 6 argued as follows:

(6.22) 有人名最不好接受，A、B难以接受，针对性太强。
It's difficult to accept person names here, and A and B [in general] are unacceptable because they target an individual.

Our foreign learners of Chinese rated utterance (A) as far the most acceptable among the various addressing realisations. Many of these respondents found the co-occurrence of the RFIE *qing* and the person's name to be an amiable way of communicating in a potential classroom conflict. For example, Respondent 3 stated the following:

(6.23) The fact that the teacher politely requests the students shows that he or she is respectful to the student – which I find very nice, and I wish our own lecturers talked like this.

When we followed up with her on this evaluation, Respondent 3 also stated that she does not

(6.24) … think that this student has done any major disruption in the class, as otherwise the teacher would not use such *nice words* [our emphasis] to her or him.

In summary, similar to Task 1 the outcomes of Task 2 pointed to a contrastive pragmatic difference resulting in varying evaluations of disciplinary criticising in the Chinese classroom context: unlike native speakers of Chinese, foreign learners found the use of a person's name to be acceptable and personal pronominal addressing also relatively acceptable. Paradoxically then, our foreign learners were unable to properly evaluate the most *aggressive* realisations of disciplinary criticising. Similar to the RFIE *qing*, pragmatic transfer may once again be responsible for this problem: in many 'Western' linguacultures, the use of person name in [+P] settings is normally considered to be a sign of amiability (see also Cotterill, 2020).

Task 3

Table 6.6 shows our respondents' evaluations of the speech acts presented in Task 3.

Table 6.6 *Chinese and foreign respondents' evaluations of the speech acts presented in Task 3*

		Native speakers of Chinese			Foreign learners of Chinese		
		Most acceptable	Acceptable	Least acceptable	Most acceptable	Acceptable	Least acceptable
(A)	好好听课！ 'Follow the class carefully!'	3	4	3	6	4	0
(B)	上课不许玩手机！ 'No mobile phones are tolerated in the class!'	5	4	1	8	2	0
	这课堂也太欢脱了！ 'This class is overly happy today!'	5	1	4	0	2	8

The Chinese speakers in our sample evaluated Request, Tell and Opine relatively similarly in the context of disciplinary criticising. For example, Respondent 7 argued as follows:

(6.25) A、B、C都是3，都可以接受，1是大学课堂最常见的，感觉约束作用最强。b语气有点过于委婉，显得老师特别软，可能起不到约束作用；c有点阴阳怪气，但是也可以接受。
I rate all A, B and C as 3. A is how most typically a lecturer would speak in a classroom, it feels authoritative. B is quite indirect, it is how a softer teacher would speak, it sounds less disciplinary. C is a bit sarcastic but also quite acceptable.

Our foreign respondents found Tell to be the most acceptable speech act, and more importantly they found Opine to be largely unacceptable. The interviews revealed that most respondents found the style of the Opine utterance 'patronising'. For example, Respondent 4 stated the following:

(6.26) While I like the Chinese, as otherwise I wouldn't have chosen Chinese as my foreign language, I find it so typically Chinese that a lecturer talks to adult students like children. From what I gather from previous of your tasks, is that all these utterances are actually meant to be reminders for students to behave in class, but lecturers in other cultures would not talk to students like children – especially if there is a trouble in the class – because this would compromise the lecturer's integrity.

While this response is of course based on a cultural overgeneralisation, it shows that linguacultural differences between the perceived rights and obligations of lecturers in the ritual space of the classroom may influence evaluations of speech acts in disciplinary criticising. In particular, Opine – which is one of the conventionalised speech act types in our data – turned out to be perceived as 'patronising' by many foreign learners of Chinese.

6.5 Conclusion

In this chapter, we have ventured beyond the relationship between expressions and speech acts, by considering how interactional acts tend to be realised by expressions and speech acts. We have put the framework presented in Chapter 3 to use in a fully-fledged way, i.e. we described an opening L2 problem, which in turn led us to conduct a bipartite inquiry.

We argued that in the study of criticising one should go beyond its traditional interpretation as a speech act. On the basis of our typology (see Chapter 3), we broke down criticising as an interactional act into the smaller components of expressions and speech acts through which this act tends to be realised in Chinese classrooms. While criticising represents language behaviour in a specific situation, this situation can be argued to be particularly important in a foreign student's life. Not being able to recognise instances of criticism in Chinese may even irritate many long-term foreign learners of this language, including the second author of this book. We believe that this is a teaching-induced error, which needs to be addressed in Chinese teaching programmes. This is all the more so because certain issues triggered by pragmatic transfer in our study – such as interpreting the RFIE *qing* as a 'politeness expression' and the use of person names as 'amiable' – may be experienced by students from many different linguacultural backgrounds in other contexts as well.

6.6 Recommended reading

Alcón, Eva and Pilar Safont Jordà. (2008). Pragmatic awareness in second language acquisition. In Jasone Cenoz and Nancy H. Hornberger (eds), *Encyclopedia of Language and Education*. New York: Springer, pp. 193–204.
In this chapter we reported on L2 learners' awareness and assessment of the use of RFIEs, other expressions and speech acts relating to the interactional act of criticising. Readers interested in metapragmatic awareness and assessment may consult the work of Alcón and Safont Jordà. In the following excerpt, Alcón and Safont Jordà discuss contrastive issues relating to L2 pragmatics:

> Pragmatic awareness is the conscious, reflective, explicit knowledge about pragmatics. It thus involves knowledge of those rules and conventions underlying appropriate language use in particular communicative situations and on the part of members of specific speech communities ... Analysing language use in context has provided language teachers and learners with a research-based understanding of the language forms and functions that are appropriate to the many contexts in which a language may be used. From this perspective, research ... has provided information on the interactive norms in different languages and cultures. Cross-cultural studies with a focus on speakers' pragmatic performance aim to determine whether the same speech act can be found in different cultures, and if so, to what extent it is performed. Likewise, explanations that account for those differences are provided. Among them, pragmatic transfer at the level of formal, semantic and speakers' perception of contextual factors seems to explain some of the differences between L1 and L2 [native and non-native] speakers' use of the language. In addition to transfer, learning effects, which may be of a formal or informal nature have been reported to cause a deviation from the target language norm. Examples of types of learning effects include overgeneralization, hypercorrection, or responses that do not reflect reality. (Alcón and Safont Jordà, 2008: 193, 195)

Note

1. In the English translations of the examples, we provide the original RFIEs in Pinyin Romanisation because these expressions are not readily translatable (see House, 2015).

CHAPTER 7

Speech acts and interactional acts 2: the case of ritual congratulating

7.1 Introduction

In this chapter, we continue exploring the relationship between speech acts and interactional acts in L2 pragmatics, by interconnecting our inquiry with the applied linguistic field of study abroad, as well as interaction ritual theory. More specifically, we examine how and why the realisation of a non-quotidian ritual interactional act – congratulating – triggers realisation difficulties for foreign learners of Chinese in **study abroad** programmes in China. The rationale behind examining such a non-quotidian and essentially ritual interactional act like congratulating is the following. Due to the notorious absence of complex ritual behaviour in teaching materials, students may never encounter such interactional acts when they learn Chinese in their home country. This knowledge gap can make itself painfully felt when a learner stays in China. For example, it put the second author of this book into an awkward situation when a friend told him that his father had turned eighty, and he was left dumbfounded because he had never been taught exactly what to say in such a ritual situation, although he knew that the eightieth birthday is an important ritual event in the Chinese linguaculture. What makes congratulating and other ritual acts more important than meets the eye is that they are not only used when someone participates in an actual ritual event. For example, ritual congratulating is also needed in ordinary events like workplace meetings when someone casually mentions a ritual family event, as shown by the above example. In such a case, there is practically as much pressure on the foreign learner to act appropriately as if he were actually participating in the event.

Similar to the previous chapter, we approach congratulating as an interactional act by breaking it down into the realisation of different conventional speech acts. Our approach is critically different from a body of research in which ritual congratulating and other forms of ritual behaviour are often analysed through non-replicable *ad hoc* speech act categories. Furthermore, we use interaction ritual theory, by bringing together Turner's (1969) concept

Speech acts and interactional acts 2 109

of 'liminality', Goffman's (1974) seminal notion of 'frame' and Kádár's (2017) interaction ritual pragmatic methodology. More specifically, we focus on congratulating realised in the context of liminal ritual events. Typical types of such liminal ritual events, which bring the participants into a new phase of life, include weddings and important birthdays, such as the eighteenth and eightieth birthday in many linguacultures. Following Goffman, we argue that congratulating for such liminal ritual events evokes a particular frame, in which the interactants are constrained by conventionalised obligations.

This chapter has the following structure. First, we present selected previous studies, then we describe our methodology and data, which will be followed by data analysis and conclusion.

7.2 Selected previous studies

Our research on study abroad is somewhat different from the mainstream literature in this area, in that the latter has mostly focused on how study abroad influences the acquisition of the target language. We consider an understudied issue, namely why and how ritual pragmatic phenomena can become problematic for learners in their target country.

Considering that study abroad has been a very popular area in applied linguistics, in the following we will only mention a few studies. Freed (1995, 1998) examined how to assess the effect of study abroad on foreign language learners. Similarly, Tanaka and Ellis (2003) focused on the assessment of L2 language proficiency in study abroad contexts, and also how learners' beliefs about language learning influence the efficiency of acquiring the target language. Kinginger (2011) considered how studying abroad influences language learners' competence, by arguing that one should consider the important role of individual differences when assessing such an impact. Isabelli-García et al. (2018) provided a general overview of the field of study abroad, dividing research into quantitative, qualitative and mixed method approaches. Taguchi (2018) also provided an overview of study abroad, examining views on the concept of 'context'.

We can see that scholars in the field of study abroad mainly pursued an interest in pragmatic phenomena which are generally important for any foreign learner group in any target country, such as speech acts, formulaic language, tonal accuracy, and so on. This interest in generally important phenomena has also been present in the narrower field of pragmatic aspects of study abroad in China. For example, Du (2013) conducted longitudinal research on the development of pragmatic competence of foreign students in China, and Kim et al. (2015) examined the development of foreign learners' tonal accuracy, vocabulary acquisition and task fulfillment. Wang and Halenko (2022) also studied how foreign students' competence evolves over time in Chinese study abroad programmes, by focusing on formulaic language use. In contrast, we focus on the less studied phenomenon of ritual, which, however, we believe constitutes a very important problem for foreign learners of Chinese when they are in China.

Wang and Halenko (2022) criticised speech act-anchored research on study abroad in China, arguing that speech act triggers an overly narrow focus on the acquisition of pragmatic phenomena in study abroad contexts. While we do not fully agree with this view, we believe that the criticism of Wang and Halenko (2022) is valid in that many scholars in the field have studied the acquisition of one particular speech act only. For example, Jin (2012, 2015) examined how foreign students develop skills in complimenting in Chinese study abroad programmes, Yang and Ke (2021) studied how foreigners learn to realise Request and Apology in China, and so on. We agree with Ren (2019) that speech acts need to be kept on the agenda of research on study abroad, and we believe that our bottom-up take on speech acts is particularly useful in this respect. In this approach, we do not zero in on the learning of one particular speech act, but rather we conduct an applied linguistic examination of an interactional phenomenon, which we break down to recurrent speech acts following our framework outlined in Chapter 3.

A body of research has focused on ritual congratulating, by associating the ritual event of congratulating with the speech act Congratulate (see e.g. Ide, 1998; Kampf, 2016). While we agree with the assumption that certain ritual contexts indeed trigger the speech act Congratulate, in accordance with our framework we approach the interactional act of congratulating in a decidedly interactional and bottom-up way, by considering exactly which speech acts may co-occur with – or substitute – Congratulate in such settings. This view helps us also to provide an alternative for previous applied linguistic research on the acquisition of ritual congratulating in the study of other 'exotic' languages, such as Arabic (see e.g. Pishghadam and Morady Moghaddam, 2011; Al-Hour, 2019).

7.3 Methodology and data

In this case study, we follow the research design outlined in our framework. First, we compiled a DCT corpus, involving a group of ten Chinese speakers. The respondents were requested to complete tasks relating to congratulating someone for the following liminal rites of passage:

- Birth of a child
- Eighteenth birthday
- Eightieth birthday
- Marriage

The reason why we included not only the different rites of passage of birthday and marriage, but also a variation between different types of ritual birthday congratulation in our DCTs, is that the Chinese linguaculture is often described as an 'age-respecting' one. While we disagree with such overgeneralisations, we believe that it is valid to argue that in the Neo-Confucian ideology, which heavily influences Chinese formal social rituals, age seems to be a central value (see Pan and Kádár, 2011).

The DCTs featured the standard sociolinguistic parameters Social Distance and Power [+/–SD, +/–P], and they included the following tasks:

Birth of a child

1. 你好朋友家的孩子满月，你会说什么表示祝贺？
   Your friend's child grew one-month-old. How would you congratulate? [–P/–SD]
2. 你邻居家（点头之交）的孩子满月，你会说什么表示祝贺？
   Your neighbour's (whom you only know to greet) child grew one-month-old. How would you congratulate? [–P/+SD]
3. 你领导家的孩子满月，你会说什么表示祝贺？
   Your manager's child grew one-month-old. How would you congratulate? [+P/–SD]
4. 你爱人领导家（点头之交）的孩子满月，你会说什么表示祝贺？
   The child of your spouse's manager (whom you only know to greet) grew one-month-old. How would you congratulate? [+P/+SD]

Eighteenth birthday

1. 你的好朋友（或好朋友家孩子）今天过 18 岁生日，你会说什么表示祝贺？
   Your friend (or the child of your friend) has turned eighteen years old. How would you congratulate. [–P/–SD]
2. Etc.
3. Etc.
4. Etc.

Eightieth birthday

1. 你好朋友家的老人今天过 80 大寿，你会说什么表示祝贺？
   Your friend's parent turned eighty. How would you express your congratulation? [–P/–SD]
2. Etc.
3. Etc.
4. Etc.

Wedding

1. 你的好朋友结婚，你会说什么表示祝贺？
   Your friend got married. How would you congratulate? [–P/–SD]
2. Etc.

3. Etc.
4. Etc.

The results of the DCTs enabled us to identify the most frequent expressions, mostly RFIEs, and speech acts through which congratulating is realised in the four ritual events.

Second, we administered another DCT set, asking a group of ten advanced learners of Chinese who had not visited China at the time of the experiment to perform the interactional act of congratulating in the context of the above four rituals. Our goal here was to observe whether the foreign learners' performance is similar to or different from the pragmatic conventions we were able to extract from the Chinese DCTs. We then selected the most frequent realisation patterns of congratulating from their DCT responses, which we used to ask a group of ten native speakers of Chinese to reflect on. The Chinese participants were not told that the utterances presented to them were produced by foreign learners of Chinese because we wanted to see their unbiased reactions to these utterances in the form of an evaluation task.

At this point, it is worth revisiting the typology of speech acts we are using in our framework (see also Chapter 3):

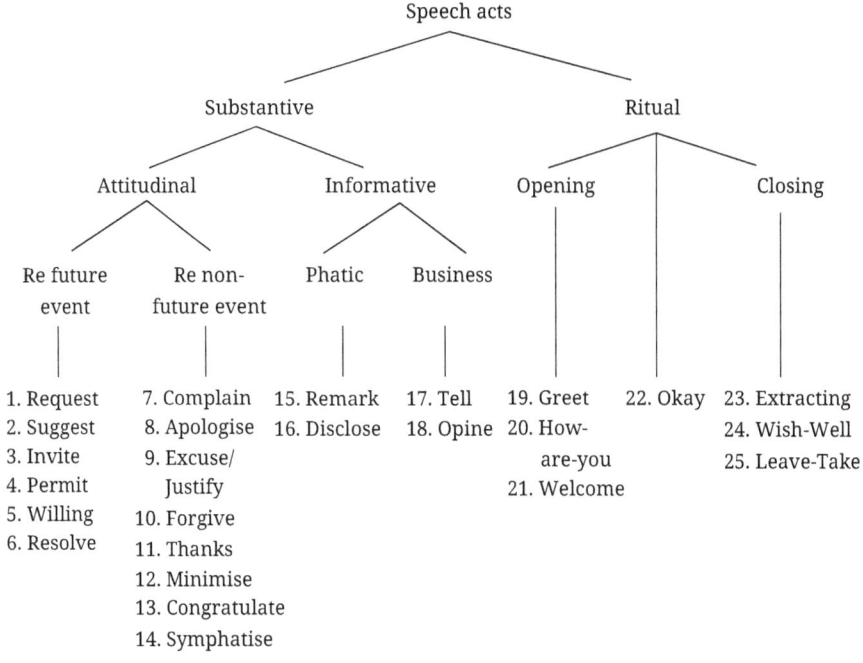

Figure 7.1 Our typology of speech acts (displayed again)

As we already noted in Chapter 3, 'Ritual' in the typology indicates an interactional slot, i.e. those phases of an interaction in which social symbolic communication is compulsory. In other words, this system does not predetermine which speech acts are ritual. For example, Congratulate is a typically Attitudinal speech act, which however is often ritual in nature:

> Congratulations are called for when the hearer has achieved some success, goal, or good fortune, or, more ritually, when he celebrates some event to which our social customs attach significance in a positive way – a specific birthday, a wedding anniversary, an engagement, the birth of a grand-child, and so on. (Edmondson and House, 1981: 167)

An important part of analysing the results of our DCT corpora is that we did not assume that responses amount to the speech act Congratulate, but rather we used the above-displayed typology to interpret the DCTs. Here we were inspired by a problem often faced by Asian learners of English, illustrated by the following extract from an EFL website:

> *Don't Say Congratulations to Wish Someone a Happy Birthday*
> How to say your birthday wishes to someone in English? Congratulations? Happy Birthday? A lot of English learners get stuck on this, because birthday greetings in some languages get translated into English as Congratulations. But, don't say congratulations when it's someone's birthday: Oh, it's your birthday! Congratulations. (https://www.myhappyenglish.com/free-english-lesson/2022/02/23/dont-say-congratulations-to-wish-someone-a-happy-birthday/)

We were interested in whether any similar problem emerges in the current study.

As mentioned above, the case study presented in this chapter is embedded in interaction ritual theory. The interaction ritual view implies that along with the standard terminology of pragmatics we use the notions of 'liminality' and 'frame', borrowed from Turner (1969) and Goffman (1974) respectively. Interaction ritual behaviour normally manifests itself through a frame triggering conventionalised patterns of language use (often indicated by RFIEs). A key advantage of studying pragmatic behaviour in a ritual frame is that it allows one to ignore idiosyncrasies. As part of studying pragmatic conventions in the interaction ritual act of congratulating, we not only study speech acts but also honorific expressions and other formulae which belong to conventional realisations of the various speech act used in this interaction ritual act.

7.4 Analysis

Here we present our analysis by dividing this section into two parts, following our bipartite research design.

7.4.1 Results of the Chinese DCTs

Congratulating for the birth of a child

Table 7.1 summarises the results of the DCTs featuring the interaction ritual act of congratulating for the birth of a child.

Table 7.1 *The results of the DCTs featuring the interaction ritual act of congratulating for the birth of a child*

Interpersonal scenario 1 [–P/–SD]	Interpersonal scenario 2 [–P/+SD]	Interpersonal scenario 3 [+P/–SD]	Interpersonal scenario 4 [+P/+SD]
Congratulate 7 [Formulae/ Honorifics 3; Intensifiers 1]	Congratulate 7 [Formulae/ Honorifics 4; Intensifiers 1]	Congratulate 8 [Formulae/ Honorifics 4; Intensifiers 2]	Congratulate 9 [Formulae/ Honorifics 4; Intensifiers 1]
Wish-Well 3	Wish-Well 4	Wish-Well 4	Wish-Well 2
Remark 2	Remark 3	Remark 1	
Opine 1			

Before interpreting the results shown in Table 7.1, the terms used here need to be defined. According to Edmondson and House (1981) and Edmondson et al. (2023), the speech act categories in the table are defined as follows. We defined Opine already in the previous chapter, but in various chapters of this book we present a number of speech act definitions, sometimes in a repetitive way, to facilitate the reader's work.

- Wish-Well: In this illocutionary act a speaker expresses his positive attitude towards his hearer by 'wishing him well' for the future, either in general terms, or with respect to some specific forthcoming event.
- Remark: Remarks are essentially phatic in nature, and H-supportive in intent. In making a Remark, a speaker shows himself favourably disposed towards the hearer. The topic of Remark is likely to be derived from the immediate context of situation.
- Opine: Through an Opine a speaker voices what he believes to be a fact in a clearly subjective way.

As part of interpreting our DCT corpus, we also quantified uses of honorifics and formulae, as well as intensifiers (see Blum-Kulka et al., 1989).

As Table 7.1 shows, the most frequent speech act in this ritual event is clearly Congratulate, followed by Wish-Well, Remark and Opine. The only meaningful variation across different interpersonal scenarios is that the number of Congratulates somewhat increases and Remark and Opine decrease in [+P] and [+SD] scenarios. An important outcome of the DCTs displayed in Table 7.1 is that Congratulate in Chinese ritual congratulating transpires to be at least as important as Wish-Well, unlike in many 'Western' linguacultures such as English.

Speech acts and interactional acts 2

Congratulate is often realised through the expression *gongxi* 恭喜 (lit. 'expressing respect for someone's happiness'), and less frequently by *zhuhe* 祝贺 (lit. 'respectfully congratulate'). The following utterances from our DCTs illustrate the use of these expressions:

(7.1) 恭喜喜得贵子。
Congratulations for the happiness of the birth of your noble son.
CONGRATULATE [HONORIFICS] ([–P/–SD])

(7.2) 祝贺祝贺。
Congratulations.
CONGRATULATE [INT.] ([–P/–SD])

(7.3) 祝贺人丁兴旺。
Congratulations for the glorious increase of males in your family.
CONGRATULATE [HONORIFICS] ([–P/–SD])

As these examples show, even in the [–P/–SD] scenario Congratulate realisations often include honorific expressions, such as *guizi* 贵子 ('noble son') in example (7.1), as well as archaic set phrases such as *rending-xingwang* 人丁兴旺 (lit. 'the glorious rise of males in someone's family', i.e. the birth of a son) in example (7.3). *Rending-xingwang* is such a specific formula that it is used only at the event of the birth of a child. Also, as example (7.2) shows, Congratulate expressions are often intensified through repetition. Intensification can be made stronger by emotive particles, as in the following example:

(7.4) 吐，宝宝太可爱了，恭喜恭喜啊
Wow, the baby is so cute, congratulations.
REMARK / CONGRATULATE ([–P/–SD])

Here *gongxi* is not only repeated but it is followed by the emotional *a* 啊 particle.

The speech act Wish-Well in this ritual event can be either realised by the more formal verb *zhu* 祝 ('wish') or the more colloquial *xiwang* 希望 ('I hope that'), with the former being more preferred than the latter. The following examples show the use of these two expressions:

(7.5) 宝宝真可爱，祝宝宝健康快乐
The baby is so cute. Wish the baby become healthy and happy.
REMARK / WISH-WELL ([–P/–SD])

(7.6) 希望宝宝健健康康成长。前途无量，有一个美好的未来。
Wish the baby will grow up in health. His prospects are myriad, he has a beautiful future.
WISH-WELL / OPINE ([–P/–SD])

In example (7.5), the Wish-Well which follows a Remark is realised with the verb *zhu*, while in (7.6) it is realised with *xiwang*. The above examples also show how Remark and Opine operate in ritual congratulating.

All the above examples represent ritual congratulating in the [–P/–SD] scenario. As noted above, Opine and Remark decrease in [+P] and [+SD] scenarios, and this tendency correlates with the fact that these speech acts occur in our data in relatively colloquial congratulating realisations (see examples (7.5) and (7.6)).

Congratulating for an eighteenth birthday
Table 7.2 summarises the results of DCTs featuring the interaction ritual act of congratulating for an eighteenth birthday.

Table 7.2 *The results of DCTs featuring the interaction ritual act of congratulating for an eighteenth birthday*

Interpersonal scenario 1 [–P/–SD]	Interpersonal scenario 2 [–P/+SD]	Interpersonal scenario 3 [+P/+SD]	Interpersonal scenario 4 [+P/+SD]
Wish-Well 5 [Formulae/ Honorifics 2]	Wish-Well 6 [Formulae/ Honorifics 2]	Wish-Well 5 [Formulae/ Honorifics 3]	Wish-Well 5 [Formulae/ Honorifics 2]
Congratulate 4 [Formulae/ Honorifics 4, Intensifiers 1]	Congratulate 4 [Formulae/ Honorifics 4, Intensifiers 1]	Congratulate 4 [Formulae/ Honorifics 4, Intensifiers 1]	Congratulate 4 [Formulae/ Honorifics 4, Intensifiers 1]
Opine 4 [Formulae 3]	Opine 5 [Formulae 2]	Opine 4 [Formulae 3]	Opine 4 [Formulae 3]
Suggest 2	Remark 1	Remark 3	Remark 3
Remark 1			

The speech act category Suggest in Table 7.2 can be defined as an illocution in which a speaker communicates that he is in favour of H's performing a future action as in H's own interest.

There is a major pragmatic difference between ritual congratulating for the birth of a child and for someone's eighteenth birthday: in the latter, the most frequented speech act is Wish-Well, while the frequency of Congratulate is lower. This difference in our view correlates with the fact that the rite for congratulating for someone's eighteenth birthday is a foreign ritual, which was imported into Chinese through the global impact of English as a lingua franca. The following example represents an informal Wish-Well:

(7.7) 生日快乐！
Happy birthday!
Wish-well

This four-character set phrase is used in all the four interpersonal scenarios in this ritual, mostly without the verb *zhu* ('wish'). Our interpretation

Speech acts and interactional acts 2   117

is that *shengri-kuaile* 生日快乐 ('happy birthday') is a formulaic expression of foreign origin, which can be used 'on its own' without any deferential verb.

Interestingly, one of our Chinese respondents 'Sinicised' this foreign formulaic expression by adding the verb *zhuhe* (lit. 'respectfully congratulate'), hence transforming the Wish-Well into Congratulate:

(7.8) 终于长大成人了。首先<u>祝贺生日快乐</u>！别辜负你爸妈对你的辛勤付出。
You have grown up. First, <u>I congratulate you on your happy birthday!</u> Don't ever let your parents down after they have invested hard work in bringing you up.
REMARK / WISH-WELL / SUGGEST   ([–P/–SD])

Our native speaker consultants pointed out that this use is not idiosyncratic.

Congratulating for an eightieth birthday
Table 7.3 summarises the results of DCTs featuring the interaction ritual act of congratulating for an eightieth birthday:

Table 7.3 *The results of DCTs featuring the interaction ritual act of congratulating for an eightieth birthday*

Interpersonal scenario 1 [–P/–SD]	Interpersonal scenario 2 [–P/+SD]	Interpersonal scenario 3 [+P/–SD]	Interpersonal scenario 4 [+P/+SD]
Opine 5 [Formulae 5]	Opine 6 [Formulae 6]	Opine 5 [Formulae 5]	Opine 6 [Formulae 6]
Wish-Well 5 [Formulae/ Honorifics 4]	Wish-Well 4 [Formulae/ Honorifics 4]	Wish-Well 5 [Formulae/ Honorifics 4]	Wish-Well 4 [Formulae/ Honorifics 4]
	Remark 1		

As Table 7.3 shows, the pragmatic patterns of ritual congratulating for someone's eightieth birthday are very different from that of the previous rituals: in this ritual event, Opine and Wish-Well are the two dominant speech acts.

Opines are always realised with a particular set phrase, as illustrated by the following example:

(7.9) 福如东海，寿比南山！
Happiness is like the east China Sea, longevity is like the South Mountain.
OPINE [FORMULAIC]   ([–P/–SD])

This particular formula is used without variation in all role relationships. While the two-times-four-characters layout of this phrase reminds one of

Classical Chinese written language, our native speaker respondents confirmed that this expression is frequented in spoken colloquial Chinese.

In [+P] relationships, longer poetic set forms of Opine may also be used:

(7.10) 日月昌明，松鹤长春，后福无疆，富贵安康。
The sun and moon are shining brightly, the pine and the white crane bring longevity, future fortune will have no boundary, will be blessed with health and prosperity.
OPINE [FORMULAIC]   ([+P/–SD])

Along with Opine, the other standard speech act in this ritual event is Wish-Well. Unlike Wish-Wells in the rituals described above, Wish-Wells in the current ritual congratulating are always formularised:

(7.11) 祝老人家健康长寿！
Wish the old person longevity and health!
WISH-WELL [FORMULAIC]   ([–P/–SD])

(7.12) 祝老人家身体健康，万寿无疆！
Wish the old person good health, his longevity may have no limit!
WISH-WELL [FORMULAIC]   ([+P/+SD])

In these Wish-Well realisations, the person who receives the congratulation is addressed/referred to with the honorific *laorenjia* 老人家 (lit. 'old, i.e. higher-ranking person'). Many Wish-Wells also include the formulae *changshou* 长寿 ('longevity') and *wanshou* 万寿 ('ten-thousand-years-longevity').

Congratulating for a wedding
Table 7.4 summarises the results of DCTs featuring the interaction ritual act of congratulating for a wedding.

Table 7.4 *The results of DCTs featuring the interaction ritual act of congratulating for a wedding*

Interpersonal scenario 1 [–P/–SD]	Interpersonal scenario 2 [–P/+SD]	Interpersonal scenario 3 [+P/–SD]	Interpersonal scenario 4 [+P/+SD]
Wish-Well 6 [Formulae/ Honorifics 6]	Wish-Well 6 [Formulae/ Honorifics 6]	Wish-Well 6 [Formulae/ Honorifics 6]	Wish-Well 5 [Formulae/ Honorifics 5]
Congratulate 4 [Formulae 4, Intensifiers 2]	Congratulate 4 [Formulae 4, Intensifiers 2]	Congratulate 4 [Formulae 4, Intensifiers 1]	Congratulate 5 [Formulae 5, Intensifiers 1]
Opine 1	Opine 1	Opine 2	

Speech acts and interactional acts 2

Wish-Well appears to be the most important speech act in this ritual event, and it tends to be realised with the formula *xinhun-kuaile* 新婚快乐 ('happy marriage'). While this formula is of foreign origin, just like the previously discussed formula *shengri-kuaile*, unlike the latter it is often Sinicised with the ensuing Chinese honorific Wish-Well form *zaosheng-guizi* 早生贵子 ('may you have a noble son early'):

(7.13) 新婚快乐，早生贵子
Happy marriage, may you have a noble son early.
WISH-WELL / WISH-WELL   ([+P/+SD])

The speech act Congratulate is also frequent in this ritual event:

(7.14) 新婚大喜，恭喜恭喜，早生贵子
Happy marriage, congratulations, may you have a lovely son early.
WISH-WELL / CONGRATULATE [INTENSIFIED] / WISH-WELL   ([–P/–SD])

(7.15) 恭喜喜结良缘
Congratulations for tying your auspicious destinies together.
CONGRATULATE   ([+P/+SD])

Example (7.14) represents an intensified Congratulate (*gongxi* repeated), co-occurring with Wish-Wells, and (7.15) is a typical set Congratulate form used in the specific rite of a wedding ritual.

In summary, our analysis reveals the following:

- There is relatively little variation between the realisation patterns of all the four types of congratulating across different interpersonal scenarios. This accords with the conventionalisedness of social rituals (see Kádár's 2017 discussion on the fixedness of ritual patterns).
- All ritual events, except congratulating for one's eighteenth birthday, are highly immersed in the Chinese linguaculture.
- The speech act Wish-Well is either used in a preset way, or rarely used at all. Wish-Well in congratulating often includes complex honorifics.
- Congratulate is arguably the most important speech act in the liminal ritual events analysed. An exception is the case of congratulating for one's eighteenth birthday, which is a rite of foreign origin.
- There is no single and uniform pragmatic pattern for realising congratulating across these various ritual events.
- Formal forms – including complex poetic Opines like those we could observe in the ritual of congratulating for someone's eightieth birthday – are frequented.

Given these results, foreign learners of Chinese in study abroad contexts may be faced with a pragmatic phenomenon which is different from what they are familiar with in their home linguaculture.

7.4.2 Results of the learner DCTs

Here, we administered DCTs to ten European learners of Chinese who had not visited China at the time. The only difference between these DCTs and those presented to native Chinese speakers was that we did not provide different interpersonal scenarios for our foreign participants. We decided to proceed in this way for two reasons: (1) we found little variation between the realisation of ritual congratulating across different interpersonal scenarios, (2) because of this we wanted to avoid overwhelming our foreign respondents. Our goal here was to select a single 'typical' foreign realisation of congratulating in each ritual event in the DCTs. We then presented the results of these DCTs to a control group of ten native speakers of Chinese whom we asked to assess the appropriateness of what was presented to them.

Congratulating for the birth of a child
Five out of our ten foreign respondents produced a simple Wish-Well, by using the standard solution *zhu-shengri-kuaile* 祝生日快乐 ('Wish Happy Birthday'). Two of our respondents also added complimenting Remarks about the child, in forms such as *(ni de) xiaohaizi hen/zhen ke'ai* （你的）小孩子真/很可爱 ('(your child) is very/really cute'). Only three foreign learners used the Congratulate expression *gongxi*. Based on these responses, we selected the following utterance to be shown to our Chinese native speakers:

(7.16) 你小孩子真可爱，祝他生日快乐！
Your child is really cute, wish him happy birthday!
REMARK / WISH-WELL

Here we did not include *gongxi* because only few respondents used this expression, and also because such uses do not differ from what our Chinese respondents provided in the same scenario.

Congratulating for an eighteenth birthday
Here all our foreign respondents produced the standard Wish-Well form *zhu-shengri-kuaile* 祝生日快乐 ('Wish happy birthday'). Four respondents also realised follow-up Wish-Wells, including two informal realisations, such as *Xiwang ni hui you henduo chenggong* 希望你会有成功 ('I hope you will have plenty of fortune') and two formal realisations, including *xingyun chenggong* 幸运成功 ('good fortune and success') and *wanshi-ruyi* 万事如意 ('all matters should be according to how you wish'). Two respondents also realised a Remark in the form of *Ni-chengren/chengda le* 你成人/成大了 ('you've grown up'). Based on these responses, we selected the following utterance to be shown to Chinese native speakers:

Speech acts and interactional acts 2 121

(7.17) 你成人了，祝你生日快乐，幸运成功！
You've grown up, wish you happy birthday, good luck and success!
REMARK / WISH-WELL / WISH-WELL

Congratulating for an eightieth birthday
All foreign respondents realised Wish-Well in this act of congratulating, and eight out of ten also used honorifics, either by modifying the standard formula with *jing* 敬 ('respectfully'), or by using an honorific form of address such as the V pronoun *nin*, or both. Nine out of ten respondents zeroed in on the standard form *shengri-kuaile,* and three respondents used additional Wish-Well formulations, such as *jiankang-xingfu* 健康幸福 ('health and happiness') below. On the basis of these responses, we selected the following utterance to be shown to our Chinese respondents:

(7.18) 敬祝您生日快乐，健康幸福。
Respectfully wish you [V form] Happy Birthday, health, happiness and luck.
WISH-WELL / WISH-WELL

Congratulating for a wedding
Eight out of ten foreign participants used the simple Wish-Well form *jiehun-kuaile* 结婚快乐 ('happy marriage') in this ritual event, or some other less formulaic Wish-Well solutions including the word *jiehun*, such as *Zhu nimen gaoxing-de jiehun* 祝你们高兴的结婚 ('Wish you happy marriage'). Some respondents modified *jiehun-kuaile* with the verb *zhu*. Three of these eight respondents also used complimentary Remarks such as *Nimen zhen piaoliang* 你们真漂亮 ('you are really beautiful'). Finally, two respondents provided repeated *gongxi*-s. In our DCTs, we selected the above-mentioned Wish-Well form *jiehun-kuaile* to be shown to our Chinese native speakers, due to its frequency.

Chinese native speaker reflections
Our ten Chinese native speakers unanimously stated that all the above utterances presented to them must have been produced by foreign speakers of Chinese. In the following, we describe their assessments in more detail.

Congratulating for the birth of a child
Six out of ten Chinese respondents argued that example (7.16) above sounds 'alien' because no Congratulate is realised here. This assessment accords with the findings of our Chinese DCTs shown in Table 7.1 above, i.e. Congratulate is a key speech act in an interaction act of congratulating for the birth of a child. For example, one of the respondents argued as follows:

(7.19) Usually, the congratulations will be given to the child's parents, like:
恭喜（祝贺）你(们)，喜得贵子。

Here the respondent suggested that the Congratulate expression *gongxi* should be used together with the formula *xide-guizi* ('happiness of the birth of your noble son'). What various respondents also argued is that it is not the child who needs to be congratulated but rather his parents. Various respondents also argued that since it is the parents who are congratulated, the child should be referred to by using forms of endearment, such as *xiaomeinü* 小美女 ('little beauty') and *xiaoshuaige* 小帅哥 ('little handsome older brother').

Three respondents argued that zero-Congratulate would be a safe solution here. These respondents took up an etic attitude, putting themselves into the shoes of a foreigner. Also, one of the Chinese respondents suggested code-switching as a solution:

(7.20) '我会说 "Happy birthday, baby, 你真可爱, 生日快乐！"'
I would say, 'Happy birthday, baby, you are very cute, happy birthday!'

Congratulating for an eighteenth birthday

Example (7.17) was assessed relatively positively by our Chinese respondents, which coincides with the fact that here we have a foreign ritual which allows congratulating with the standard Wish-Well form *(zhu-)shengri-kuaile*. While the Chinese respondents raised problems with the utterance presented to them, unanimously arguing that it sounds 'foreign', these criticisms were not centred on the lack of Congratulate, but rather on the inappropriacy of the opening Remark and closing Wish-Well form which we had included in the utterance. Several respondents suggested 'more Chinese' solutions, such as the following one:

(7.21) 生日快乐！你十八岁了，是个成年人了，希望你幸运和成功！
Happy birthday! You became 18 years old, you are now an adult, wish you happiness and success in the future.

Here a Chinese respondent suggested colloquial formulations through which foreigners could more easily cope with congratulating in this situation.

Congratulating for an eightieth birthday

Interestingly, four out of ten Chinese respondents argued that the utterance featured as example (7.18) above is acceptable for them, even though this is the most complex ritual in our Chinese DCTs. All these Chinese respondents made it clear that it was the utterance's respectful style which made them asses it as appropriate. The following extract illustrates this type of assessment:

Speech acts and interactional acts 2 123

(7.22) 书面语比较适合。对长辈会用'您',如果是书面语或是短信等会用'敬祝'。
This would be relatively acceptable in a written form. Here the [V pronominal form] *nin* is used towards a senior person, and the [verbal form] 'respectfully wish' (*jingzhu*) suggests that this [utterance] is made is writing or in an SMS.

While this Chinese speaker noted that the utterance does not necessarily accord with how she herself would realise the congratulating in spoken interaction, she assessed it as 'relatively acceptable'.

It was a less surprising outcome that six out of ten Chinese respondents argued that the congratulating presented to them is inappropriate because it does not include the Opine formula *furu-Donghai, shoubi-Nanshan* ('Happiness is like the east China Sea, longevity is like the South Mountain'). The following bilingual response illustrates this point:

(7.23) This congratulation will not be appropriate even it starts with the honorific '敬祝' ['respectfully wish']. The problem also lies in the expression of '生日快乐' [*shengri-kuaile*]. In Chinese, '生日快乐' will not be used to people who is [sic!] at a high age like 80, because it is kind of impolite. However, there is no clear-cut definition or standard of 'high age'. Personally speaking, it is safe to use '生日快乐' to people who are under 60, to those who beyond 60, please think twice. Actually, in Chinese we have lots of polite formula for someone's 80th birthday, such as: 祝您福如东海,寿比南山 ['Happiness is like the east China Sea, longevity is like the South Mountain'] … .

One respondent also suggested a relatively colloquial solution, combining the above Opine formula with a Remark:

(7.24) 今天是您八十大寿!祝您福如东海,寿比南山!
You [V pronoun] are having the auspicious 80th birthday today! Happiness is like the east China Sea, longevity is like the South Mountain

Congratulating for a wedding

All our ten Chinese respondents recognised a pragmatic transfer in the utterance presented to them: while our foreign respondents provided the form *jiehun-kuaile* 结婚快乐, which translates as 'Happy marriage', in Chinese the appropriate form to be used in wedding congratulations is *xinhun-kuaile* 新婚快乐 (lit. 'new wedding happiness'). Only five Chinese respondents argued that something is 'missing' from the congratulating presented to them, which reflects what we found in our Chinese DCTs, namely that Wish-Well is the most important speech act in ritual wedding congratulation (see Table 7.4). Two out of the above-mentioned five respondents argued that the congratulation presented to them was inappropriate because it did not include the traditional Wish-Well form *zaosheng-guizi* ('may you have a noble son early') (see example (7.13) above). Three other respondents argued that a Congratulate is missing, as illustrated by the following extract:

(7.25) '恭喜'或'恭喜恭喜'是中国人的通用祝福语，适用于祝福对方喜事的场合。
Gongxi (lit. 'expressing respect for someone's happiness') or *gongxi-gongxi* is how we Chinese ordinarily express wish-well, it is used whenever we congratulate to the other on a happy occasion.

The Chinese native speakers' above-outlined assessments show that congratulating at different ritual occasions triggers a variety of types of inappropriateness and rates of inappropriacy. While the absence of associating the speech act Congratulate with the interactional act of congratulating is a general problem for foreign learners of Chinese, not all of the difficulties experienced by foreign learners can be readily explained by this simple cross-cultural pragmatic difference.

7.5 Conclusion

In this chapter, we have provided another case study where we investigated an L2 pragmatic problem by bringing together the units of speech act and interactional act, and also by incorporating RFIEs in the scope of our analysis. In our case study, we have examined how and why the realisation of the non-quotidian ritual act of congratulating is difficult for foreign learners of Chinese. To the best of our knowledge, textbooks and teaching programmes rarely cover such rituals, presumably because foreigners may seldom take part in such ritual events even when they stay in China. We argued that this, however, does not mean that foreigners can afford to be ignorant about such rituals because they may easily find themselves in mundane situations such as workplace meetings where congratulating or other rituals are needed. We have shown that studying rituals is important because their use can trigger a complex cluster of problems for foreign learners of Chinese. While Chinese participants involved in our study have turned out to be tolerant – i.e. they did not evaluate foreigners' failures of appropriately realising congratulating as 'impolite, 'offensive' and so on – they unanimously sensed that something was clearly 'wrong' with the learners' congratulations.

After having studied the speech act–interactional act interface, in the following chapters we move towards the highest unit of analysis in our framework: Types of Talk.

7.6 Recommended reading

Celeste Kinginger. (2011). Enhancing language learning in study abroad. *Annual Review of Applied Linguistics* **31, 58–73.**
In this chapter, we have discussed the important L2 pragmatic area of study abroad. Readers with additional interest in this area may consult the above-mentioned overview by Kinginger. In the following excerpt, Kinginger discusses the practical L2 issue of how engagement in learning abroad can be enhanced and how students should be prepared for a sojourn abroad:

> Clearly, students' interest and investment in language learning is not guaranteed, and there will always be a variety of ways in which study abroad is approached and interpreted. In the interest of students who truly desire language competence, however, it follows from the preceding findings that language educators have a number of crucial roles to play: promoting educationally relevant engagement in the practices of host communities, providing guidance in the interpretation of these practices, and preparing students to take specific advantage of language learning opportunities.
>
> Before students go abroad, they can be guided towards the practice of unbiased observation, participate in informal dialogs with members of their host communities, articulate appropriate goals, and prepare to make the most of their sojourn. While students are abroad, they can engage in informal ethnographic inquiry through tasks and projects, and they can participate in service learning, internships, or independent research. When students return from their in-country experience, much depends on how their experience is received within their home institution: whether or not it is integrated into the curriculum, with ongoing attention to their need for instruction in language and advanced literacy practices. [...]
>
> There are several ways in which language educators can help students to prepare for a language-focused sojourn abroad. First among these is the provision of guidance in selecting a program prioritizing language learning. Subsequently, students may benefit from enhanced understanding of both what and how they may learn while they are abroad. Concerning the former, many students may hold "folk-linguistic theories" (Miller & Ginsburg, 1995, p. 293), in which, for example, language is analogous to architecture, with words as building blocks and grammar as mortar. Absent from such portrayals are the social interactive abilities (sociolinguistic, discourse, or pragmatic) best learned in extensive interactive contact with expert speakers (Miller & Ginsburg, 1995). A short course in language awareness, such as the one outlined in Kinginger (2009b) or participation in an online pragmatics course ... might help students to recognize and cultivate these abilities.

Kinginger (2009b) also noted the commonalities between the goals of language learners abroad and those of scholars in the ethnography of communication ... Observation, participation, and reflection or introspection are among the main modes of learning languages in study abroad settings, as revealed in the Hassall (2006) study already reviewed here. These modes are also the key techniques used by ethnographers of communication as they attempt to understandwhat a speaker needs to know in order to communicate appropriately within a given community, and as they carry out field work "observing, asking questions, participating in group activities, and testing the validity of one's perceptions against the intuitions of natives" (Saville-Troike, 2003, p. 3). Kinginger (2009b) and Jackson (2008) offered suggested tasks for training in ethnographic observation for the predeparture stage. Through computer-mediated communication, it is possible to offer students occasions to practice informal, intercultural dialog (Tudini, 2007), virtual visits to their future host country (Pertusa-Seva & Stewart, 2008), and telecollaborative exchanges in which they interact directly with their peers at institutions abroad (Kinginger & Belz, 2005). Telecollaborative exchanges provide a sheltered opportunity to participate in socially consequential interactions, discover the social significance of linguistic choices, and begin crafting an appropriate foreign-language-mediated identity. Finally, the findings of DeKeyser's (2010) study suggest careful consideration and cultivation of students' predeparture language proficiency. Other studies, including Kinginger (2008), offer evidence for the benefit of study abroad to students of quite varied initial proficiency. However, if students' aspiration is to quickly and efficiently develop speaking abilitywhile abroad for a typical sojourn of a semester or less, guidance in preparing for this challenge is in order. (Kinginger, 2011: 67–68)

CHAPTER 8

Types of Talk in L2 pragmatics 1: greeting in English as a foreign language

8.1 Introduction

In this chapter, we move towards the largest unit in our system, namely Types of Talk. As we argued in Chapter 1, Types of Talk represents discourse as a finite unit in our system, which unlike other definitions of discourse can be replicably studied in a contrastive pragmatic way. An advantage of focusing on this highest unit of analysis is that it allows us to bring together all the other units, including RFIEs, speech acts and interactional acts, in a single comprehensive analysis.

In this chapter we investigate the interactional act of greeting in English, which can be surprisingly challenging for speakers of other languages. Specifically, we approach the challenges which greeting in English can pose for speakers of Chinese, by exploring deep-seated differences between English and Chinese greeting conventions. By 'greeting' we mean the seemingly 'simple' interactional act of choosing conventionalised expressions and related speech acts at the Opening Talk of an encounter.

Just as in the previous chapters, in this chapter we first describe selected previous research, followed by a section on methodology and data, as well as our analysis and a conclusion.

8.2 Selected previous research

In order to systematically analyse greeting and its perceptions, it is worth considering how greeting was defined in different fields of inquiry. In 1971, Goffman proposed a definition for greeting, distinguishing 'passing greetings' from other more interactionally involved greeting types:

> When two acquaintances pass close by each other on their separate daily rounds in consequence of what is seen as the routine intersecting of their activities, they are likely to exchange "passing greetings," often

without otherwise pausing. (In rural areas, something like these social-recognition rituals may be performed between passing strangers.) Often these displays will be relatively muted and fully exhaust the encounter to which they give rise; nonetheless, the spontaneous impulse to perform them is very strong. (Goffman, 1971: 75)

Goffman here refers to an Anglophone context where the instinct to greet even 'passing strangers' is strong. In the study described in this chapter we will consider whether this instinct also holds for Chinese.

In his influential study, Duranti (1997) proposed the following classification of approaches to greeting:

1. Ethology: greeting is interpreted as a means of conflict avoidance (e.g. Eibl-Eibesfeldt, 1977).
2. Ethnography: focusing on cultural patterns of greeting (e.g. Goody, 1972).
3. Conversation analysis: examines greeting mainly through the lens of adjacency pairs (Schegloff and Sacks, 1973).
4. Speech act theory: greeting is approached as a speech act (e.g. Searle and Vanderveken, 1985).

We follow the fourth approach above, i.e. we pursue a speech act-anchored analysis of greet expressions and approach greeting as an interactional act. In such research, the following definition of greet by Searle and Vanderveken (1985: 215–216) has often been referred to:

"Greet" is only marginally an illocutionary act since it has no propositional content. When one greets someone, for example, by saying 'Hello', one indicates recognition in a courteous fashion. So we might define greeting as a courteous indication of recognition, with the presupposition that the speaker has just encountered the hearer.

This definition has been criticised by many because it dismisses Greet as an act devoid of propositional content. Various scholars argued that the speech act Greet is meaningful in many non-Anglophone linguacultures. For example, Agyekum (2008) provided an in-depth study of the rich variety of meaningful Greet expressions in Akan.

Many scholars have interpreted Greet as an interactionally 'extended' speech act (e.g. Ide, 1998; de Kadt, 1998; Segun Olaoye, 2018; Nilsson et al., 2018). This interpretation relates to the ritual nature of Greet. For instance, Agyekum (2008: 498) proposed the concept of 'Complex greetings' to describe clusters of adjacency pairs through which opening encounters are managed in various relationships. We here adopt a different approach to Greet, based on our speech act typology which allows us to divide the Opening phase of an interaction into discrete speech act units, and without pre-assuming that what the interactants say at the beginning of an interaction is definitely a Greet.

Previous research on Chinese Greets frequently categorised different speech acts through which Chinese speakers open an interaction under the umbrella of 'greeting'. However, this is an overly broad usage considering that the phatic Opening phase of an interaction in Chinese can be realised in very diverse ways (Bardovi-Harlig and Su, 2018; Ying and Ren, 2021), i.e. greeting as an interactional act in Opening is subject to significant linguacultural variation. Also, as Chen (1988) noted, many expressions associated with the speech act Greet such as *Ni-hao* 你好 (T-pronoun-greeting) are relatively new coinations, while others such as *Nin-hao* 您好 (V-pronoun-greeting) are loanwords. So, in many Chinese contexts such expressions may be less important in the Opening phase of an interaction than those associated with speech acts like How-are-you. An oft-quoted example is *Ni chifan le ma* 你吃饭了吗 ('Have you eaten already?'; e.g. Zhang, 2014). The use of expressions occurring in the Opening phase of Chinese interactions has often puzzled researchers (e.g. Sheridan, 2018) and it has also triggered overgeneralising descriptions, e.g. the claim that speakers of Chinese 'do not greet each other' in many spheres of life (e.g. Ye, 2007; Huang, 2008). Interestingly, far less attention has been devoted to how speakers of Chinese perceive the interactional act of greeting in Anglophone or other linguacultures (but see e.g. Zhu, 2000). While scholars such as Zhang (2004), Li (2009) and Gong (2018) have shown differences between Chinese and English greeting conventions, few attempts have been made to investigate contrastive pragmatic differences between the conventions of using 'simple' expressions, such as *Ni-hao* versus *Hello*, i.e. forms which realise the speech act Greet itself. The present chapter fills the research gaps described above.

Our case study also contributes to previous research on the acquisition of English as a foreign language. As the recent overview of Baratta (2020) has shown, while the interactional act of greeting has certainly been studied in second language acquisition, most studies have approached it through the lens of routine formulae (see e.g. Weinert, 1995; also Wray, 2000).

8.3 Methodology and data

In this study we again proceed according to the framework we outlined in Chapter 3. That is, we first identified an L2 pragmatic problem – on this occasion through pilot interviews with Chinese learners of English. We then conducted our main analysis, by first doing a contrastive analysis, which was followed by an L2 pragmatic inquiry.

We conducted interviews to elicit Chinese learners' perceptions of English Greet conventions. We recruited a group of ten advanced Chinese learners of English who had spent at least one year in an English-speaking country. They were asked the following questions:

1. In your opinion, is how speakers of English greet each other similar to, or different from, how you prefer greeting others in Chinese?
2. In your opinion, how and why are English and Chinese greeting customs similar or different?

Eight out of ten respondents thought that greeting in English is different from how they would greet others in Chinese. Six respondents also expressed a sense of puzzlement by English greeting conventions. The following excerpts reflect this perception:

(8.1) I found greeting customs in English robotic. Chinese people are emotional, and they only greet someone either if they know him, or if there's a specific reason to greet him. In English this is different: there is always a sense of pressure to say hello to everyone.

(8.2) When I was an exchange student, I was reluctant to greet the clerk when I entered the small shop where I used to do my grocery. The clerk always shouted 'hiya' at me as if he wanted something from me, which I found intimidating, particularly because I felt he expected me to respond. This greeting would be really strange and unexpected in China. In some Chinese shops like convenience stores they may shout a welcome [the interviewee here refers to the honorific greeting *Huanying-guanglin* 欢迎光临, lit. 'Welcome your glory'], but this greeting is impersonal and you are not expected to return it.

The puzzlement expressed in examples (8.1) and (8.2) leads us to assume that greeting in English appears to be ubiquitous for speakers of Chinese. However, 'ubiquity' is too broad a concept to allow us to understand exactly which aspects of greeting in English puzzle speakers of Chinese. So, we used our twofold approach in the main part of our framework to capture what 'ubiquity' here involves in a differentiated and language-anchored way.

Our analysis is centred on expressions associated with the speech act Greet in a narrower sense. The rationale behind this approach is that, while phatic expressions such as 'Have you eaten?' (equalling the speech act How-are-you) tend to be preferred in Opening Talk in various Chinese contexts, they do not 'substitute for' Greet expressions. Even if verbal Greet expressions are absent from an interaction in Chinese, some form of ritual recognition of the other always precedes a phatic exchange, i.e. the interactional act of greeting may happen in some form. Thus, equating expressions like 'Have you eaten?' with Greet expressions is like comparing apples with pears, and we rather need to focus on expressions realising Greet specifically.

In order to explore contrastive differences (and similarities) between English and Chinese Greet expressions, we follow our standard twofold procedure:

Types of Talk in L2 pragmatics 1

1. We use corpora to investigate pragmatic differences/similarities between conventionalised uses of English and Chinese comparable Greet expressions, first by examining them separately and then conducting a contrastive analysis. This step helps us model the contextual spread of Greet expressions in English and Chinese.
2. We elicit production data from speakers of English and Chinese to investigate their behaviour in the opening phase of an interaction in various contexts, including both greeting itself and phatic interaction following greeting. Step 1 does not reveal information about the relationship between greeting and follow-up phatic interaction because corpus search is limited to either the study of Greet or other phatic expressions, but neither the combination of these two nor absences of verbal Greet realisations can be reliably studied with the aid of corpora, as far as we are aware. Hence the need for this second step.

In this inquiry, we use our typology of speech acts as shown in Figure 8.1.

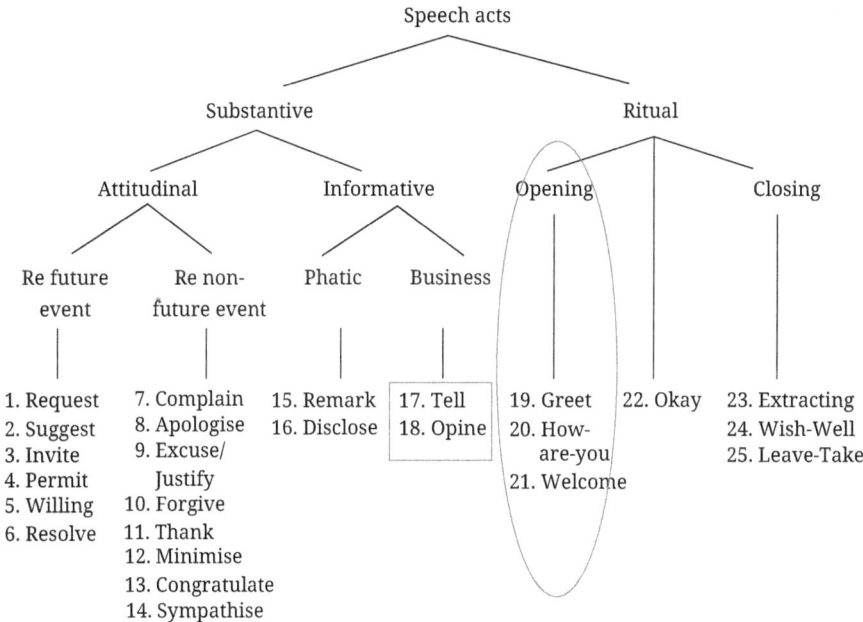

Figure 8.1 Our typology of speech acts, with focal points added

In our typology of speech acts, the Opening phase (circled) is a typically Ritual part of an interaction, consisting by default of Greet, How-are-you and Welcome. However, other speech acts like Remark may also become conventionally important in the Opening phase of an interaction. Still, the two speech acts (boxed) Tell (inform someone) and Opine (expressing an opinion) are related by default to what we define as the Business phase of an interaction, typically representing what happens between interactional opening and closing. While such speech acts may follow a Greet, they normally move the interaction immediately into Business Talk.

Let us now outline the methodological steps we follow in this study and the data used in these steps.

8.3.1 Step 1

Considering that we are interested in how Chinese learners of English perceive the interactional act of greeting in Anglophone contexts, we first compare two sets of three common English and Chinese Greet expressions with increasing degree of formality.

Table 8.1 *The Greet expressions compared*

English	Chinese
Hi	*Ni-hao* 你好 (T-pronoun-greeting)
Hello	*Nin-hao* 您好 (V-pronoun-greeting)
Good morning/afternoon/evening	*Zaoshang/xiawu/wanshang* 早上/下午/晚上好 ('good morning/afternoon/evening')

These two sets of three Greet expressions were provided by groups of ten English and Chinese speakers, whom we asked to list comparable expression sets with increasing degrees of formality on a scale of three. We chose the most frequently named expression in each slot. While we understand that there is a larger stylistic gap between *Ni-hao* and *Nin-hao* than between *Hi* and *Hello*, we believe that frequency of use should overrule this style difference in a contrastive pragmatic study like ours.

As in several chapters, we again examined uses of these expressions by annotating our data according to the following pairs of variables:

1. The standard sociolinguistic parameters Social Distance and Power [+–SD/ +/–P].
2. The Private versus Public ([Priv/Pub]) nature of an encounter.

In this case study, we examined the broader context of each utterance and annotated our data as [Priv/Pub] accordingly. For example, many of our Chinese examples may seem to occur in dyadic encounters but we annotated them as [Pub] because they originally occurred in TV programmes where listeners are inherently present. To provide another example, we typically annotated interactions between policemen and suspects as [Pub] because a policeman typically animates the voice of an institution, i.e. here a community is symbolically and ritually present.

We sampled two times 100 valid cases of each of the English and Chinese Greet expressions.[1] Typical examples of 'invalid' cases are translations, which were frequent in the Chinese data. We first sampled 100 valid examples of 'stand-alone' uses of our two sets of English and Chinese Greet expressions, i.e. cases when Greets are not followed by other speech acts in a fleeting encounter. We then sampled another 100 valid cases where Greets are followed by other speech acts in the same turn (marked as →Speech Act). Our goal here was to explore which speech act types tend to follow Greets in the two linguacultures and to interpret such tendencies by using our model of speech acts, along with the above variables.

In Step 1, we collected data from Mandarin Chinese and British English corpora. Our Chinese data were sampled in a parallel and balanced way from two corpora: the Modern Chinese General Balanced Corpus and the Peking University Corpus.[2] We relied on two Chinese corpora because each of them is smaller than their British English counterpart – the British National Corpus.

8.3.2 Step 2

Our production tasks followed Step 1, by building on the above-outlined variable pairs. Here we investigated two issues:

1. Do members of a group of ten British speakers and of a comparable Chinese group realise Greet in various relationships/interpersonal scenarios?
2. Which speech acts and expressions do such speakers frequent in the opening phase of an encounter?

We explored if and how the outcomes of Step 2 relate to Step 1.

All interviewees were university students with at least undergraduate educational background. Their age was between 19 and 25 years. All their personal information was removed.

8.4 Analysis

8.4.1 Step 1

We first present the outcome of our monolingual English and Chinese corpus analysis of Greet expressions, followed by a contrastive analysis.

English expressions
Hi
Table 8.2 shows *Hi* uses occurring in a batch of 100 stand-alone Greets, annotated with the variables ['+/–SD, +/– P'] and [Priv/Pub]:

Table 8.2 *Stand-alone uses of* Hi

	Priv	Pub
[–P/–SD]	44	5
[–P/+SD]	29	2
[+P/–SD]	11	–
[+P/+SD]	–	9

As Table 8.2 illustrates, *Hi* in fleeting encounters is [–P/–SD/Priv]-leaning; see example (8.3):

(8.3)   'Hi, Robin', I murmured as I passed.   [–P/–SD/Priv]

Table 8.3 summarises *Hi* uses in a second sample of 100 examples where the Greets realised by *Hi* are followed by another speech act in the same turn (the subsequent speech acts are included in a decreasing order of frequency):

Table 8.3 *Uses of* Hi *in Greet→Speech act*

Hi (Greet)	→Disclose	→How-are-you	→Request	→Complain	→Invite
[–P/–SD] 56	1 [Pub] 21 [Priv]	5 [Pub] 13 [Priv]	7 [Priv]	5 [Priv]	4 [Priv]
[–P/+SD] 39	2 [Pub] 12 [Priv]	3 [Pub] 7 [Priv]	12 [Priv]	2 [Priv] 1 [Pub]	–
[+P/–SD] 5	–	5 [Priv]	–	–	–
[+P/+SD] 0	–	–	–	–	–

Commonly known speech act categories like Request do not need introduction. However, the following two speech acts may (again) need definition:

- *Disclose:* This speech act gives biographical information through which the hearer 'knows one better'.
- *How-are-you:* In using a How-are-you, a speaker asks after the hearer, expressing a ritual interest in his welfare.

The use of *Hi* in Greet→Speech act is also [–SD/–P/Priv]-leaning. Speech acts following *Hi*-Greets in the same turn fall into the following three categories:

1. Speech acts (here: How-are-you) which by default belong to the opening phase (see Figure 8.1) following a Greet:

    (8.4)   Hi Paul, how're you doing?
            GREET / HOW-ARE-YOU   [–P/–SD/Priv]

How-are-you is conventionally connected to the speech act Greet, and so normally it cannot move the interaction into the Business phase.

Types of Talk in L2 pragmatics 1

2. Speech acts, such as Disclose, Request and Invite, which do not belong to the Opening phase of interaction in our typology can 'migrate' into the Opening phase:

   (8.5)   'Hi,   my name's Dave.'
            GREET /DISCLOSE   [–P/+SD/Priv]

   (8.6)   Hi John, tell me what you do.
            GREET / REQUEST   [–P/–SD/Priv]

   (8.7)   Hi, Tiffany, come in.
            GREET   /   INVITE   [–P/–SD/Priv]

When these speech acts follow a Greet, the interaction often remains in the Opening phase, with the other interactant being required to adjacently respond in turn.

3. Cases when speech acts not by default belonging to the Opening phase occur in the Opening and bring the interactants into the Business phase of an interaction. For example, Complain may immediately bring the interactants into the Business phase. Compare the following:

   (8.8)   'Hi,   you're late', said Jonquil airily …
            GREET /COMPLAIN   [–P/–SD/Priv]

   (8.9)   '"Hi!   you can't go off like that", he called after her, and ran to catch her up.'
            GREET / COMPLAIN   [–P/+SD/Pub]

While the Complain in (8.8) is part of casual Opening, in (8.9) it definitely is not.

Hello
Table 8.4 summarises uses of *Hello* in a batch of 100 stand-alone Greets:

Table 8.4 *Stand-alone uses of* Hello

	[Priv]	[Pub]
[–P/–SD]	51	2
[–P/+SD]	42	3
[+P/–SD]	–	–
[+P/+SD]	2	–

As Table 8.4 illustrates, similar to *Hi*, the use of *Hello* is [–P/–SD/Priv]-leaning.

Table 8.5 summarises *Hi* uses in Greet→Speech act sequences in a second sample of 100 examples:

Table 8.5 *Uses of* Hello *in Greet→Speech act*

Hello (Greet)	→Disclose	→Request	→Invite	→How-are-you	→Welcome	→Remark	→Complain	→Tell
[–P/–SD] 56	3 [Pub] 17 [Priv]	1 [Pub] 12 [Priv]	9 [Priv]	7 [Priv]	4 [Priv]	3 [Priv]	–	–
[–P/+SD] 33	12 [Priv]	4 [Pub] 2 [Priv]	5 [Priv]	4 [Priv]	2 [Priv]	2 [Priv]	2 [Priv]	–
[+P/–SD] 1	–	–	–	1 [Priv]	–	–	–	–
[+P/+SD] 10	–	–	–	–	5 [Priv]	–	3 [Pub]	2 [Pub]

The following speech acts in Table 8.5 may need explanation (again):

- *Remark:* Through this phatic speech act the speaker shows herself favourably disposed towards the hearer. The topic of a Remark is likely to be derived from the immediate context of situation, which is obvious to all participants.
- *Tell:* Tell is a typically informative illocution through which the speaker announces information in a matter-of-fact way. Tell typically occurs in the business phase.

Uses of *Hello* in Greet→Speech act tend to be [–P/–SD/Priv]-leaning. Such Greets tend either to be followed by speech acts which naturally belong to the Opening phase, like How-are-you and Welcome, or by others which often migrate into the Opening phase without moving the interaction into the Business phase, like Disclose, Request, Invite and Remark. Here we only provide examples of Welcome and Remark which do not occur in our *Hi* sample above:

(8.10) Well, hello, Mrs – er – Machin, this is an honour
 GREET / WELCOME [+P/+SD/Priv]

(8.11) Hello, seen you before haven't I?
 GREET / REMARK [–P/+SD/Priv]

Greets realised with *Hello* may also be followed by the speech act Tell, although such sequences are relatively infrequent (see Table 8.5). Tell by default immediately takes the interactants into the business phase:

(8.12) Hello, you are under arrest.
 GREET / TELL [+P/+SD/Pub]

Good morning/afternoon/evening

Table 8.6 summarises uses of *Good morning/afternoon/evening* in a batch of 100 stand-alone Greets:

Table 8.6 *Stand-alone uses of* Good morning/afternoon/evening

	[Priv]	[Pub]
[–P/–SD] 19	19	–
[–P/+SD] 57	54	3
[+P/–SD] 10	10	–
[+P/+SD] 14	9	5

As Table 8.6 shows, the use of *Good morning/afternoon/evening* in 'fleeting encounters' is different from that of *Hi* and *Hello* in that *Good morning/afternoon/evening* are more frequent in [+SD] than [–SD] settings. This may relate to the fact that this expression group is generally more formal than the other two Greet expressions, which may also explain why *Good morning/afternoon/evening* are slightly more frequent in [+P] contexts than the other two Greet expressions. However, similar to *Hi* and *Hello*, *Good morning/afternoon/evening* are far more frequent in [Priv] than [Pub] one-off Greets. Example (8.13) illustrates a [+P/–SD/Priv] stand-alone use of *Good morning* (second utterance in the example):

(8.13) His uncle turned stiffly round in the chair. 'Good morning, my boy.'
'<u>Good morning</u>, sir.'

Table 8.7 summarises Greet→Speech act uses of *Good morning/afternoon/evening* in a second sample of 100 examples:

Table 8.7 *Uses of* Good morning/afternoon/evening *in Greet→Speech act*

Good morning/ afternoon/ evening (Greet)	→Welcome	→Request	→Disclose	→Thanks	→Tell	→Con-gratulate	→How-are-you
[–P/–SD] 12	–	4 [Priv]	2 [Priv]	2 [Priv]	1 [Priv]	3 [Priv]	–
[–P/+SD] 77	26 [Priv]	14 [Priv]	2 [Pub] 11 [Priv]	1 [Pub] 8 [Priv]	9 [Priv]	2 [Priv]	4 [Priv]
[+P/–SD] 4	–	2 [Priv]	–	2 [Priv]	–	–	–
[+P/+SD] 7	1 [Pub]	3 [Pub]	–	1 [Pub]	2 [Pub]	–	–

As Table 8.7 illustrates, Greets realised by *Good morning/afternoon/evening* are often followed by speech acts that either naturally belong to the Opening phase, such as Welcome and How-are-you, or those that often migrate into the Opening phase without bringing the interaction into the Business phase, including Request, Disclose, Thanks and Congratulate. Tell may also follow Greets realised by *Good morning/afternoon/evening*, and in such cases the interaction immediately enters the Business phase:

(8.14) Good morning, sir, last man just collecting his weapon
         GREET / TELL   [+P/+SD/Pub]

Chinese expressions
Ni-hao (T-pronoun-greeting)
Table 8.8 summarises *Ni-hao* uses in a sample of 100 stand-alone Greets:

Table 8.8 *Stand-alone uses of* Ni-hao

	[Priv]	[Pub]
[–P/–SD] 3	2	1
[–P/+SD] 62	19	43
[+P/–SD] 6	2	4
[+P/+SD] 29	7	22

As Table 8.8 illustrates, the use of *Ni-hao* is [+SD]-leaning, and also it is far more frequent in [Pub] encounters than any of the English Greet expressions. Thus, *Ni-hao* is a relatively formal expression, notwithstanding that *Ni* is a second person T-pronoun. The formality of *Ni-hao* is also evidenced by the fact that in our sample many stand-alone uses of *Ni-hao* follow deferential address forms:

(8.15) 罗老师,   你好!
        Professor Luo, *Ni-hao*!   [–P/+SD/Pub]

Table 8.8 also shows that *Ni-hao* in stand-alone Greets is relatively frequent in [+P] settings; see example (8.16):

(8.16) 李宗仁先生激动地说："总理你好,总理你好!"
        Li Zongren said in an excited voice: "Prime Minister, *Ni-hao*, Prime Minister, *Ni-hao!*"   [+P/–SD/Pub]

Table 8.9 summarises Greet→Speech act uses of *Ni-hao* in a second sample of 100 examples where the Greets realised with *Ni-hao* are followed by another speech act in the same turn:

Table 8.9 *Uses of* Ni-hao *in Greet→Speech act*

Ni-hao (Greet)	→Tell	→Request	→Disclose	→Welcome	→Remark
[–P/–SD] 6	1 [Priv]	2 [Priv]	–	–	3 [Priv]
[–P/+SD] 57	17 [Pub] 3 [Priv]	10 [Pub] 6 [Priv]	6 [Pub] 5 [Priv]	3 [Pub]	7 [Priv]
[+P/–SD] 4	–	1 [Priv]	–	–	3 [Pub]
[+P/+SD] 33	9 [Pub] 2 [Priv]	6 [Pub] 4 [Priv]	8 [Pub]	4 [Pub]	–

Types of Talk in L2 pragmatics 1   139

Table 8.9 shows that in Greet→Speech act uses *Ni-hao* is [+SD]-leaning and is relatively frequent in [+P] and [Pub] encounters. Furthermore, *Ni-hao* Greets are most frequently followed by Tell in our sample, i.e. *Ni-hao* is not only formal but also often implies that the speaker wishes to move into the Business phase:

(8.17) 你好，今天我只是来看看江河出事的地方。
Ni-hao, today I just came to see the place of the Jiang He incident.
GREET / TELL   [–P/+SD/Pub]

(8.18) "喂，你好，"一个女护士说。"我们这里有个女的，她有一只小旅行包要交给病人"
"Hello, *Ni-hao*", a female nurse said. "We have a woman here with a small travel bag to give to the patient"
GREET / GREET [Ni-hao]   /   TELL   [–P/+SD/Pub]

When Greets realised by *Ni-hao* are followed by speech acts other than Tell in our sample, the interaction usually remains in the Opening phase. Here *Ni-hao* is often ceremonial. Example (8.19) below illustrates the use of *Ni-hao* in a Greet followed by a Welcome, which conventionally belongs to the Opening phase, while examples (8.20)–(8.22) illustrate its uses in Greet→Speech act sequences where the speech act following Greet migrates into the Opening phase without bringing the interactants into the business phase:

(8.19) 你好！ 欢迎你！
Ni-hao! Welcome here!
GREET   /   WELCOME   [–P/+SD/Pub]

(8.20) "你好，" 她说，"请问尊姓大名？"
"*Ni-hao*", she said, "your respected name [honorific] is?"
GREET   /   REQUEST (FOR-INFORMATION)   [+P/+SD/Pub]

(8.21) 你好！ 我是王耀先。
Ni-hao! I am Wang Yaoxian.
GREET   /   DISCLOSE   [–P/+SD/Priv]

(8.22) 姐，你好！你也来家了！
Older Sister, *Ni-hao*! You also came home!
GREET /   REMARK   [–P/–SD/Pub]

Nin-hao (V-pronoun-greeting)
Table 8.10 summarises *Nin-hao* uses occurring in a sample of 100 stand-alone Greets:

Table 8.10 Stand-alone uses of Nin-hao

	[Priv]	[Pub]
[–P/–SD] 2	2	–
[–P/+SD] 53	15	39
[+P/–SD] 7	7	–
[+P/+SD] 38	6	32

The comparison of Table 8.10 with Table 8.8 shows no significant variation between the use of *Ni-hao* and *Nin-hao*: both are [+SD]-leaning and frequent in [+P] and [Pub] interactions. This finding runs counter to the popular belief that *Nin-hao*, unlike *Ni-hao*, is a 'politeness expression' (e.g. Chen, 1988).

Table 8.11 summarises *Nin-hao* Greet→Speech act uses in a second sample of 100 examples:

Table 8.11 Uses of Nin-hao in Greet→Speech act

Nin-hao (Greet)	→Disclose	→Tell	→Request	→Remark
[–P/–SD] 0	–	–	–	–
[–P/+SD] 63	21 [Pub]	16 [Pub]	3 [Pub]	5 [Pub]
	7 [Priv]	9 [Priv]	2 [Priv]	
[+P/–SD] 4	4 [Priv]	–	–	–
[+P/+SD] 33	17 [Pub]	5 [Pub]	5 [Pub]	2 [Pub]
	2 [Priv]	2 [Priv]		

Table 8.11 not only shows that the use of *Nin-hao* is formal, but also that, similar to *Ni-hao*, it is often followed by Tell, immediately bringing the interaction into the Business phase. Since we have shown Greet→Speech act uses of the various speech act types featured in Table 8.11, here we only provide a single example, illustrating the use of *Nin-hao* in a Greet→Tell sequence in a [Pub] interaction:

(8.23) 您好！孙夫人。我知道早晨散步，是一种有益健康的锻炼。难道孙夫人喜欢中午散步吗？
Nin-hao! Mrs Sun. I know that a morning walk is a healthy exercise. Does Mrs Sun also like walking at noontime?
GREET/ TELL / REQUEST-(FOR-INFORMATION)   [–P/+SD/Pub]

Zaoshang/Xiawu/Wanshang-hao ('Good morning/afternoon/evening')
These Greet expressions are infrequent in both Chinese corpora, and so obtaining a valid sample of 100 examples of stand-alone Greets realised with *Zaoshang/Xiawu/Wanshang-hao* was difficult in comparison to the sampling of other Greet expressions. Table 8.12 illustrates uses of *Zaoshang/Xiawu/Wanshang-hao* in stand-alone Greets:

Table 8.12 *Stand-alone uses of* Zaoshang/Xiawu/Wanshang-hao

	[Priv]	[Pub]
[–P/–SD] 1	1	–
[–P/+SD] 61	19	42
[+P/–SD] 0	–	–
[+P/+SD] 38	11	27

As Table 8.12 shows, although *Zaoshang/Xiawu/Wanshang-hao* are more formal than either *Ni-hao* or *Nin-hao*, essentially all the Chinese Greet forms studied are [+SD]-leaning and frequent in [+P] and [Pub] interactions.

Our sample of *Zaoshang/Xiawu/Wanshang-hao* Greet→Speech act sequences only included seventy-three valid examples. This low frequency may be due to the high formality of these Greet expressions, which reduces their frequency in oral encounters featured in the particular Chinese corpora we used.[3] Table 8.13 summarises Greet→Speech act uses of *Zaoshang/Xiawu/Wanshang-hao* in our sample:

Table 8.13 *Uses of* Zaoshang/Xiawu/Wanshang-hao *in Greet→Speech act*

Zaoshang/Xiawu/Wanshang-hao (Greet)	→Tell	→Welcome	→Request
[–P/–SD] 0	–	–	–
[–P/+SD] 61	21 [Pub]	19 [Pub]	6 [Pub]
	5 [Priv]	2 [Priv]	8 [Priv]
[+P/–SD] 0	–	–	–
[+P/+SD] 12	8 [Pub]	3 [Pub]	1 [Priv]

Table 8.13 illustrates that, similar to the other Chinese Greet expressions, *Zaoshang/Xiawu/Wanshang-hao* are often followed by the speech act Tell. The table also shows that *Zaoshang/Xiawu/Wanshang-hao* are [+SD]-leaning and frequent in [+P] and [Pub] encounters. The following example illustrates a Greet realised by *Xiawu-hao* followed by a Tell:

(8.24) 大家下午好！　　前一个论题，他们都听到了…
   Good afternoon, everyone! They've all heard the previous topic …
   Greet   /   Tell   [–P/+SD/Pub]

Contrastive analysis
We now compare the outcome of the monolingual English and Chinese analyses presented above.

As the examination of the English Greet forms shows, the least formal *Hi* is [–SD]-leaning, while both *Hello* and *Good morning/afternoon/evening* are frequented in both [–SD] and [+SD] relationships, with the latter having a higher [+SD] frequency than *Hello*. We observed a similar tendency with regard to the variable [+/–P], although all the English Greet expressions occur most frequently in [–P] settings. Every English Greet expression studied is

[Priv]-leaning. Important to our analysis, Tells infrequently follow Greets in the English dataset. Also, while some speech acts such as Complain following a Greet can immediately bring the interaction into the Business phase, such uses are infrequent, i.e. English Greet forms conventionally keep the interaction in the Opening phase.

The analysis of the Chinese Greet expressions has shown that they are [+SD]-leaning – and to a lesser degree [+P]-leaning – and also that they are frequent in [Pub] encounters. Another linguacultural difference between English and Chinese is that the Chinese Greet expressions may often be followed by a Tell, which means that they can take the interaction directly into Business Talk.

Thus far we have presented the outcomes of our first procedural step. These outcomes relate to only one aspect of the problem studied in this chapter, i.e. they reveal that there are multiple aspects of differences between English and Chinese conventions of the interactional act of greeting, all of which potentially contributing to the puzzlement reported in the pilot interviews. However, such corpus work is limited to either the study of Greet expressions (as in our case) or expressions associated with other phatic speech acts, but neither the combination of these two nor absences of verbal Greet realisations can be reliably studied with the aid of corpora. We therefore triangulated our research by using the following production tasks.

8.4.2 Step 2

In our production tasks, we first examined whether members of a British and a Chinese group of ten speakers realise a Greet in various relationships and interpersonal scenarios (first question), and if yes, which expressions and speech acts they use in the Opening phase (second question). We presented two sets of four situations to our respondents. These situations represented the [+/–P, +/–SD] and [Priv/Pub] variables. As regards the latter variables, in the first set we exposed the respondents to a situation in which they enter into someone else's private space, while in the second set they accidentally bump into another person on the street. All the situations were constructed on the basis of their relevance for the students' day-to-day lives. We did not reveal information about our research objectives to the respondents. The respondents were provided with the following sets of production task:

Production task set 1 [Priv]
1. You meet a friend in a dormitory when nobody is around. Would you greet him? [first question] If yes, what would you say initially? [second question] [–P/–SD] setting.
2. You meet a friend's friend in a dormitory when nobody is around. Etc. [–P/+SD]
3. You meet a lecturer in a classroom when nobody is around. Etc. [+P/+SD]
4. You meet an administrative staff member in a university office when nobody else is around. Etc. [+P/+SD]

Types of Talk in L2 pragmatics 1 143

Production task set 2 [Pub]
1. You accidentally bump into a friend in a dormitory. Would you greet him? If yes, what would you say initially? [–P/–SD]
2. You accidentally bump into a friend's friend who you don't know very well on the street. Etc. [–P/+SD]
3. You are in a company and accidentally bump into your lecturer on the street. Etc. [+P/–SD]
4. You accidentally bump into an administrative staff member of your university on the street. Etc. [+P/+SD]

Results of the English production tasks
As regards the first question in our task, the British responses were the following:

Table 8.14 *British responses to the first [Priv] question*

Task-1 [–P/–SD]	Task-2 [–P/+SD]	Task-3 [+P/–SD]	Task-4 [+P/+SD]
Greet (10)	Greet (10)	Greet (10)	Greet (10)

Table 8.15 *British responses to the first [Pub] question*

Task-1 [–P/–SD]	Task-2 [–P/+SD]	Task-3 [+P/–SD]	Task-4 [+P/+SD]
Greet (10)	Greet (3) Non-Greet (7)	Greet (6) Non-Greet (4)	Greet (3) Non-Greet (7)

As Tables 8.14 and 8.15 show, private space triggers unanimous verbal Greet realisation in English. This accords with Goffman's (1971) argument that in Anglophone linguacultures sharing someone's space makes it impossible to 'ignore' their presence. The situation is different in public where the lack of familiarity may allow language users to not acknowledge the presence of the other.

Our British respondents produced the following expression types shown in Tables 8.16 and 8.17 in response to the second question in the task:

Table 8.16 *British responses to the second [Priv] question*

Speech act types	Task-1 [–P/–SD]	Task-2 [–P/+SD]	Task-3 [+P/–SD]	Task-4 [+P/+SD]
Greet	*Hi* (4) *Hello* (3) *Hiya* (2) *Sup* (1)	*Hi* (5) *Hello* (4) *Good morning/ afternoon* (1)	*Hello* (5) *Good morning/ afternoon* (4) *Hi* (1)	*Good morning/ afternoon/evening* (7) *Hello* (2) *Hi* (1)

Table 8.17 *British responses to the second [Pub] question*

Speech act types	Task-1 [–P/–SD]	Task-2 [–P/+SD]	Task-3 [+P/–SD]	Task-4 [+P/+SD]
Greet	*Hi* (5) *Hello* (3) *Howdy* (1) *Hiya* (1)	*Hello* (7) *Hi* (2) *Good morning/ afternoon* (1)	*Hello* (6) *Hi* (3) *Good morning* (1)	*Good morning/ afternoon* (8) *Hello* (2)

The results of the English production tasks are comparable to the outcome of our corpus analysis, in that the choice of English Greet expressions correlates with the presence or absence of formality. Even more importantly, our respondents only produced the speech act Greet.

The production tasks also revealed that the Greet forms *Hi* and/or *Hello* occur in practically all interpersonal scenarios, albeit to varying degrees. Greet in English in the opening phase may therefore be ubiquitously present. This is why *Hi/Hello* may suffice in [+P/+SD] situations:

(8.25) Hello, erm, is it now a good time for you to talk?   [+P/+SD/Priv]

(8. 26) Hello, are you also getting stuff at Sainsbury's?   [+P/+SD/Pub]

Nevertheless, in formal contexts most of the British respondents provided *Good morning/afternoon/evening*:

(8.27) Good morning, I am looking for the person in charge of formative assignments.   [+P/+SD/Priv]

What interconnects all such Greet realisations is that every British respondent started the interaction with a Greet expression. This indicates that the recognition of the other triggers an expression associated with the speech act Greet regardless of the formality of the scenario.

Results of the Chinese production tasks
Our Chinese respondents provided the following responses to the first question in the production task:

Table 8.18 *Chinese responses to the first [Priv] question*

Task-1 [–P/–SD]	Task-2 [–P/+SD]	Task-3 [+P/–SD]	Task-4 [+P/+SD]
Greet (5) Non-Greet (5)	Greet (2) Non-Greet (8)	Greet (10)	Greet (10)

Types of Talk in L2 pragmatics 1 145

Table 8.19 *Chinese responses to the first [Pub] question*

Task-1 [–P/–SD]	Task-2 [–P/+SD]	Task-3 [+P/–SD]	Task-4 [+P/+SD]
Greet (4) Non-Greet (6)	Greet (1) Non-Greet (9)	Greet (10)	Greet (10)

As Tables 8.18 and 8.19 show, in [–P/–SD] settings in Chinese Greet is non-compulsory, and is even less so in [–P/+SD] settings. The private–public nature of an encounter only slightly influences this tendency. However, the situation changes dramatically in [+P] environments, which necessitate the realisation of a verbal Greet.

Our Chinese respondents produced the following expressions and speech acts in response to the second question of the production task:

Table 8.20 *Chinese responses to the second [Priv] question*

Speech act types and realisation patterns	Task-1 [–P/–SD]	Task-2 [–P/+SD]	Task-3 [+P/–SD]	Task-4 [+P/+SD]
Greet (formal)	–	*Ni-hao* 你好 (T-pronoun-greeting) (5)	*Ni-hao* 你好 *Title+hao* 好 (lit. title + 'wish-you-good') (10)	*Nin-hao* 您好 (V-pronoun) *Title+hao* 好 (lit. title + 'wish-you-good') (9)
Greet: code-switching (to English)	*Haluo* 哈喽 (for English 'hello') *Hai* 嗨 (for 'hi') (3)	*Hei* 嘿 (for 'hey') (2)	–	–
Zero-Greet + Request (for-information)	–	Name + *zai ma* Name + 在吗 ('is "Name" here?') (3)	–	–
Address form only	*Qin'ai-de* 亲爱的 ('Darling') (1)	–	–	Using the addressee's title only (1)
Migrated speech act (Remark)	*Zai ne* 在呢 ('You're here') *Ni zai ya* 你在呀 ('You're here') (6)	–	–	–

Table 8.21 *Chinese responses to the second [Pub] question*

Speech act types and realisation patterns	Task-1 [–P/–SD]	Task-2 [–P/+SD]	Task-3 [+P/–SD]	Task-4 [+P/+SD]
Greet (formal)	–	*Ni-hao* 你好 (2)	*Title+hao* 好 (title + 'wish-you-good') (10)	*Ni-hao* 你好 *Nin-hao* 您好 (10)
Greet: code-switching (to English)	*Halou* 哈喽 (for English 'hello') *Hai* 嗨 (for 'hi') (8)	*Hai Hei* (8)	–	–
Migrated speech act (Remark)	*Qu nar* 去哪儿? ('Where are you going?') *Zenmele* 怎么了? ('How are things?') (2)	–	–	

As Tables 8.20 and 8.21 show, formal Greet realisations are practically non-existent in [–P/–SD]/[Priv/Pub] encounters. The following expressions and speech act types occur in such settings:

1. Many respondents used code-switching, by uttering a Chinese version of informal English Greet expressions:

   (8.28) 嗨兄弟，不好意思打扰下 ...
   <u>Hi</u>, brother, sorry for disturbing you but ...

Loanwords such as *Hai* 嗨 ('Hi') are frequent in informal settings because they may not sound as formal as a 'proper' *Ni-hao*, not mentioning other more deferential Chinese Greet expressions. The young age and learner background of the respondents may explain the frequency of code-switching in the dataset.

2. In a relatively large number of cases, in particular in [Priv], respondents provided a Remark migrating into the place of Greet, hence substituting for – rather than complementing – the Greet:

   (8.29) 你在呀！我给你带了点儿茶来，不知道你喜欢这个不？
   <u>Ah, you're here</u>! I brought you some tea, do you like it?

3. We received a single [–P, –SD] answer where the respondent uttered a feminine form of endearment only (*Qin'ai-de* 亲爱的, 'Darling').

As these examples show, there is no pressure on Chinese language users to formally Greet one another in [–P/–SD] settings. Also, in such situations, non-Greet phatic speech acts such as Remark (e.g. *Zai ne* 在呢, 'You're here') typically occur.

Greet realisations are less varied in [–P/+SD] settings. Here our respondents either used the Greet form *Ni-hao* or code-switching. Another pattern that three of our respondents followed is *Zero-Greet+Request-(for-information)* – a case in which the speaker directly moves the interaction into the Business phase:

(8.30)   小王在吗？
         Is Little Wang there?

Here the speaker opens the interaction with a Request(-for-information). Such usage not only shows that Greet is non-ubiquitous in Chinese, but also that skipping it in certain interpersonal relationships is not necessarily inappropriate. In particular, in [+SD/–P] settings Chinese language users may easily omit a formal Greet.

In the presence of [+P], Greet patterns dramatically change. In [+P/–SD] settings respondents unanimously provided either the Greet form *Ni-hao* or Title + *hao* (lit. 'Title wish-you-good'). Greeting in [+P/+SD] settings is similar, apart from a variation between the T/V Greet pronominal forms *Ni-hao/Nin-hao*. The following examples are typical utterances in [+P/–SD/Priv] and [+P/+SD/Pub] situations:

(8.31)   老师好，请问您有时间吗？
         Teacher-*hao*, may I ask whether you (V-pronoun) have time?
         [+P/–SD/Priv]

(8.32)   您好，请问 ...
         Nin-hao, may I respectfully ask ...   [+P/+SD/Pub]

The above examples illustrate what Tables 8.20 and 8.21 already showed, i.e. the [Priv/Pub] nature of a setting tends to be of secondary importance in the opening phase of interactions in Chinese. So, it is the presence of [+P] and [+SD] which primarily triggers formal Greet realisations in Chinese. In informal settings, the Chinese respondents provided solutions such as code-switching, presumably to avoid using conventional Greet expressions.

Contrastive analysis

The comparison of the English and Chinese production tasks reveals that conventions of the interactional act of greeting are very different in the two linguacultures. Greet in English is normally compulsory in [Priv] encounters. This is different in [Pub] encounters, which tend to allow the speaker to not ritually notice the other's presence (see 'civil inattention' in Goffman, 1963). In Chinese it is not so much the [Priv/Pub] nature of an interaction but rather interpersonal relationships which decide whether a Greet is required or not.

As Tables 8.18 and 8.19 have shown, in [–P/–SD] relationships practically no Greet is required. Furthermore, verbal realisations of Greet ubiquitously spread over all role constellations. While the formality of an interaction certainly influences the choice of expressions in English, ultimately all Greet expressions (and *only* Greet expressions) can be used to acknowledge the other's presence in an encounter. In Chinese, the other's presence can be acknowledged either through less conventional Greet forms, such as code-switching to English, or via non-opening speech acts migrating into the opening phase and substituting for Greets.

Figures 8.2 (below) and 8.3 (opposite page) summarise our findings:

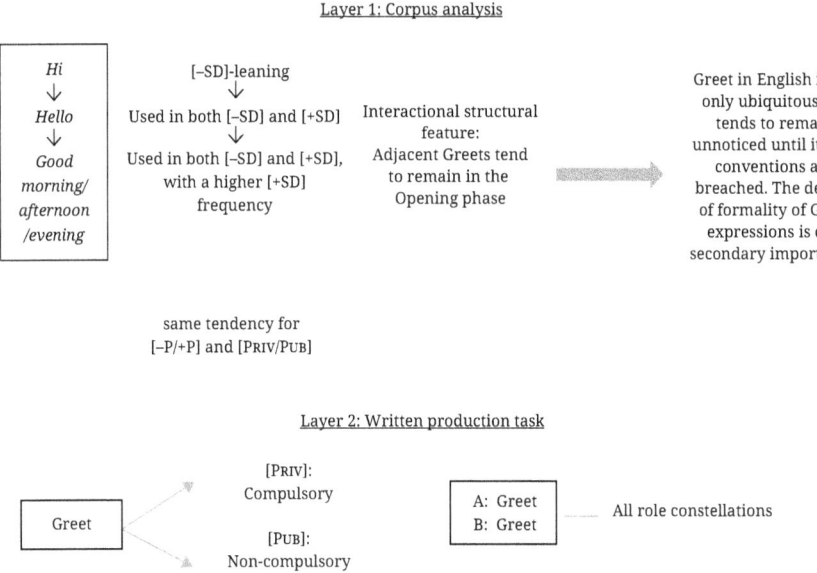

Figure 8.2 Outcome of our twofold analysis – English

Let us revisit the pilot interviews from which we departed in this study in light of these outcomes. It may be insufficient to describe differences between English and Chinese conventions of the interactional act of greeting simply by arguing that the former is ubiquitous, and the latter is not. Rather, we need to consider exactly why and how English greeting conventions may appear ubiquitous for Chinese speakers. Let us here revisit the following excerpt from one of the pilot interviews reported above (Example 8.2):

"The clerk always shouted 'hiya' at me <u>as if he wanted something from me,</u> which I found intimidating …"

As the underlined section illustrates, one of the things that this interviewee found puzzling about English Greet conventions was that there seemed to

Types of Talk in L2 pragmatics 1

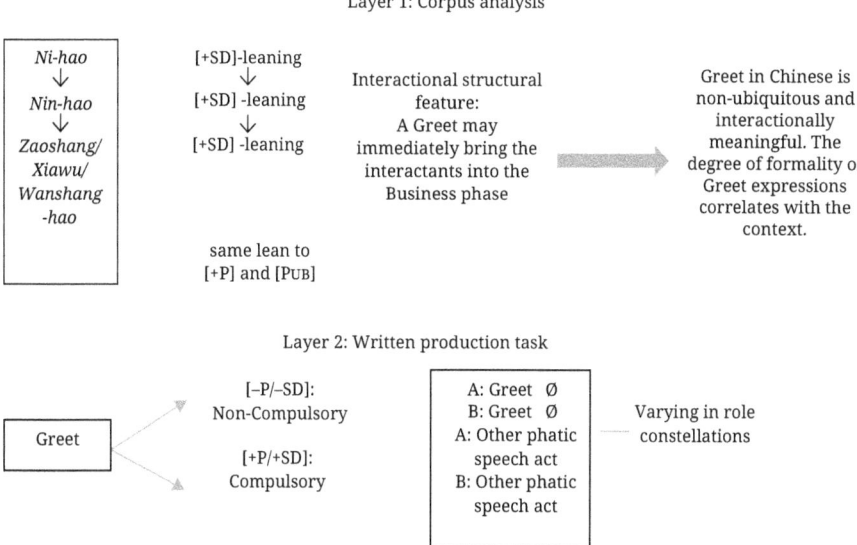

Figure 8.3 Outcome of our twofold analysis – Chinese

be an 'underlying agenda' behind exchanging Greets in this situation. The problem is not simply that the interviewee in his role as a customer was expected to return a shop assistant's greeting, but also that he seemed to perceive returning such a greeting as a move leading to further unwanted interaction. Differently put, if we want to get to the bottom of this interviewee's puzzlement, we need to consider various factors identified in our analysis above, i.e. not only linguacultural differences between the role constellations involved in conventions of greeting, but also differences between the way in which the speech act Greet relates to the Business phase of an interaction in Chinese and English.

As we stated before, we believe that an advantage of the analytic framework we propose in this book is that it provides a strictly language-anchored (rather than cultural) and multi-componential way to systematically explain reasons behind the types of puzzlement, such as those that greeting in English may trigger for Chinese speakers. Thus, our analytic design helps one avoid gross overgeneralisations, such as 'in English everyone always greets one another' and 'in Chinese people do not do this'. Our monolingual and subsequent contrastive analyses have shown that the situation is far more complex than that, and we believe that it is exactly this complexity which is responsible for the feelings of puzzlement reported by our respondents.

8.5 Conclusion

In this chapter, we have moved to the highest unit in our analytic system, i.e. Types of Talk. We have shown that the study of Types of Talk not only provides insight into interesting L2 pragmatic issues, but also that in the analysis of Types of Talk we need to rely on all the various units of analysis that we have discussed in this book. In the following chapter, we will continue discussing the relevance of Types of Talk to contrastive L2 pragmatic research by looking at the other end of interaction, i.e. L2 pragmatic issues emerging in the Closing phase of interactions.

8.6 Recommended reading

Goffman, Erving. (1983). The interaction order: American Sociological Association, 1982 Presidential Address. *American Sociological Review* **48(1), 1–17.**
In the present chapter we have referred to the work of the renowned sociologist Erving Goffman whose view on encounters heavily influenced the way in which we approached greeting in Opening Talk. The following is a relevant excerpt from Goffman's work:

> When one turns to "deeper" relationships, knowership and its obligations remain a factor, but now not the defining one. However, other links between relationships and the interaction order appear. The obligation to exchange passing greetings is extended: the pair may be obliged to interrupt their independent courses of action so that a full-fledged encounter can be openly dedicated to display of pleasure at the opportunity for contact. During this convivial pause, each participant is constrained to demonstrate that she or he has kept fresh in mind not only the name of the other but also bits of the other's biography. Inquiries will be in order regarding the other's significant others, recent trips, illness if any, career outcomes, and sundry other matters that speak to the questioner's aliveness to the world of the person greeted. Correspondingly, there will be the obligation to update the other regarding one's own circumstances. Of course these obligations help to resuscitate relationships that might otherwise have attenuated for want of dealings: but they also provide both the grounds for initiating an encounter and an easy initial topic. So one might have to admit that the obligation to maintain an active biography of our acquaintances (and ensure that they can sustain the same in regard to us) does at least as much for the organization of encounters as it does for the relationship of the persons who encounter each other. This service to the interaction order is also very evident in connection with our obligation to retain our acquaintance's personal name immediately in mind, allowing us always

to employ it as a vocative in multiperson talk. After all, personal name in utterance-initial position is an effective device for alerting ratified hearers as to which of them is about to be addressed. (Goffman, 1983: 13)

Notes

1. We collected 100 hits by randomly sampling batches of ten examples in our corpora. In our data sampling we first collected an initial dataset, and then replaced the invalid examples with valid ones that occurred before the batches of ten examples.
2. See: http://bcc.blcu.edu.cn/; http://ccl.pku.edu.cn/.
3. E.g. in the Chinese Media Language Corpus (https://ling.cuc.edu.cn/RawPub/) instances of *Zaoshang/Xiawu/Wanshang-hao* Greet→Speech act sequences are very frequent.

CHAPTER 9

Types of Talk in L2 pragmatics 2: the case of extracting

9.1 Introduction

In this chapter, we present yet another case study where we use our framework to study an L2 pragmatic issue through the unit of Types of Talk. Here we focus on the interactional act of extracting, which describes the behaviour of one speaker who wants to end the conversation, while the other goes on talking relentlessly. Similar to the interactional act of greeting which occurs in the Opening phase, extracting is an act which occurs in the Closing phase of an interaction, and it tends to be conventionally realised by various speech acts across linguacultures. Considering that in this chapter we proceed in a similar way as in the previous chapter to illustrate how our framework can be put to use, here we do not provide a detailed review of previous research but start directly with the case study, especially since to the best of our knowledge the phenomenon of extracting has not been studied in L2 pragmatics at all.

9.2 Case study

The problem investigated in this study was raised when the first author visited the second author in China. As we have already noted elsewhere, the second author is a foreign resident in China. He told the first author that despite his fluency in Chinese, he still found it difficult, even after having learnt the language for a lifetime, to appropriately extract himself from an interaction while the other person keeps on talking. In a subsequent discussion, we hypothesised that this may well point to a linguacultural difference between Chinese and English which is worth examining further. Considering the important role of English as a global lingua franca, we decided to look at this problem from a reverse angle, i.e. to investigate whether the conventions of extracting oneself in Closing *in English* can cause frustrations for *Chinese* learners of English.

We define the speech act Extractor – rather than extracting as a broader interactional phenomenon – as follows:

> The Extractor is a strategic signal anticipating a Leave-Take: in using an Extractor a speaker wishes to legitimize or justify his imminent leave-taking by giving reasons for it, or by excusing his intention to leave, i.e. he "extracts" himself from the ongoing conversation. Extractors tend to appear when an encounter has not yet led to a natural point of closure. (Edmondson and House, 1981: 194–195)

Since we distinguish the speech act Extractor from the interactional act of extracting in the Closing phase of an interaction, our definition of Extractor is radically minimal in the sense that it covers the very specific act of explicitly announcing the necessity of leaving. While announcing this necessity can take many different forms, such forms are interconnected by their common function and explicit formulation. For example, an Extractor can be realised in the form of 'I must go now'. While one could argue that this is an implicit Apology, such an utterance is nevertheless an Extractor in our system due to its pragmatic function and form, whereas in the interactional act of extracting several other speech acts may have a place, and among such speech acts a typical Apologise such as 'I am sorry' may easily accompany the speech act Extractor or substitute for it.

It is also worth noting that what we describe as extracting has been referred to in conversation analysis (CA) as 'pre-leave taking'. As we argued in Chapter 3, while we definitely agree with the importance of the CA approach, we take a different path by using our strictly speech act-related analysis and defining speech acts within broader interaction acts and phases. In our view, extracting is not simply a pre-leave taking act realised in the Closing phase, but also a cluster of different speech acts surrounding or substituting for an Extractor.

Similar to what we have done in other studies presented in this book, we began our investigation with a lead-in study, by interviewing ten Chinese learners of English living in the UK. All the interviewees had spent at least two years in the UK at the time of the interviews. We asked them the following questions:

1. Do you find the way in which one ends a conversation in English while the other keeps on talking similar to, or different from, Chinese?
2. If yes, why? If not, why not? Please explain your response in some detail.

As regards the first question, nine out of ten interviewees responded that ending a conversation in English is rather different from Chinese. This response itself simply confirmed what we described as the experience of the second author. However, what surprised us is that in response to the second question, the majority of these nine respondents voiced strong feelings about conventions of extracting in English, arguing that the British tend to be 'robotic' and that they 'coldly disregard' the feelings of others. For example, the following is a typical response:

(9.1) The Brits do not seem to care much when they want to get out of a chat. Basically, they just say 'I have to go now'. Maybe they add a simple 'sorry', but that doesn't really mean a lot. So, I don't think they actually consider the feelings of others. This would certainly not be the case in Chinese where we treat the other with respect and care, as we usually explain why we interrupt the other, and in general we are simply nicer to the other when we have to end a chat.

Many other respondents also reported irritations triggered by the perceived 'abruptness' of how their British interlocutors extracted themselves in the Closing phase. For example, our respondent quoted in Example (9.2) experienced such abruptness when, during a rather pleasant get-together, a British friend suddenly announced that she had to leave, without 'properly' apologising:

(9.2) When I was with my British friend chatting about something, she suddenly interrupted and announced that she had to leave now, telling me that she must be running to the restaurant where she worked as a waitress. While I perfectly understood her reason, she should have properly apologised or at least pretended to be sorry about ending our chat so abruptly.

On the basis of these interviews – which we duly anonymised – we concluded that extracting oneself in the Closing phase of an interaction in English can cause puzzlement and irritation even for advanced Chinese learners of English who have lived in an English-speaking environment for some time. We zeroed in on the use of extracting in dyadic dialogues, bearing in mind that extracting oneself can become much more complex in multiparty scenarios than in dyadic ones.

9.2.1 Contrastive research

In the second step of our case study in this chapter, we compiled a DCT corpus, involving two groups of ten Chinese and ten British students who had never been in the other country. The respondents were requested to complete tasks relating to extracting themselves in the Closing phase in their native tongues. We designed the DCTs by involving the standard sociolinguistic parameters Social Distance and Power [+/–SD, +/–P], which we also used in our other case studies in this book. Our DCTs included the following tasks, distributed to both groups in their native tongues:

Types of Talk in L2 pragmatics 2

1. You are chatting with your best friend, and you suddenly remember that it's your mother's birthday. You really must leave right now, but your friend keeps on talking. What do you say in order to reach a closure of the talk? [–P/–SD]
2. You are chatting with an acquaintance whom you don't know very well, and you suddenly remember that you have a doctor's appointment right now. You really must leave, but your acquaintance keeps on talking. What do you say in order to reach a closure of the talk? [–P/+SD]
3. You are talking to your supervisor, and you suddenly remember that you have an appointment right now with another professor whom you don't know very well. You really must leave, but your supervisor keeps on talking. What do you say in order to reach a closure of the talk? [+P/–SD]
4. You are talking to a professor whom you don't know very well, and you suddenly remember you have an appointment with your supervisor right now. You are desperate to leave, but the professor keeps on talking. What do you say in order to reach a closure of the talk? [+P/+SD]

Analysis of the Chinese DCT data
Table 9.1 displays both the realisations of the speech act Extractor and various other speech acts in our Chinese DCTs:

Table 9.1 *Frequency of Extractor and other speech acts in the Closing phase in our Chinese DCT corpus*

	[–P/–SD]	[–P/+SD]	[+P/–SD]	[+P/+SD]	Total number
Extractor	10	10	7	5	32
Excuse/justify	4	5	10	10	29
Apologise	1	5	9	9	24
Willing/Offer of compensation	5	6	6	7	24
Request	2	3	8	9	22
Thank	0	0	3	4	7
Opine	0	0	2	2	4

As Table 9.1 shows, while Extractor is the most frequent speech act type in the interactional act of extracting, in Chinese it is possible to realise extracting without an Extractor (see below).

In the Chinese DCT corpus, the speech act Extractor is often indicated by honorifics. Here we do not provide a detailed description of the pragmatic features of all such expressions in our corpus – readers with interest in this area are advised to consult He and Ren (2016). As our corpus shows, such honorifics tend to co-occur with non-honorific Extractor realisations, which make the honorific Extractor sound more tolerable in colloquial interaction.[1] In our data two honorifics were found:

1. *Nin-xian-mang* 您先忙 (lit. 'you (V-pronoun) busy first', meaning 'please carry on first with the matter that keeps you busy').

Example:

(9.3) 老师不好意思，我跟导师定的一会见面，<u>我得先走了</u>，下次再来向您请教，<u>您先忙</u>。
Professor, it is embarrassing, but I have an appointment and <u>I must go now</u>. I will respectfully ask for your teaching (honorific expression referring to consultation) on another occasion, <u>please be busy first</u>.

Here the first non-honorific Extractor (*wo dei xian zou-le* 'I must go now') is followed by the honorific Extractor *nin-xian-mang*.

2. *Xian-gaoci-le* 先告辞了 (lit. 'I must first announce my leave', i.e. 'I am afraid I need to go now').

Example:

(9.4) 老师，对不起，我刚想起来今天和导师约了见面，<u>有点儿来不及了</u>，那我就<u>先告辞了</u>！
Professor, my apologies, I just realised that I have a meeting with my supervisor, so <u>I must run now, please let me first announce my leave</u>.

Here again a non-honorific Extractor (*youdiar laibuji-le* 'I must run now') is followed by the honorific Extractor *xian-gaoci-le*.

In our Chinese corpus, such honorific forms are only used in [+P] relationships and they are not meant to substitute for a realisation of the speech act Leave-Take. Table 9.2 shows the frequency of such honorific forms in the ten DCTs:

Table 9.2 *Frequency of Extractor-indicating honorifics in our Chinese DCT corpus*

	[–P/–SD]	[–P/+SD]	[+P/–SD]	[+P/+SD]
Nin-xian-mang 您先忙 (lit. 'you (V-pronoun) are busy first')	0	0	5	6
Xian-gaoci-le 先告辞了 (lit. 'I must first announce my leave')	0	0	0	2

Along with Extractor honorifics, other deferential address forms also appear in our Chinese DCT corpus. It is not surprising that the participants used deferential forms of address in [+P] situations. Here we asked participants to provide utterances in university settings involving a lecturer, and they unanimously used the deferential address form *laoshi* 老师 ('teacher', i.e. 'Professor') in the [+P] scenarios. However, various respondents also used deferential forms of address in [–P] settings, mainly including affective quasi-familial forms of address, illustrated by the following examples:

Types of Talk in L2 pragmatics 2 157

(9.5) 兄弟，<u>我实在得走了</u>，我妈今天过生日在等我，之后再聊哈。
Brother, <u>I really must leave now</u>. It's my mom's birthday today and she's waiting for me, let's catch up on another day.

(9.6) 亲爱的，<u>我得走了</u>，今天我妈过生日。
Darling, <u>I have to go home</u>. Today is my mother's birthday.

Xiongdi 兄弟 ('brother') in example (9.5) is a deferential masculine address form, while *qin'ai-de* 亲爱的 ('darling') in example (9.6) is a feminine one. Such forms of address tend to be used in [–P/–SD] situations, and they tend to be followed by non-honorific Extractors. Table 9.3 summarises the frequency of deferential and quasi-familial forms of address in our Chinese DCT corpus:

Table 9.3 *Frequency of deferential and quasi-familial forms of address in our Chinese DCT corpus*

	[–P/–SD]	[–P/+SD]	[+P/–SD]	[+P/+SD]
Deferential forms of address	0	0	10	10
Quasi-familial forms of address	7	0	0	0

As our Chinese data also show, extracting in Chinese can occasionally be realised without the speech act Extractor. Example (9.7) illustrates such a case – here the Extractor is absent in a [+P/+SD] situation and is substituted by other speech acts:

(9.7) 老师，不好意思哈，您记得之前给我们做讲座的教授嘛，正好他一会有时间给我们答疑，我想先过去一下，等结束了再回来找您，也把论文问题和您反馈一下。
I'm sorry, professor, do you remember the professor who gave us a lecture? He happens to have time to answer questions now and I'd like to go over to his place and come back to you when that meeting is over. I also plan to further discuss my thesis questions with you.

Here, our respondent realised an Apologise, a Request (for information) and an Excuse/Justify, followed by a Willing (Offer of compensation).

Let us now discuss the finding that in our Chinese DCTs (see Table 9.1) other speech acts are also frequently realised in the Closing phase of an interaction. At this point, we only discuss the three most frequent speech acts which occurred in our corpus along with Extractor: Excuse/Justify, Apologise, and Willing (Offer of compensation). As Table 9.1 above shows, it is particularly the [+P] scenario that triggers different speech acts in the Closing phase – this correlates with the fact that in [+P] scenarios the face-threat triggered by extracting is comparatively high.

Among the speech acts realised in the Closing phase, the speech act Excuse/Justify appears to be the most important one. The figures in Table 9.1 show that all our respondents realised Excuse/Justify in [+P] situations. This implies that in the Chinese linguaculture getting out of a meeting with a higher-ranking interactant while the other is still talking is a very difficult interactional act, which needs mitigatory justification.

Along with Excuse/Justify, another frequent speech act in our corpus is Apologise, already illustrated by the above example (9.7). The speech act Apologise appears to be all but 'compulsory' in [+SD] settings, as Table 9.3 shows. Example (9.8), representing a [+P/+SD] situation, illustrates a triple use of apology forms in extracting oneself during a Closing:

(9.8) 对不起，对不起，非常抱歉！医生约我，我可以先走吗？今天见到您非常开心，我希望以后可以继续与您相约。
I apologise, I apologise, I am extremely sorry. I have an appointment with my doctor, so may I take my leave? I was delighted to be having an opportunity to see you, and I hope I will have the pleasure of continuing our discussion on another occasion.

Willing (Offer of compensation) is also a frequent speech act type in our corpus – the following example (9.9) illustrates its use in a [+P/+SD] scenario:

(9.9) 老师不好意思，我跟导师定的一会见面，我得先走了，下次再来向您请教，您先忙。
Professor, it is embarrassing, I have a meeting with my supervisor so I must leave. I will come again to ask for your respected teaching, please be busy first.

The relative frequency of such Willing (Offer of compensation) realisations surprised us because from a cultural outsider point of view the [+P] variable generally does not encourage the inferior party to offer a compensation.

Following this analysis of our Chinese DCT data, let us now move onto the analysis of the English DCT data.

Analysis of the English DCT data
Table 9.4 includes the various speech act types realised in the Closing phase in our English DCT corpus:

Table 9.4 *Frequency of speech act types in the Closing phase in our English DCT corpus*

	[–P/–SD]	[–P/+SD]	[+P/–SD]	[+P/+SD]	Total number
Extractor	10	10	10	10	40
Excuse/Justify	7	9	10	10	36
Apologise	3	5	6	6	20
Opine	7	4	2	4	17
Thank	0	0	4	5	9

Types of Talk in L2 pragmatics 2

The speech act Extractor seems to be ubiquitous when it comes to extracting oneself in the Closing phase in our English data. Furthermore, an Extractor may appear on its own without any other speech acts surrounding it, as in the following utterance realised in the [–P/–SD] scenario:

(9.10) Whoops, I must be off now.

Here the respondent only realised an Alerter ('Whoops') before the Extractor. Such Extractor realisations with no accompanying speech acts only emerge in [–P/–SD] scenarios. Yet, their occurrence shows that extracting oneself in the Closing phase can be realised in a minimal way in English.

Our English DCTs also show that the speech act Extractor tends to be realised by routine formulae (Coulmas, 1979). The following formulae are preferred in our English DCT corpus:

1. I must/have to/got to do x
2. I'd better do x

Examples (9.11) and (9.12) illustrate the use of these routine formulae:

(9.11) Sorry, Dr Smith, <u>I really must leave now</u>. I have an appointment with my supervisor in a couple of minutes.

(9.12) Hey, David, <u>I'd better hit the road now</u>. It's my mum's birthday and I still have to buy her a present.

As these examples show, routine formulae are at the heart of realising the Extractor in English. The fact that the speech act Extractor is ubiquitous in English and tends to be realised in a formulaic way accords with what the first author of this book found in her previous research (see House, 2006): in the realisation of many speech acts, English speakers seem to rely more heavily on routine formulae than speakers of various other languages, such as German. Routine formulae indicating the speech act Extractor tend to be used in all role relationships. Table 9.5 shows the overwhelming frequency of these routine formulae in our English corpus of ten DCTs:

Table 9.5 *Frequency of Extractor-indicating routine formulae in our English DCT corpus*

	[–P/–SD]	[–P/+SD]	[+P/–SD]	[+P/+SD]
Routine formulae indicating Extractor	10	10	10	10

Let us now examine other speech acts in our English DCT corpus. As Table 9.4 shows, while Extractor is by far the most frequent speech act type when one realises extracting in the Closing phase of an interaction in English, the speech act Excuse/Justify frequently co-occurs with Extractor. The following examples illustrate the realisation of Excuse/Justify in a [–P/+SD] and a [+P/+SD] situation:

(9.13) Ugh, I must rush <u>because I have to prepare for my mum's birthday</u>.

(9.14) Erm, Dr Smith, <u>I have a meeting with my supervisor in a sec</u>, so I'm afraid I must go now.

Another frequent speech act type in our corpus is Apologise, illustrated by example (9.15):

(9.15) <u>I'm sorry for interrupting</u>, but I have a meeting with my supervisor, I must take my leave now.

What frequently happens in our corpus of English DCTs is that an Apologise is made for *interrupting* the other rather than for the act of *leaving* the interlocutor.

In our English DCT corpus, Opine is also frequently used. The following examples show [–P/–SD] and [–P/–SD] uses of this speech act:

(9.16) Hey, <u>I'd love to go on talking to you</u>, but I must be off now because there is a family event.

(9.17) Gosh, <u>I really profited from this conversation,</u> and I am sorry for interrupting, but I have an appointment with Dr Josephson, so I need to run now.

The speech act Thank is relatively infrequent in our corpus, only appearing in [+P] constellations. The following example illustrates its use:

(9.18) <u>I'm grateful for this consultation</u>, it was really useful, but I must be off now.

Contrastive analysis
We first describe a similarity and then the contrastive pragmatic differences between English and Chinese conventions of extracting oneself in the Closing phase of an interaction:

1. In both our corpora, Excuse/Justify is the most frequent speech act realised apart from Extractor itself. This contrastive similarity is not surprising because excusing and justifying oneself for the act of extracting suits this situation very well, necessitating an explanation of some form.

2. In Chinese, but not in English, it is possible to extract oneself in the Closing phase of an interaction without realising the speech act Extractor. This absence of an Extractor in the Closing phase can typically be observed in our Chinese corpus in [+P] scenarios, where the lack of an Extractor mitigates the face-threat triggered by extracting oneself from an interaction while one's superior keeps on talking. Such a non-realisation of the speech act Extractor appears to be not possible in English: the use of an Extractor is conventionalised to such an extent in English that speakers may realise Extractor without other accompanying speech acts. This ubiquity of Extractor correlates with the fact that this speech act is practically always realised by routine formulae. In Chinese, on the other hand, the Extractor is not only non-compulsory, but is also often realised by various types of honorifics in both [+P] and [–P] relationships. This contrastive pragmatic difference indicates that extracting oneself while one's interlocutor is still talking is more face-threatening and less routinised in Chinese than in English. This outcome should not be interpreted as a case of stronger indirectness and increased 'politeness' by speakers of Chinese – as we already pointed out in Chapter 3, we are decidedly against such essentialist overgeneralisations (see also Leech, 2007). Rather, we should simply interpret this linguacultural difference through the cold eye of the researcher, analysing in detail the *exact* differences between Chinese and English conventions of extracting oneself in the Closing phase of an interaction.

3. In Chinese, the realisation of an Extractor generally involves more frequent and diverse realisations of other speech acts than is the case in English. In our Chinese corpus, we found six different speech acts co-occurring with, or substituting for, Extractor: the most commonly used speech acts Apologise and Willing (Offer of compensation) had a frequency rate of 72.5 per cent and 62.5 per cent respectively. In our English corpus, on the other hand, there are only four speech act types co-occurring with Extractor. In English, even the most frequent speech acts Apologise and Opine have a somewhat lower frequency rate: 50 per cent and 42.5 per cent respectively. This contrastive pragmatic difference can be interpreted as follows: due to the easy availability of routine formulae resulting in a more strongly ritualised pragmatic convention of extracting oneself in English, much less interactional work needs to be done to realise extracting.

As Kádár (2017) argues, the ritualisation of face-threatening speech acts implies less mitigation work because a ritualised pragmatic convention operates with an underlying sense of moral order, i.e. the speaker needs to invest less mitigatory work, amounting to less 'beating around the bush'. In Chinese, on the other hand, one can witness a scarcity of routine formulae in interactions where honorification is needed. We also found a lower frequency of Extractor-indicating honorifics in comparison with the high frequency of routine formulae in English. These pragmatic conventions imply that, in Chinese, more interactional work is needed in extracting oneself in the Closing phase because of the dearth of routine formulae characterising English (see House, 2006, who found a comparable contrast between English and German).

These linguacultural differences highlight a sharp pragmatic contrast when we compare two poignant realisations of extracting oneself in the Closing phase in the [+P/+SD] scenario presented in our DCTs:

(9.19) 对不起，对不起，非常抱歉！医生约我，我可以先走吗？今天见到您非常开心，我希望以后可以继续与您相约。
I apologise, I apologise, I am so sorry. I have an appointment with my doctor. May I take my leave now? I am so happy that we could see each other today and I do hope that we can continue our meeting on another occasion.

In example (9.19), the Chinese respondent offered an intensified Apologise, including three expressions (*duibuqi* 对不起 realised twice and *feichangdaoqian* 非常抱歉), which unlike the English expression *sorry* are 'speech act-anchored', i.e. they practically always realise the speech act Apologise (see Chapter 4). The multiple Apologise realisations are followed by an Excuse/Justify, a Request for permission, as well as an Opine and a Willing (Offer of compensation). As this example illustrates, in Chinese [+P/+SD] situations in particular one may witness the absence of an Extractor and the presence of a multitude of other speech acts. The following example highlights how very differently extracting oneself from an interaction tends to be realised in English from what we have seen in Chinese:

(9.20) Thank you for all your time. As I have an appointment with my GP I have to run now, but I will be in touch soon if I may.

Unlike in the comparable Chinese example (9.19), in the English example (9.20) the respondent realised a 'proper' Extractor ('I have to run now'), even though the Extractor is prefaced by the speech acts Thanks and Excuse/Justify and is followed by a Willing (Offer of compensation).

9.2.2 Discussion

Let us revisit the sense of irritation reported by Chinese learners of English living in the UK. These irritations might now be explained through the pragmatic differences identified in our case study. As mentioned above, our Chinese interviewees mainly complained about the 'abruptness' and 'robotic' character of extracting oneself from an interaction in English, and also about the lack of 'proper' apologies offered by the person who extracts herself. 'Abruptness' may correlate with the comparatively lower frequency of other speech acts surrounding Extractor in English. The perceived 'robotic' character may relate to the general preference for routine formulae in English, which, as we can see, is very different from the preference for honorific forms by speakers of Chinese. Finally, while the speech act Apologise was found to be present in both our corpora, our analysis has shown that speakers of English often apologise for *interrupting* rather than *leaving* the other. So, it may be likely that speakers of Chinese feel that there is a lack of 'proper' apology in instances of extracting in English because they perceive that the Apologise offered by the British interlocutors actually missed the point. Let us reiterate our warning that these differences are not be interpreted through the lens of sweeping overgeneralisations, such as 'British speakers of English are direct and coldly businesslike', 'speakers of Chinese are polite and considerate', and so on. Rather, one should systematically investigate contrastive pragmatic differences (and similarities) between linguistic realisation patterns of the phenomena studied. One should also carefully consider the potential implications such differences might have for learning and teaching a foreign language such as English.

9.3 Conclusion

In this chapter, we again demonstrated how to use our framework in L2 pragmatic research involving Types of Talk. As a case study, we examined the interactional act of extracting in the Closing phase of an interaction, which may be surprisingly irritating and challenging for foreign language learners. Paradoxically, phases of interaction such as Opening and Closing are often presented in an overly simple fashion in English language programmes, and we hope that through the current discussion we can trigger more interest in Opening and Closing Talk in foreign language learning and teaching.

In the following Chapter 10, we will provide the reader with yet another case study illustrating how to use our framework in the study of Types of Talk, by moving to a type of Core Talk.

9.4 Recommended reading

Emanuel E. Schegloff and Harvey Sacks. (1973). Opening up closings. *Semiotica* 8(4), 289–327.
Readers who would like to follow up on the topic of how interactions are terminated may want to consult the above work of the conversation analysts Schegloff and Sacks, which provides an insightful discussion of this topic. The following is an excerpt from this work:

> A machinery that includes the transition relevance of possible utterance completion recurrently for any utterance in the conversation generates an indefinitely extendable string of turns to talk. Then, an initial problem concerning closings may be formulated: how to organize the

simultaneous arrival of the co-conversationalists at a point where one speaker's completion will not occasion another speaker's talk, and that will not be heard as some speaker's silence. The last qualification is necessary to differentiate closings from other places in conversation where one speaker's completion is not followed by a possible next speaker's talk, but where, given the continuing relevance of the basic features and the turn-taking machinery, what is heard is not termination but attributable silence, a pause in the last speaker's utterance, etc. It should suggest why simply to stop talking is not a solution to the closing problem: any first prospective speaker to do so would be hearable as 'being silent' in terms of the turn-taking machinery, rather than as having suspended its relevance. Attempts to 'close' in this way would be interpretable as an 'event-in-the-conversation', rather than as outside, or marking, its boundaries, and would be analyzed for actions being accomplished in the conversation, e.g., anger, brusqueness, pique, etc. (Schegloff and Harvey Sacks, 1973: 294–295)

Note

1. As Pan and Kádár (2011) argue, in colloquial Chinese (unlike, for instance, in Japanese) honorifics are often associated with written language, and in the realisation of various speech acts in spoken interaction they often have to be 'softened' by more colloquial expressions.

CHAPTER 10

Types of Talk in L2 pragmatics 3: the case of phatic Opening versus Business Talk

10.1 Introduction

In this final chapter on Types of Talk, we discuss a case study in which we conducted an experiment to find out whether Chinese learners of English are able to recognise cases when the speech act Complain is realised in a context where ritual Opening Talk may conventionally be expected. In other words, we investigated whether L2 learners can cope with a situation when one Type of Talk – Opening – is transformed into another Type of Talk, i.e. Business Talk. In real life, such transformations often occur, and as our case study will show, they can be challenging for L2 learners.

Similar to Chapter 9, the phenomenon we study in this chapter has been largely ignored in L2 pragmatics. Thus, instead of providing a review of relevant studies, we move directly to our case study.

10.2 Case study

10.2.1 Experiment

Our small experiment was conducted with two groups of ten native speakers of English and Chinese respectively. We examined whether contrastive pragmatic differences between phatic language use and the interactional act of greeting in English and Chinese (see Chapter 7) influence the ability of Chinese learners of English to adequately recognise uses of English Greet expressions to realise the speech act Complain, representing Business Talk. Our research questions were as follows:

1. How do native speakers of English evaluate unconventional and unexpected non-phatic uses of greeting in English when such uses indicate the speech act Complain?

2. How do Chinese learners of English evaluate the same unconventional and unexpected non-phatic uses of greeting in English when such uses indicate the speech act Complain?

All our Chinese respondents were advanced learners of English with a background of English as a foreign language major.

In this experiment, we constructed a set of situations in an Anglophone context in which the ubiquitous speech act Greet fails to get realised by one of the interactants, and the other interactant realises the speech act Complain in turn, by uttering 'And a very good morning to you too.' While this particular utterance often functions as a conventionalised Greet itself, in the context featured in the DCT it operates as a response to the non-occurrence of an expected Greet. Considering that interpreting the situated function of this Greet as a Complain requires a certain amount of contextual information, we provided detailed descriptions of the situations in which this utterance occurs in the written DCT form. In other words, we aimed to provide sufficient information for our respondents to be able to recognise that the utterance indicates Business Talk rather than phatic Opening. Our two groups of respondents were presented with the utterance 'And a very good morning to you too' occurring in different situations differentiated according to the standard sociolinguistic parameters Social Distance and Power [+/−SD, +/−P].

The written DCT included the following four situations:

1. You enter a friend's room in the dormitory who had said he was sick and who turns out to be completely healthy, playing computer games. You feel angry and disappointed.
   You say: ...
   Your friend responds: 'And a very good morning to you too.' ([−P/−SD] situation)
2. You meet a classmate, who you don't really know, in the common bathroom. There are only the two of you. This person used up all the hot water and you cannot take a shower. You feel angry and disappointed.
   You say: ...
   This person responds: 'And a very good morning to you too.' ([−P/+SD] situation)
3. You go to your grandparents' house. You sleep there, and in the morning you find them already eating breakfast with no food left for you. You feel angry and disappointed.
   You say: ...
   Your grandfather responds: 'And a very good morning to you too.' ([+P/−SD] situation)
4. You go to the administrative office in your university, after you hear that an administrator removed you from a course, without asking you at all. You feel angry and disappointed.

You say: ...
The administrator responds: 'And a very good morning to you too.'
([+P/+SD] situation)

We adopted this research design because our previous research (see Chapter 7) had revealed that in Chinese it is mainly the [+P/+SD] situation, and to a lesser degree the [+P/–SD] situation, which trigger the speech act Greet, while in other situations Chinese speakers frequent the phatic speech act Remark in the Opening phase of an interaction, hence the aforementioned weak relationship between phatic interaction and the speech act Greet in Chinese. In other words, the four situations in the task represent a broader spectrum of contexts than those in which phatic interaction conventionally necessitates Greet in Chinese. We did not reveal the goal of the experiment to our respondents. Following the completion of the above-outlined written DCT, the respondents were asked to explain the reasons for providing their responses.

10.2.2 Outcome

The following Table 10.1 summarises the responses of our British respondents:

Table 10.1 Choices of our British respondents

Respondent	[–P/–SD]	[–P/+SD]	[+P/–SD]	[+P/+SD]
1	✓	✓	✓	✓
2	✓	✓	✓	✓
3	✓	✓	✗	✓
4	✓	✓	✓	✓
5	✓	✓	✓	✓
6	✓	✓	✗	✓
7	✓	✓	✓	✓
8	✓	✓	✗	✓
9	✓	✓	✓	✓
10	✓	✓	✓	✓

As Table 10.1 shows, nearly all our British respondents assessed the utterance 'And a very good morning to you too' as a realisation of the speech act Complain. That is, they interpreted the context as essentially conflictive primarily because no phatic Greet occurs in the first turn where they felt it should have occurred. The directness of these utterances varied in all situations, as the following responses to the first [–P/–SD] task show:

(10.2) What the heck, mate, you are not ill at all.

(10.3) Shouldn't you be in hospital right now?

The first of these utterances is direct, while the response in (10.3) realises irony by being more indirect. Notwithstanding this difference, both respondents successfully recognised that something 'odd' must have been going on in the first turn, in order for the response to become a Complain regarding the lack of a Greet.

We only received three 'inappropriate' responses from the British participants in our DCT. All of them relate to the third situation. Here, our respondents provided speech act sequences, consisting of a Complain followed by a Greet, or the other way around:

(10.4) For heaven's sake, Grampa, why didn't you wait for me. Good morning anyway! (Complain→Greet)

(10.5) Good morning! What am I supposed to eat now? (Greet→Complain)

The follow-up explanations provided by our respondents made clear that all of them felt that the emotional tie one normally has with one's grandparents necessitates some form of greeting. It is worth noting that even though we classified these responses as 'inappropriate', they might as well be appropriate because there is a Complain element realised either before or after the Greet in them, showing that these respondents also perceived that a conflict must be present in turn 1 of the interaction provided. As the following summary of choices of our Chinese respondents shows, even such so-called 'inappropriate' responses turn out to be legitimate in comparison to the types of recognition failures by the majority of our Chinese respondents.

The responses of our Chinese group were radically different from their British peers:

Table 10.2 *Choices of our Chinese respondents*

Respondent	[–P/–SD]	[–P/+SD]	[+P/–SD]	[+P/+SD]
1	✗	✗	✗	✗
2	✓	✓	✗	✗
3	✗	✓	✓	✗
4	✗	✗	✗	✗
5	✗	✗	✗	✗
6	✗	✗	✗	✗
7	✓	✓	✗	✓
8	✓	✓	✓	✓
9	✓	✗	✗	✗
10	✗	✗	✗	✗

As Table 10.2 shows, a significant majority of our Chinese respondents were not able to recognise that the second responsive utterance in the task is simply meant to be a Complain about the lack of an occurrence of a Greet in the first turn, in spite of their very advanced level of English. That is, they frequently provided a Greet expression in the empty line they were requested to fill in, even when they recognised that the second utterance in some way relates to something 'inappropriate' that happened in the first turn. Also, they rarely produced a Complain along with the Greet (see examples (10.4) and (10.5) above). The high rate of recognition failure on the part of our Chinese respondents relates to the fact that in Chinese the use of 'proper' Greet forms has only a weak relationship with phatic interaction, i.e. they apparently did not associate the conflict in turn 2 with a breach of phatic interaction *per se*. Differently put, they did not recognise that here they have an instance of Business Talk on hand.

In what follows, we present two of our Chinese subjects' responses to the [–P/–SD] task, followed by their explanations. Example (10.6) represents an appropriate response and Example (10.7) represents an inappropriate response.

(10.6) Oh, that must be a completely good morning for you.

Explanation: In this situation, I might feel being fooled. Since this person is my friend, I may say 'Oh, that must be a completely good morning for you' to be ironic. This irony would show my feelings of anger and disappointment, while it would also help me to avoid further conflict owing to the indirect nature of how I speak.

This respondent appropriately interpreted that the source of the responsive Complain in the second turn in the task was the lack of Greet in the first turn. The second respondent quoted below initially seemed to provide an appropriate utterance in the task, hence performing better than various other respondents involved in our experiment. However, her subsequent explanation revealed that she misunderstood the situation presented in the task:

(10.7) I knew it! You've got to cover me next time.

Explanation: In this situation, I would feel angry and disappointed, and I would want the favour I made to my friend to be returned. This is why I would ask my friend to return my favour.

As the explanation here shows, the utterance produced in turn 1 was meant to convey a relationally positive message in spite of the initial criticism ('I knew it!'). Such a relationally positive message may not have the capacity to trigger the speech act Complain.

We can now proceed to answer our two research questions:

1. How do native speakers of English evaluate unconventional and unexpected non-phatic uses of greeting in English when such uses realise the speech act Complain?

2. How do Chinese learners evaluate the same unconventional and unexpected non-phatic uses of greeting in English when such uses realise the speech act Complain?

Regarding the first question, it is clear that for native speakers of English it is easy to recognise the source of Complain in the second turn in the tasks. This relates to the fact that Greet is ubiquitous in English (see Chapter 7), and so in the phatic Opening phase of an interaction its non-realisation is marked. As regards the second question, our Chinese respondents often struggled with interpreting what was going on in the tasks. This interpretative difficulty is, in our view, related to pragmatic transfer. More specifically, according to what we could see in Chapter 7, fully-fledged realisations of the speech act Greet are not 'compulsory' in phatic Openings in certain interpersonal scenarios in the Chinese linguaculture. In such scenarios in particular, it is generally the speech act Remark which is associated with Opening in many interpersonal relationships.

10.3 Conclusion

In this final short case-study chapter, we have presented an experimental way in which our concept of Type of Talk and our broader framework can be put to use in L2 pragmatics.

Through our various case studies in Chapters 4–10 we have shown the reader how our framework operates, by involving all our units of analysis presented in Chapter 1. In the following and final chapter, we will conclude this book.

10.4 Recommended reading

Schegloff, Emanuel E. (1968). Sequencing in conversational openings. ***American Anthropologist* 70, 1075–1095.**
Readers with a further interest in the Opening of interactions may want to consult the above-cited classic work of the conversation analyst Schegloff. In the following, we present an excerpt of this work:

> A first rule of telephone conversation, which might be called a "distribution rule for first utterances," is: the answerer speaks first. Whether the utterance be "hello," "yeah," "Macy's," "shoe department," "Dr. Brown's office," "Plaza 1-5000," or whatever, it is the one who picks up the ringing phone who speaks it. This rule seems to hold in spite of a gap in the informational resources of the answerer. While the caller knows both his own identity, and, typically, that of his intended interlocutor (whether a specific person or an organization is being phoned), the answerer, at

least in most cases, knows only who he is and not specifically who the caller is. That is not to say that no basis for inference might exist, as, for example, that provided by time of day, the history of a relationship, agreed upon signaling arrangements, etc. To the question "whom are you calling?" a caller may give a definitive answer, but to the question "who's calling?" the answerer, before picking up the phone, can give only a speculative answer.

[...]

It may help to gain insight into the working of the distribution rule to consider, speculatively, what might be involved in its violation, and the reader is invited to do so ... One possible violation would involve the following: The distribution rule provides that the answerer normally talks first, immediately upon picking up the receiver. To violate the rule and attempt to have the other person treated as the one who was called, he would not talk, but would remain silent until the caller spoke first. Suppose after some time the caller says "Hello?" This might be heard as an attempt by the caller to check out the acoustic intactness of the connection. In doing so, the caller employs a lexical item, and perhaps an intonation, that is standardly used by called parties in answering their home phones. This would provide the violator (i.e., the answerer acting as a caller) with a resource. Given the identity of the lexical items used by persons to check out and to answer in this case, the violater may now treat the checking out "hello" as an answering "hello." Continuing the role reversal, he would be required to offer a caller's first remark. (Schegloff, 1968: 1076–1077)

CHAPTER 11

Conclusion

11.1 Retrospect

In the following, we provide short synopses of the chapters of this book:

- Chapter 1 provided an introduction to the book, including the units of analysis of our framework.
- Chapter 2 introduced the reader to the field of cross-cultural pragmatics, by giving a general overview of how the field has developed, its key concepts, and the very possibility of contrastively examining two comparable units of language use.
- Chapter 3 presented our framework and our replicable research methodology, and provided two key figures to visualise the core of the framework and the methodology.
- Chapter 4 looked at how expressions as the smallest pragmatic unit of analysis can indicate speech acts, and the L2 pragmatic issues arising from this indication.
- Chapter 5 discussed the relationship between expressions and speech acts in L2 pragmatics by exploring the phenomenon of altered speech act indication, including three key types of such altered speech act indication.
- Chapter 6 investigated speech acts and interactional acts from an L2 pragmatic point of view, by examining the interactional act criticising in the classroom.
- Chapter 7 revisited the relationship between speech acts and interactional acts in L2 pragmatics, and also connected it with the applied linguistic field of study abroad and interaction ritual theory, by examining the realisation of the ritual interactional act of congratulating.
- Chapter 8 examined the unit of Types of Talk, the largest unit of analysis in our system, by studying L2 pragmatic difficulties, which the interactional act of greeting in English in Opening Talk triggers for L2 learners.
- Chapter 9 examined an L2 pragmatic issue in another Type of Talk, namely Closing Talk, by looking at the interactional act of extracting.

Conclusion

- Chapter 10 provided yet another case study of L2 pragmatic research involving Types of Talk, by examining cases when the speech act Complain transforms Opening Talk into another Type of Talk, i.e. Business Talk.

11.2 Prospect

Before concluding this book, let us present various areas where we believe further contrastive L2 pragmatic research would be particularly beneficial.

As we have said repeatedly in this book, we are absolutely against culturally motivated (over)generalisation of L2 pragmatic issues. Many such (over)generalisations stem from the use of non-linguistic notions, which also often trigger top-down approaches to one's data. Such notions include, for example, 'values', 'sensitivity', the so-called 'East–West divide', 'individualism versus collectivism', and so on. As we argued in Chapter 3, a particular problem with relying on such notions is that they prompt the researcher to only seek to confirm their validity, instead of approaching her or his data in a more neutral way, i.e. by attempting to identify exactly what may trigger an L2 pragmatic problem, and also whether this claimed problem exists at all. We believe that L2 pragmatic research needs to be strictly language anchored, and in this book we have proposed a replicable framework through which such language-anchored pragmatic research can be carried out. A disadvantage of our framework is that it is largely incompatible with any culturally and psychologically based pre-assumptions of differences between linguacultures and related L2 pragmatic issues. Its advantage, however, is that it allows us to resolve puzzles which we would not be able to resolve otherwise, as we could see in many case studies, such as that of greeting. Obviously, what we can offer in this book is somewhat limited, in that we only looked at Chinese and English, partly because they are important languages and partly because one of the authors is fluent in Chinese. A key advantage of using these two languages is that they are typologically distant, and so their contrastive study offers a rich reservoir for study. In future, it would be advisable to look at many different linguacultures in contrastive L2 pragmatic research, with a particular focus on the aforementioned notion of typological distance (see House and Kádár, 2021a, where we outlined 'typological distance' as a contrastive pragmatic principle). Interesting language pairs would be, for example, English–Japanese, German–Japanese, Korean–Chinese, and so on. The reader may have noted that not all the above-mentioned examples of language pairs include English, and this is for a good reason: while English is arguably the most important lingua franca worldwide and can be expected to occupy this position in the foreseeable future, there is no reason why contrastive L2 pragmatic research should always include English in its repertoire.

Another important task for future contrastive L2 pragmatic research would be to venture beyond dyadic linguacultural pairs and include at least two or even three comparable L2 learner groups. We use the expression 'comparable' (see also Chapter 2) to highlight the fact that it is productive in contrastive pragmatic research to simultaneously compare data drawn from speakers of typologically close and distant linguacultures. In House and Kádár (2021a: 204) we visualised this more complex comparison procedure as shown in Figure 11.1.

Linguaculture 1 (typologically close date 1)

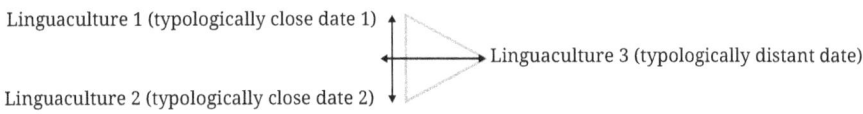

Linguaculture 3 (typologically distant date)

Linguaculture 2 (typologically close date 2)

Figure 11.1 The typological distance-based contrastive approach

As Figure 11.1 illustrates, an advantage of such an approach where we include typologically distant linguacultures is that, paradoxically, it often helps us to learn more about contrastive pragmatic similarities and differences between typologically close linguacultures than their typologically distant counterpart. In Figure 11.1, the vertical axis represents typological closeness, and it refers to an analytic focus whereby we investigate research questions relating to data drawn from typologically close linguacultures. The horizontal axis represents typological distance, and it refers to an analytic focus whereby we examine data drawn from typologically distant linguacultures. In future research, it would be intriguing, for example, to simultaneously study L2 pragmatic issues faced by German and British learners of Chinese, not only to examine L2 pragmatic issues relating to Chinese as a foreign language but also to learn more about pragmatic *similarities* and differences between the language use by these groups of L2 learners.

In this book, the phenomenon of ritual emerged in two different respects. On the one hand we defined certain speech acts as Ritual, following our typological model outlined in Chapter 3. According to this model, Opening and Closing Talk typically triggers ritual speech acts, and we have shown that the study of these seemingly 'simple' speech acts can trigger intriguing and complex L2 pragmatic difficulties. On the other hand, we also examined certain ritual interactional acts like congratulating, and we have shown that these often non-quotidian ritual interactional acts are very relevant to L2 pragmatics. In future research, ritual in both these senses should ideally be more visibly featured in contrastive L2 pragmatic enquiries. Regarding what we defined as ritual illocutionary acts, the study of How-are-you, Welcome, Okay, etc. would be beneficial for L2 pragmaticians because they occur relatively frequently, and also they are used in many linguacultures to lubricate the social machinery of interaction. While of course research on these individual speech acts has often been conducted in the field, to the best of our knowledge their relation to both one another and to the broader flow of interaction has remained regretfully understudied. We believe that the typology of speech acts, the notion of altered speech act interaction, and the broader research procedure we proposed in this book might give momentum to such enquiries. As regards ritual interactional acts, there are many such acts which would be interesting to study. For example, we are presently engaged in the study of the interactional act of condolencing, involving foreign learners of Chinese. Condolencing – just like congratulating – is clearly non-quotidian and highly important in any society. For example, the question may rightly be asked: Can anything be more embarrassing than not being able to provide an appropriate utterance when an acquaintance of a learner suffers a bereavement in the family? We hope that future contrastive L2 pragmatic research will pay more attention to this underresearched area.

In this book, we have devoted comparatively little attention to the practical matter of teaching pragmatics in the foreign language classroom. This is a definite gap, and all we can do at this point is to admit our shortcomings in this area. We sincerely hope that in future we will witness attempts to use the contrastive L2 pragmatic framework proposed in this book in actual teaching, involving a rich repertoire of languages. Our dear and deeply respected colleague, Willis Edmondson, whose thought has inspired our thinking, was both a scholar and an enthusiastic language teacher, and in another volume (Edmondson et al., 2023) we considered at least some ways in which parts of the framework presented here can be put into classroom practice. However, the framework we offered in the current book still needs to be experimented with in the foreign language classroom.

To conclude this book, we would like once again to emphasise the need for a strictly language-anchored research procedure in L2 pragmatics. In a recent position paper (House and Kádár, 2023), we not only pointed out why there is a clear need in the field for our radically minimal, finite and interactional system of speech acts, but we also argued for the necessity of consistently foregrounding language rather than culture and psychology in the field. While the research we recommended in this book may appear to be less grandiose and alluring than more culturally and psychologically motivated enquiries, we hope we have shown that it is worth doing and intriguing to engage in contrastive L2 pragmatic research.

Glossary

'Altered speech act-indication': Many RFIEs (*see also* RFIEs) can conventionally indicate more than just one speech act, or completely lose their speech act-indicating function.

Bottom-up: Involves research starting from inductively studying data, rather than studying data to prove the validity of one's assumption.

Contextualisation cue: Those forms in an utterance that alert the speaker to contextually important information, such as who the speaker is, where she came from, her social class, age, and so on, as well as the contextual meaning of the utterance.

Contrastive pragmatics: Involves research through which scholars systematically compare language use across different languages and language varieties, in order to understand a particular phenomenon concerning language use.

Conventionalisation: The degree of recurrence of a particular pragmatic phenomenon in the language use and evaluations of members of a social group or a broader linguaculture.

Cooperative Principle: Paul Grice's principle stating that participants expect that each will make a conversational contribution such as is required, at the stage at which it occurs, by the expected purpose or direction of the talk exchange (adapted from Grice, 1975).

Corpus: A searchable collection of machine-readable texts of varying size.

Cross-cultural pragmatics: This term is a synonym for contrastive pragmatics (*see* contrastive pragmatics). However, while 'contrastive' is more often used to describe a pragmatic methodology, the expression 'cross-cultural'

Glossary   177

refers to a broader field in which the researcher engages in both basic contrastive research and other non-contrastive methodologies. In other words, 'cross-cultural' is a more comprehensive expression than 'contrastive'.

Cross-Cultural Speech Act Realisation Project (CCSARP): A foundation project through which cross-cultural pragmatics came into existence and which continues to have a significant methodological impact on both pragmatics and second language learning.

Discourse Completion Tests (DCTs): DCTs consist of scripted dialogues that represent socially differentiated situations in particular linguacultures. Each dialogue is preceded by a short description of the situation.

'East–West divide': An overgeneralising view attributing contrastive pragmatic differences to a deep-seated cultural gap between so-called 'Eastern' and 'Western' cultures.

Emic: The linguistic and cultural insider's view on certain phenomena.

Etic: The linguistic and cultural outsider's perspective on certain phenomena.

Exoticisation: To attribute an exotic meaning to forms that may trigger puzzlement and irritation for foreign language learners.

Expression: We prefer 'expression' to 'word' because here we are talking about a pragmatic rather than linguistic unit, which may include forms of varying size.

Interactional act: A unit of analysis, which can be realised by various speech acts.

Interpersonal scenario: The participation structure of an interaction, which we divide in our framework into the three basic scenarios of 'dyadic', 'multi-party' and 'public'.

L2 pragmatics: Focuses on the pragmatic aspects of second and foreign language learning.

Linguaculture: Culture manifested through patterns of language use.

Mixed method approaches: We propose relying on different analytic approaches in order to triangulate our data.

Modified speech act-indicating use: RFIEs (*see also* RFIEs) may indicate various speech acts simultaneously.

'Native speaker': A controversial term in applied linguistics referring to people who were born in one particular country, and who are thus automatically considered as expert speakers of a language spoken in this country. This term is used in a critical way in the present book.

Non-speech act-anchored use: RIFEs (*see also* RFIEs) may lose their speech act-indicating function entirely and be used in non-speech act-anchored ways.

Private versus Public: An interaction is defined as Private when there are clearly no bystanders/overhearers around and when it is uttered for the hearer only, while it qualifies as Public when bystanders/overhearers are present either physically or symbolically.

Qualitative research: Research whereby one engages in a detailed examination of individual interactions, in order to gain a deeper understanding of the phenomenon studied.

Quantitative research: Examination of the data whereby one looks into the frequency of occurrence of a pragmatic phenomenon; such research involves measuring, counting and analysing data.

Radical minimalism: This term refers to the system of speech acts proposed in this book, according to which we operate with an interactionally defined and radically minimal and replicable set of speech acts, which allows us to pin down more complex phenomena that we define as interactional acts (*see also* interactional act).

Replicability: The aim of contrastive L2 pragmatic research as represented in this book is to study data beyond idiosyncratic cases, in a way which can be repeated with comparable outcomes in different data types.

Ritual: In this book the term 'ritual' is used in two different but interrelated ways. Firstly, it describes certain speech acts like Greet which seemingly have no meaning but in fact have important social meanings. Secondly, it describes language behaviour in settings in which rights and obligations prevail and pragmatic conventions prompt language users to follow preset pragmatic realisation patterns.

Ritual frame indicating expressions (RFIEs): Expressions indicating that the speaker is aware of who and where he is, i.e. awareness of the rights and obligations and related pragmatic conventions holding for a particular standard situation.

Scalar approach: A view according to which many seemingly bipolar pragmatic phenomena should be seen as ends of a scale; this view was created by Leech (1983).

Social Distance and Power: Two key sociopragmatic parameters in contrastive L2 pragmatic research.

Speech act: A speech act is an utterance considered to be an action.

Speech act migration: The use of a speech act in a different and less conventionalised way than its default conventional use.

Standard situation: "A situation qualifies as 'standard' for language users if the speaker assumes with a fair amount of certainty that the partner is able and willing to perform act A" (from Hoppe-Graff et al., 1985: 90).

Study abroad: An applied linguistic area focusing on learners' L2 development during their stay in their target country.

Transformed speech act-indicating use: RFIE (*see also* RFIEs) may indicate an entirely different speech act than the one they are normally associated with.

Types of Talk: The building blocks of an interaction, which include conventionalised sequences of speech acts.

References

Agyekum, K. (2008) The pragmatics of Akan greetings. *Discourse Studies* **10**(4), 493–516. doi.org/10.1177/14614456080918

Al-Gahtani, S., Roever C. (2015) The development of requests by L2 learners of Modern Standard Arabic: A longitudinal and cross-sectional study. *Foreign Language Annals* **48**(4), 570–583. doi.org/10.1111/flan.12157

Al-Hour, I. I. (2019) *The Speech Act of Congratulation in Palestinian Society: Positive Politeness and Gender Differences*. Doctoral thesis, Hebron University.

Alcón, E., Safont Jordà, P. (2008) Pragmatic awareness in second language acquisition. In Cenoz, J., Hornberger, N. (eds), *Encyclopedia of Language and Education*. New York: Springer, 193–204. doi.org/10.1007/978-0-387-30424-3_149

Allami, H., Eslamizadeh, A. (2022) Self-sacrifice expressions in Persian. *International Journal of Language and Culture* **9**(1), 151–172. doi.org/10.1075/ijolc.21072.all

Austin, J. L. (1962) *How to Do Things with Words*. Oxford: Oxford University Press.

Baratta, A. (2020) A fine 'How-do-you-do': Contextual factors within English greetings. In Vyas, M., Patel, Y. (eds), *Teach English as a Second Language: A New Pedagogy for a New Century*. Delhi: PHI Learning, 62–179.

Bardovi-Harlig, K. (2012) Formulas, routines, and conventional expressions in pragmatics research. *Annual Review of Applied Linguistics* **32**, 206–227. doi.org/10.1017/S0267190512000086

Bardovi-Harlig, K., Su, Y. (2018) The acquisition of conventional expressions as a pragmalinguistic resource in Chinese as a foreign language. *The Modern Language Journal* **102**(4), 732–757. doi.org/10.1111/modl.12517

Bardovi-Harlig, K., Vellenga, H. (2012) The effect of instruction on conventional expressions in L2 pragmatics. *System* **40**(1), 77–89. doi.org/10.1016/j.system.2012.01.004

Barron, A. (2003) *Acquisition in Interlanguage Pragmatics: Learning How to Do Things with Words in a Study*. Amsterdam: John Benjamins. doi.org/10.1075/pbns.108

Blum-Kulka, S., Olshtain, E. (1984) Requests and apologies: A cross-cultural study of speech act realization patterns (CCSARP). *Applied Linguistics* **5**(3), 196–213. doi.org/10.1093/applin/5.3.196

Blum-Kulka, S., House, J., Kasper, G. (1989) *Cross-Cultural Pragmatics: Requests and Apologies*. Norwood, NJ: Ablex.

Bou-Franch, P., Garces-Conejos Blitvich, P. (2003) Teaching linguistic politeness: A methodological proposal. *International Review of Applied Linguistics in Language Teaching* **41**(1), 1–22. doi.org/10.1515/iral.2003.001

Brown, J. D. (2018) Assessing pragmatic competence. In Liontas, J., DelliCarpini, M. (eds), *The TESOL Encyclopaedia of English Language Teaching*. New York: Wiley. doi.org/10.1002/9781118784235.eelt0384

Brown, P. (2017) Politeness and impoliteness. In Huang, Y. (ed.), *The Oxford Handbook of Pragmatics*. Oxford: Oxford University Press, 383–399. doi.org/10.1093/oxfordhb/9780199697960.013.16

Brown, P., Levinson, S. P. (1987) *Politeness: Some Universals of Language Usage*. Cambridge: Cambridge University Press.

Bull, P., Fetzer, A., Kádár, D. Z. (2020) Calling Mr Speaker 'Mr Speaker': The strategic use of ritual references to the Speaker of the UK House of Commons. *Pragmatics* 30(1), 64–87. doi.org/10.1075/prag.19020.bul

Burdelski, M. (2010) Socializing politeness conventionals: Action, other-orientation, and embodiment in a Japanese preschool. *Journal of Pragmatics* 42(6), 1606–1621.

Busse, U. (2002) Changing politeness strategies in English request: A diachronic investigation. In Fisiak, J. (ed.), *Studies in English Historical Linguistics and Philology: A Festschrift for Aiko Izumi*. Bern: Peter Lang, 17–35.

Byon, A. S. (2002) Pragmalinguistic features of KFL learners in the speech act of request. *Korean Linguistics* 11(1), 151–182. doi.org/10.1075/kl.11.09asb

Byon, A. S. (2004) Learning linguistic politeness. *Applied Language Learning* 14(1), 37–62.

Chen, S. C. (1988) The social distribution and development trend of Chinese greetings [in Chinese]. *Language Planning* 4, 27–29.

Cohen, A. (2005) Strategies for learning and performing L2 speech acts. *Intercultural Pragmatics* 2(3), 275–301. doi.org/10.1515/iprg.2005.2.3.275

Cohen, A. (2008) Teaching and assessing L2 pragmatics: What can we expect from learners? *Language Teaching* 41(2), 213–235. doi.org/10.1017/S0261444807004880

Cook, V. (1999) Going beyond the native speaker in language teaching. *TESOL Quarterly* 32(2), 185–209. doi.org/10.2307/3587717

Cotterill, S. (2020) Call me Fei: Chinese-speaking students' decision whether or not to use English names in classroom interaction. *Language, Culture & Curriculum* 33(3), 228–241. doi.org/10.1080/07908318.2019.1614598

Coulmas, F. (1978) Kontrastive Pragmatik. In von Faber, H., Kreifels, B., Siegrist, L. (eds), *Technologie und Medienverbund, Sprachtests, kontrastive Linguistik und Fehleranalyse, IRAL Sonderband GAL'78*. Heidelberg: Groos, 53–60.

Coulmas, F. (1979) On the sociolinguistic relevance of routine formulae. *Journal of Pragmatics* 3(3/4), 239–266. doi.org/10.1016/0378-2166(79)90033-X

Coulmas, F. (1981) Introduction: Conversational routine. In Coulmas, F. (ed.), *Conversational Routine: Explorations in Standardized Communication Situations and Prepatterned Speech*. Berlin: Mouton de Gruyter, 1–18.

Croft, W. (1994) Speech act classification, language typology and cognition. In Savas, S., Tsohatzidis, L. (eds), *Foundations of Speech Act Theory: Philosophical and Linguistic Perspectives*. London: Routledge, 460–477.

Culpeper, J., Pat, K. (2021) Compliment responses in Hong Kong: An application of Leech's pragmatics of politeness. *Text & Talk* 41(5/6), 667–690. doi.org/10.1515/text-2020-0047

Cunningham, J. D. (2017) Methodological innovation for the study of request production in telecollaboration. *Language Learning & Technology* 21(1), 75–98. dx.doi.org/10125/44596

Davies, A. (2004) The native speaker in applied linguistics. In Davies, A., Elder, C. (eds), *The Handbook of Applied Linguistics*. Oxford: Wiley, 431–450. doi.org/10.1002/9780470757000.ch17

Davies, E. E. (1987) A contrastive approach to the analysis of linguistic formulas. *Applied Linguistics* **8**(1), 75–88. doi.org/10.1093/applin/8.1.75

de Kadt, E. (1998) The concept of face and its applicability to the Zulu language. *Journal of Pragmatics* **29**(2), 173–191. doi.org/10.1016/S0378-2166(97)00021-0

Drew, P. (2013) Conversation analysis and social action. *Journal of Foreign Languages* **37**(3), 2–19.

Drew, P., Walker, T. (2010) Citizens' emergency calls requesting assistance in calls to the police. In Coulthard, M., Johnson, A. (eds), *The Routledge Handbook of Forensic Linguistics*. London: Routledge, 96–110. doi.org/10.4324/9780203855607

Du, H. (2013) The development of Chinese fluency during study abroad in China. *The Modern Language Journal* **97**(1), 131–143. doi.org/10.1111/j.1540-4781.2013.01434.x

Duranti, A. (1997) Universal and culture-specific properties of greetings. *Linguistic Anthropology* **7**(1), 63–97. jstor.org/stable/43103940

Edmondson, W. J. (1981) *Spoken Discourse: A Model for Analysis*. London: Longman.

Edmondson, W. J., House, J. (1981) *Let's Talk and Talk About It: An Interactional Grammar of English*. München: Urban & Schwarzenberg.

Edmondson, W. J., House, J. (2011) *Einführung in die Sprachlehrforschung*, 4th ed. Tübingen: Narr.

Edmondson, W. J., House, J., Kádár, D. Z. (2023) *Expressions, Speech Acts and Discourse: A Pedagogic Interactional Grammar of English*. Cambridge: Cambridge University Press. doi.org/10.1017/9781108954662

Edmondson, W., House, J., Kasper, G., Stemmer, B. (1982) *Kommunikation: Lehren und Lernen*. Heidelberg: Groos.

Edmondson, W., House, J., Kasper, G., Stemmer, B. (1984) Learning the pragmatics of discourse: A project report. *Applied Linguistics* **5**(2), 113–127. doi.org/10.1093/applin/5.2.113

Eibl-Eibesfeldt, I. (1977) Patterns of greetings in New Guinea. In Wurm, S. A. (ed.), *New Guinea Languages and Language Study*. Cambridge: Cambridge University Press, 209–247.

Eslami, Z. (2010) Refusals: How to develop appropriate refusal strategies. In Martínez-Flor, A., Usó-Juan, E. (eds), *Speech Act Performance: Theoretical, Empirical and Methodological Issues*. Amsterdam: Benjamins, 217–236. doi.org/10.1075/lllt.26.13esl

Félix-Brasdefer, C. (2008) *Politeness in Mexico and the United States: A Contrastive Study of the Realization and Perception of Refusals*. Amsterdam: Benjamins. doi.org/10.1075/pbns.171

Freed, B. F. (1995) *Second Language Acquisition in a Study Abroad Context*. Amsterdam: John Benjamins. doi.org/10.1075/sibil.9

Freed, B. F. (1998) An overview of issues and research in language learning in a study abroad setting. *Frontiers: The Interdisciplinary Journal of Study Abroad* **4**(1), 31–60. doi.org/10.36366/frontiers.v4i1.62

Fries, C. C. (1945) *Teaching and Learning English as a Foreign Language*. Ann Arbor: The University of Michigan Press.

Geertz, C. (1973) *The Interpretation of Cultures*. New York: Basic Books.

Goffman, E. (1955) On face-work: An analysis of ritual elements in social interaction. *Psychiatry: Interpersonal and Biological Processes* **18**(3), 213–231. doi.org/10.1080/00332747.1955.11023008

Goffman, E. (1963) *Behavior in Public Places: Notes On The Social Organization of Gatherings*. New York: Free Press.

Goffman, E. (1971) *Relations in Public*. New York: Basic Books.

Goffman, E. (1974) *Frame Analysis: An Essay on the Organization of Experience.* Cambridge, MA: Harvard University Press.
Goffman, E. (1981) *Forms of Talk.* Philadelphia: The University of Pennsylvania Press.
Goffman, E. (1983). The interaction order: American Sociological Association, 1982 Presidential Address. *American Sociological Review* **48**(1), 1–17. doi.org/10.2307/2095141
Golato, A. (2003) Studying compliment responses: A comparison of DCTs and recordings of naturally occurring talk. *Applied Linguistics* **8**(1), 90–121. doi.org/10.1093/applin/24.1.90
Gong, Z. (2018) *Situation-bound Utterances as Main Supporters of Chinese as a Second Language Learners' Conceptual Socialization.* PhD Thesis, State University of New York.
Goody, E. (1972) 'Greeting', 'Begging' and the presentation of respect. In La Fontaine, J. (ed.), *The Interpretation of Ritual.* London: Tavistock, 39–72.
Grice, H. P. (1969) Utterer's meaning and intentions. *The Philosophical Review* **78**(2), 147–177.
Grice, H. P. (1975) Logic and conversation. In Cole, P., Morgan, J. L. (eds), *Syntax and Semantics, Vol. 3.* New York: Academic Press, 41–58.
Gumperz, J. (1978) The conversational analysis of interethnic communication. In Lamar Ross, E. (ed.), *Interethnic Communication.* Athens: Georgia University Press, 14–31.
Habermas, J. (1979) *Communication and the Evolution of Society,* T. McCarthy (trans.). Boston, MA: Beacon Press.
Harris, R. (1988) *Language, Saussure and Wittgenstein: How to Play Games with Words.* London: Routledge.
He, Z., Ren W. (2016) Current address behaviour in China. *East Asian Pragmatics* **1**(2), 163–180. doi.org/10.1558/eap.v1i2.29537
Holtgraves, T. (2007) Second language learners and speech act comprehension. *Language Learning* **57**(4), 595–610. doi.org/10.1111/j.1467-9922.2007.00429.x
Hoppe-Graff, S., Herrmann, T., Winterhoff-Spurk, P., Mangold, R. (1985) Speech and situation: A general model for the process of speech production. In Forgas, J. P. (ed.), *Language and Social Situations.* New York: Springer, 81–95.
Hosni, H. R. (2020) Advice giving in Egyptian Arabic and American English: A cross-linguistic, cross-cultural study. *Journal of Pragmatics* **155**, 193–212. doi.org/10.1016/j.pragma.2019.11.001
House, J. (1989) Politeness in English and German: The functions of please and bitte. In Blum-Kulka, S., House, J., Kasper, G. (eds), *Cross-Cultural Pragmatics: Requests and Apologies.* Norwood, NJ: Ablex, 96–119.
House, J. (1996) Developing pragmatic fluency in English as a foreign language: Routines and metapragmatic awareness. *Studies in Second Language Acquisition* **18**(2), 225–252. doi.org/10.1017/S0272263100014893
House, J. (2003a) English as a lingua franca: A threat to multilingualism? *Journal of Sociolinguistics* **7**(4), 556–578. doi.org/10.1111/j.1467-9841.2003.00242.x
House, J. (2003b) Misunderstanding in intercultural university encounters. In House, J., Kasper, G., Ross, S. (eds), *Misunderstanding in Social Life. Discourse Approaches to Problematic Talk.* London: Longman, 22–56.
House, J. (2005) Politeness in Germany – Politeness in Germany? In Hickey, L., Stewart, M. (eds), *Politeness in Europe.* Clevedon: Multilingual Matters, 13–29. doi.org/10.21832/9781853597398-003
House, J. (2006) Communicative styles in English and German. *European Journal of English Studies* **10**(3), 249–267. doi.org/10.1080/13825570600967721

House, J. (2015) *Translation Quality Assessment: Past and Present.* London: Routledge.
House, J., Kádár, D. Z. (2021a) *Cross-Cultural Pragmatics.* Cambridge: Cambridge University Press. doi.org/10.1017/9781108954587
House, J., Kádár, D. Z. (2021b) Altered speech act indication: A contrastive pragmatic analysis of Thanking and Greeting. *Lingua* 264(103162). doi.org/10.1016/j.lingua.2021.103162
House, J., Kádár, D. Z. (2023) Speech acts and interaction in second language pragmatics: A position paper. *Language Teaching* (2022), 1–12. doi.org/10.1017/S0261444822000477
House, J., Kádár, D. Z. (2024 forthcoming) *Translation and Politeness: A Cross-Cultural Pragmatic Approach.* Cambridge: Cambridge University Press.
House, J., Kasper, G. (1981) Politeness markers in English and German. In Coulmas, F. (ed.), *Conversational Routine: Explorations in Standardized Communication Situations and Prepatterned Speech.* Berlin: Mouton de Gruyter, 157–186.
Huang, Y. (2008). Politeness principle in cross-culture communication. *English Language Teaching* 1(1), 96–101.
Hyland, K. (2002) Authority and invisibility: Authorial identity in academic writing. *Journal of Pragmatics* 34, 1091–1112. doi.org/10.1016/S0378-2166(02)00035-8
Hymes, D. (1962) The ethnography of speaking. In Gladwin, T., Sturtevant, W. C. (eds), *Anthropology and Human Behavior.* Washington, DC: Anthropology Society of Washington, 13–53.
Hymes, D. (1964) Directions in (ethno-)linguistic theory. In Kimball Romney, A., D'Andrade, R. G. (eds), *Transcultural Studies of Cognition.* New York: American Anthropological Association, 6–56.
Hymes, D. (1971) Sociolinguistics and the ethnography of speaking. In Ardener, E. (ed.), *Social Anthropology and Language.* London: Routledge, 47–93.
Ide, S. (1989) Formal forms and discernment: Two neglected aspects of universals of linguistic politeness. *Multilingua* 8, 223–248. doi.org/10.1515/mult.1989.8.2-3.223
Ide, R. (1998) 'Sorry for your kindness': Japanese interactional ritual in public discourse. *Journal of Pragmatics* 29(5), 509–529. doi.org/10.1016/S0378-2166(98)80006-4
Isabelli-García, C., Bown, J., Plews, J. L., Dewey, D. P. (2018) Language learning and study abroad. *Language Teaching* 51(4), 439–484. doi.org/10.1017/S026144481800023X
Ishihara, N. (2010) Compliments and responses to compliments: Learning communication in context. In Martínez-Flor, A., Usó-Juan, E. (eds), *Speech Act Performance: Theoretical, Empirical and Methodological Issues.* Amsterdam: Benjamins, 179–198. doi.org/10.1075/lllt.26.11ish
Jaworski, A. (1994) Pragmatic failure in a second language: Greeting responses in English by Polish students. *International Review of Applied Linguistics in Language Teaching* 32(1), 41–56. doi.org/10.1515/iral.1994.32.1.41
Jin, L. (2012) When in China, do as the Chinese do? Learning compliment responding in a study abroad program. *Chinese as a Second Language Research* 1(2), 211–240. doi.org/10.1515/caslar-2012-0013
Jin, L. (2015) Developing Chinese complimenting in a study abroad program. *Chinese Journal of Applied Linguistics* 38(3), 277–300. doi.org/10.1515/cjal-2015-0018
Johnson, D. (2009) *Spectacle and Sacrifice: The Ritual Foundations of Village Life in North China.* Harvard, MA: Harvard University Press.
Jucker, A. (2012) Pragmatics in the history of linguistic thought. In Allan, K., Jaszczolt, K. M. (eds), *The Cambridge Handbook of Pragmatics.* Cambridge: Cambridge University Press, 495–512. doi.org/10.1017/CBO9781139022453.027
Kádár, D. Z. (2013) *Relational Rituals and Communication: Ritual Interaction in Groups.* Basingstoke: Palgrave Macmillan. doi.org/10.1057/9780230393059

Kádár, D. Z. (2017) *Politeness, Impoliteness and Ritual: Maintaining the Moral Order in Interpersonal Interaction.* Cambridge: Cambridge University Press. doi.org/10.1017/9781107280465

Kádár, D. Z., House, J. (2020) Ritual frames: A contrastive pragmatic approach. *Pragmatics* 30(1), 142–168. doi.org/10.1075/prag.19018.kad

Kádár, D. Z., Ning, P., Ran, Y. (2018) Public ritual apology – A case study of Chinese. *Discourse, Context and Media* 26, 21–31. doi.org/10.1016/j.dcm.2018.01.003

Kampf, Z. (2016) All the best! Performing solidarity in political discourse. *Journal of Pragmatics* 93, 47–60. doi.org/10.1016/j.pragma.2015.12.006

Kasper, G. (2006) Speech acts in interaction: Towards discursive pragmatics. In Bardovi-Harlig, K., Felix-Brasdefer, C., Saleh Omar, A. (eds), *Pragmatics & Language Learning, Vol. 11.* Mānoa: University of Hawai'i at Mānoa, 281–314.

Kasper, G., Blum-Kulka, S. (eds) (1993) *Interlanguage Pragmatics.* Oxford: Oxford University Press.

Kasper, G., Rose, K. R. (1999) Pragmatics and SLA. *Annual Review of Applied Linguistics* 19, 81–104. doi.org/10.1017/S0267190599190056

Katan, D. (2009) Translation of intercultural communication. In Munday, J. (ed.), *The Routledge Companion to Translation Studies.* London: Routledge, 74–92.

Kim, J., Dewey, D. P., Baker-Smemoe, W., Ring, S., Westover, A., Eggett, D. L. (2015) L2 development during study abroad in China. *System* 55, 123–133. doi.org/10.1016/j.system.2015.10.005

Kinginger, C. (2011) Enhancing language learning in study abroad. *Annual Review of Applied Linguistics* 31, 58–73. doi.org/10.1017/S0267190511000031

Kissine, M. (2013) *From Utterances to Speech Acts.* Cambridge: Cambridge University Press. doi.org/10.1017/CBO9780511842191

Kobayashi, Y. (2011) Applied linguistics research on Asianness. *Applied Linguistics* 32(5), 566–571. doi.org/10.1093/applin/amr032

Kogan, A.-F. (2008) Social anchorage of remote assistance for elderly people: From speech acts to organizational information. *Les Enjeux de l'information et de la communication* 2008(1), 31–43. doi.org/10.3917/enic.008.0300

Kramsch, C. (1993) *Context and Culture in Language Teaching.* Oxford: Oxford University Press.

Kroeber, A., Kluckhohn, C. (1952) *Culture: A Critical Review of Concepts and Definitions.* Harvard, MA: Harvard University Peabody Museum of American Archaeology and Ethnology Papers 47.

Kubota, R. (2016) The multi/plural turn, postcolonial theory, and neoliberal multiculturalism: Complicities and implications for applied linguistics. *Applied Linguistics* 37(4), 474–494. doi.org/10.1093/applin/amu045

Lado, R. (1957) *Linguistics across Cultures: Applied Linguistics for Language Teachers.* Ann Arbor: The University of Michigan Press.

Leech, G. (1983) *Principles of Pragmatics.* London: Longman.

Leech, G. (2007) Politeness: Is there an East–West divide? *Journal of Politeness Research* 3(2), 167–206. doi.org/10.1515/PR.2007.009

Lerer, S. (2003) Hello, dude: Philology, performance, and technology in Mark Twain's 'Connecticut Yankee'. *American Literary History* 15(3), 471–503. doi.org/10.1093/ALH/AJG032

Levinson, S. J. (2017) Speech acts. In Huang, Y. (ed.), *Oxford Handbook of Pragmatics.* Oxford: Oxford University Press, 199–216. doi.org/10.1093/oxfordhb/9780199697960.013.22

Li, W. (2009) Different communication rules between the English and Chinese greetings. *Asian Culture and History* **1**(2), 72–81.

LoCastro, V. (2000) Evidence of accommodation to L2 pragmatic norms in peer review tasks of Japanese learners of English. *JALT Journal* **22**(2), 245–270. doi.org/10.37546/JALTJJ22.2-2

McConarchy, T. (2019) L2 pragmatics as 'intercultural pragmatics': Probing sociopragmatic aspects of pragmatic awareness. *Journal of Pragmatics* **151**, 167–176. doi.org/10.1016/j.pragma.2019.02.014

Maíz-Arévalo, C. (2017) Expressive speech acts in educational e-chats. *Pragmática Sociocultural/Sociocultural Pragmatics* **5**(2), 151–178. doi.org/10.1515/soprag-2017-0016

Meier, A. J. (1997) Teaching the universals of politeness. *ELT Journal* **51**(1), 21–28. doi.org/10.1093/elt/51.1.21

Meier, A. J. (2010) Culture and its effect on speech act performance. In Martínez-Flor, A., Usó-Juan, E. (eds) *Speech Act Performance: Theoretical, Empirical and Methodological Issues*. Amsterdam: Benjamins, 75–89. doi.org/10.1075/lllt.26.05mei

Nelson, C. L. (1991) New Englishes, new discourses: New speech acts. *World Englishes* **10**(3), 317–323. doi.org/10.1111/j.1467-971X.1991.tb00166.x

Nilsson, J., Norrthon, S., Lindström, J., Wide, C. (2018) Greetings as social action in Finland Swedish and Sweden Swedish service encounters – A pluricentric perspective. *Intercultural Pragmatics* **15**(1), 57–88. doi.org/10.1515/ip-2017-0030

Nilsson, J., Norrby, C., Bohman, L., Skogmyr Marian, K., Wide, C., Lindström, J. (2020) What is in a greeting? The social meaning of greetings in Sweden-Swedish and Finland-Swedish service encounters. *Journal of Pragmatics* **168**, 1–15. doi.org/10.1016/j.pragma.2020.06.007

Olshtain, E., Weinbach, L. (1993) Interlanguage features of the speech act of complaining. In Kasper, G., Blum-Kulka, S. (eds), *Interlanguage Pragmatics*. Oxford: Oxford University Press, 108–122.

Oraby, S., Harrison, V., Misra, A., Riloff, E., Walker, M. (2017) Are you serious? Rhetorical questions and sarcasm in social media dialog. In Jokinen, K., Stede, M., DeVault, D., Louis, A. (eds), *Proceedings of the 18th Annual SIGdial Meeting on Discourse and Dialogue*. Saarbrücken: Association for Computational Linguistics, 310–319.

Pan, Y., Kádár, D. Z. (2011) *Politeness in Historical and Contemporary Chinese*. London: Bloomsbury.

Pike, K. L. (ed.) (1967) *Language in Relation to a Unified Theory of Structure of Human Behavior*, 2nd ed. The Hague: Mouton.

Pishghadam, R., Morady Moghaddam, M. (2011) Towards a contrastive pragmatic analysis of congratulation speech act in Persian and English. *Journal of English Pedagogy and Practice* **4**(9), 130–151.

Ren, W. (2019) Pragmatic development of Chinese during study abroad: A cross-sectional study of learner requests. *Journal of Pragmatics* **146**, 137–149. doi.org/10.1016/j.pragma.2019.01.017

Rose, K., Kasper, G. (eds) (2001) *Pragmatics in Language Teaching*. Cambridge: Cambridge University Press. doi.org/10.1017/CBO9781139524797

Rose, K., Ono, R. (1995) Eliciting speech act data in Japanese: The effect of questionnaire type. *Language Learning: A Journal of Research in Language Studies* **45**(2), 191–223. doi.org/10.1111/j.1467-1770.1995.tb00438.x

Safont Jordà, P. (2003) Metapragmatic awareness and pragmatic production of third language learners of English: A focus on request act realizations. *International Journal of Bilingualism* **7**(1), 43–68. doi.org/10.1177/13670069030070010401

Said, E. (1978) *Orientalism*. New York: Pantheon Books.
de Saussure, F. (1916) *Course in General Linguistics*, Wade Baskin (trans.). London: Fontana/Collins.
Sbisà, M., Turner, K. (eds) (2013) *Pragmatics of Speech Actions*. Berlin and New York: Mouton de Gruyter. doi.org/10.1515/9783110214383
Schauer, G. (2022) Exploring the potential of graphic novels for L2 pragmatic teaching and learning – Focus on young learners. *The Language Learning Journal* 50(4), 491–505. doi.org/10.1080/09571736.2022.2088445
Schegloff, E. E. (1968) Sequencing in conversational openings. *American Anthropologist* 70, 1075–1095. doi.org/10.1525/aa.1968.70.6.02a00030
Schegloff, E. E., Sacks, H. (1973) Opening up closings. *Semiotica* 8(4), 289–327. doi.org/10.1515/semi.1973.8.4.289
Searle, J. R. (1969) *Speech Acts: An Essay in the Philosophy of Language*. Cambridge: Cambridge University Press. doi.org/10.1017/CBO9781139173438
Searle, J. R. (1979) The classification of illocutionary acts. *Language in Society* 8, 137–151. doi.org/10.1017/S0047404500006837
Searle, J., Vanderveken, D. (1985) *Foundations of Illocutionary Logic*. Cambridge: Cambridge University Press.
Segun Olaoye, S. (2018) Yoruba greeting culture: An anthropo-linguistic review. *Nile Journal of English Studies* 3(4), 105–117. doi.org/10.20321/nilejes.v3i4.144
Sharifian, F. (2008) Cultural schemas in L1 and L2 compliment responses: A study of Persian-speaking learners of English. *Journal of Politeness Research* 4(1), 55–80. doi.org/10.1515/PR.2008.003
Sharoff, S., Rapp, R., Zweigenbaum, P., Fung, P. (2013) *Building and Using Comparable Corpora*. New York: Springer. doi.org/10.1007/978-3-642-20128-8
Sheridan, D. (2018) 'If you greet them, they ignore you': Chinese migrants, (refused) greetings, and the inter-personal ethics of global inequality in Tanzania. *Anthropological Quarterly* 91(1), 237–265. doi.org/10.1353/anq.2018.0007
Shleykina, G. (2016) *The Speech Act of Greeting Performed by Russian EFL Learners*. Doctoral thesis, Oklahoma State University.
Simpson, S. (2008) Western EFL teachers and East-West classroom-culture conflicts. *RELC Journal* 39(3), 381–394. doi.org/10.1177/0033688208096
Sinclair, J. M. (1991) *Corpus, Concordance, Collocation*. Oxford: Oxford University Press.
Spencer-Oatey, H. (2005) (Im)politeness, face and perceptions of rapport: Unpackaging their bases and interrelationships. *Journal of Politeness Research* 1(1), 95–119. doi.org/10.1515/jplr.2005.1.1.95
Steuten, A. A. G. (1997) Structure and coherence in business conversations – A hierarchical model. In Dignum, F., Dietz, J. (eds) *The Language/Action Perspective*. Veldhoven: Proceedings of the Second International Workshop on Communication Modeling, Veldhoven, The Netherlands, 9–10 June 1997, 133–144.
Taguchi, N. (2006) Analysis of appropriateness in a speech act of request in L2 English. *Pragmatics* 16(4), 513–533. doi.org/10.1075/prag.16.4.05tag
Taguchi, N. (ed.) (2009) *Pragmatic Competence*. Berlin: Mouton de Gruyter. doi.org/10.1515/9783110218558
Taguchi, N. (2018) Contexts and pragmatics learning: Problems and opportunities of the study abroad research. *Language Teaching* 51(1), 124–137. doi.org/10.1017/S0261444815000440

Taguchi, N., Li, S. (2021) Cross-cultural pragmatics and second language (L2) pragmatics: Approaches to assessing L2 speech act production. *Contrastive Pragmatics* **2**(1), 1–23. doi.org/10.1163/26660393-BJA10014

Takahashi, S. (2019) Individual learner considerations in SLA and L2 pragmatics. In Taguchi, N. (ed.), *The Routledge Handbook of Second Language Acquisition and Pragmatics*. London: Routledge, 429–443.

Tanaka, K., Ellis, R. (2003) Study abroad, language proficiency, and learner beliefs about language learning. *JALT Journal* **25**(1), 63–85. doi.org/10.37546/JALTJJ25.1-3

Tatton, H. (2008) 'Could you, perhaps, pretty please?': Request directness in cross-cultural speech act realization. *Studies in Applied Linguistics & TESOL* **8**(2), 1–4. doi.org/10.7916/salt.v8i2.1479

Terkourafi, M. (2005) An argument for a frame-based approach to politeness: Evidence from the use of the imperative in Cypriot Greek. In Lakoff, R., Ide, S. (eds), *Broadening the Horizon of Linguistic Politeness*. Amsterdam: John Benjamins, 99–116. doi.org/10.1075/pbns.139.10ter

Terkourafi, M. (2015) Conventionalization: A new agenda for im/politeness research. *Journal of Pragmatics* **86**, 1–18. doi.org/10.1016/j.pragma.2015.06.004

Tracy, K., Van Dusen, D., Robinson, S. (1987) Good and bad criticism: A descriptive analysis. *Journal of Communication* **37**, 46–59. doi.org/10.1111/j.1460-2466.1987.tb00982.x

Turner, V. (1969) *The Ritual Process: Structure and Anti-Structure*. London: Aldine Publishing.

Vacas Matos, M., Cohen, A. (2022) Native-like performance of pragmatic features: Speech acts in Spanish. *Contrastive Pragmatics* **3**(2), 222–251. doi.org/10.1163/26660393-bja10034

Vanderveken, D. (1990) *Meaning and Speech Acts*. Cambridge: Cambridge University Press.

Wang, J., Halenko, N. (2022) Developing the use of formulaic language for study abroad: A targeted instructional intervention. *The Language Learning Journal* **50**(4), 409–426. doi.org/10.1080/09571736.2022.2088446

Weinert, R. (1995) The role of formulaic language in second language acquisition: A review. *Applied Linguistics* **16**(2), 180–205. doi.org/10.1093/applin/16.2.180

Wichmann, A. (2004) The intonation of please-requests: A corpus-based study. *Journal of Pragmatics* **36**(9), 1521–1549. doi.org/10.1016/j.pragma.2004.09.003

Wierzbicka, A. (1985) Different cultures, different languages, different speech acts: Polish vs. English. *Journal of Pragmatics* **9**(2/3), 145–178. doi.org/10.1016/0378-2166(85)90023-2

Wittgenstein, L. (1958) *Philosophical Investigations*. Oxford: Blackwell.

Wray, A. (2000) Formulaic sequences in second language teaching: Principle and practice. *Applied Linguistics* **21**(4), 463–489. doi.org/10.1093/applin/21.4.463

Yang, L., Ke, C. (2021) Proficiency and pragmatic production in L2 Chinese study abroad. *System* **98**, 102475. doi.org/10.1016/j.system.2021.102475

Ye, Z. V. (2007) La Double Vie de Veronica: Reflections on my life as a Chinese migrant in Australia. *Life Writing* **1**(1), 133–146. doi.org/10.1080/10408340308518247

Ying, J, Ren, W. (2021) Advanced learners' responses to Chinese greetings in study abroad. *International Review of Applied Linguistics in Language Teaching* **2021**(4), 1173–1199. doi.org/10.1515/iral-2020-0150

Youn, S. J. (2020) Managing proposal sequences in role-play assessment: Validity evidence of interactional competence across levels. *Language Testing* **37**(1), 76–106. doi.org/10.1177/0265532219860077

Young, R. (2011) Interactional competence in language learning, teaching, and testing. In Young, R. (ed.), *Handbook of Research in Second Language Teaching and Learning*. London: Routledge, 426–443.

Yu, M.-C. (2004) Interlinguistic variation and similarity in second language speech act behavior. *The Modern Language Journal* **88**(1), 102–119. doi.org/10.1111/j.0026-7902.2004.00220.x

Zhang, D. (2014) More than 'Hello' and 'Bye-bye': Opening and closing the online chats in Mandarin Chinese. *Computer Assisted Language Learning* **27**(6), 528–544. doi.org/10.1080/09588221.2013.776966

Zhang, L.-X. (2004) The cultural refraction in the Chinese greeting 'Have you eaten?' [in Chinese]. *Journal of Hefei University of Technology* **18**(3), 141–145.

Zhang, Y. (2021). Combining computer-mediated communication with data-driven instruction: EFL learners' pragmatic development of compliment responses. *System* **103**. doi.org/10.1016/j.system.2021.102624

Zhu, Y. (2000) Structural moves reflected in English and Chinese sales letters. *Discourse Studies* **2**(4), 473–496. doi.org/10.1177/1461445600002004000

Index

addressing, 97–8
Alerter, 17, 75, 76–9, 87, 159
Austin, John, 12, 13, 31, 91

Bardovi-Harlig, Kathleen, 22, 41, 70, 71, 129
Blum-Kulka, Shoshana, 5, 15–17, 24, 25, 29, 41, 75, 94, 114
buyao 不要, 96

code-switching, 145–6
Cohen, Andrew, 5, 28, 29
comparability, 7, 16, 19, 25, 25, 27, 34, 36, 42, 44, 74, 81, 131–3, 144, 162, 172, 174
complain, 92
congratulate, 35, 110, 113, 115
congratulating, 108–24
Coulmas, Florian, 3, 22, 24, 69–71, 73, 159
criticising, 90–106
culture, 19–20

disclose, 28, 134, 135
Discourse Completion Test (DCT), 16–18, 35, 37
Drew, Paul, 32
duibuqi and its variants, 55–8
Duranti, Alessandro, 128

Edmondson, Willis, 2, 4, 7, 13, 15, 17, 26, 28, 30–2, 37, 39, 48, 54, 55, 69–71, 92–4, 97, 113, 114, 153, 175
English as a global lingua franca, 152
excuse/justify, 157, 158, 160
extracting, 152–63
extractor, 153

Freed, Barbara, 109

Goffman, Erving, 44, 109, 113, 127, 128, 143, 147, 150, 151
good morning/afternoon/evening, 74–89, 137, 138
Greet, 74–89, 127–51, 165–70
Grice, Paul, 13
Gumperz, John, 14

hello/hallo, 74–89, 135–6
hi, 133–5
honorifics, 50, 51, 53, 58, 81, 82, 95, 114–19
Hoppe-Graff, Sigfried, 15
House, Juliane, 2, 7, 13, 15–25, 27–30, 31, 33, 37, 40, 41, 46, 48, 52, 54, 55, 71, 73, 75, 77, 92–7, 107, 113, 114, 153, 159, 162
how-are-you, 5, 129, 130–4, 136, 174
Hymes, Dell, 14, 15

idiosyncrasy, 20, 34, 35, 93, 113, 117
invite, 28, 33, 135

Kádár, Dániel Z., 2, 15, 17, 18, 23, 27, 28, 31, 33, 37, 40, 44, 52, 56, 73, 75, 93, 98, 109, 111, 119, 161, 164, 173
Kasper, Gabriele, 5, 15–21, 25, 27, 29, 31, 41, 46, 75, 94, 114
Kinginger, Celeste, 109, 125

Levinson, Stephen, 31, 89, 91
liminal rites of passage, 110–12
loanwords, 146

ni hao 你好 and its variant, 74–89, 138–40
non-quotidian ritual, 108

Index

Olshtain, Elite, 29, 92
Opine, 92, 94, 98, 99, 101, 104, 105

please and its variants 45–9
Popper, Karl, 7

qing 请 and its variants, 49–52, 94, 95

remark, 114
Ren, Wei, 129
research procedure, 34–7
request, 3, 4, 7, 14, 16, 17, 22–4, 26, 28, 29, 38, 40–53, 57, 69, 91, 92, 94–105, 110, 134–41, 145, 147
routine formulae, 3, 22, 71, 129, 159, 161, 162

Searle, John, 12, 13, 31, 91, 128
Sharoff, Serge, 36
sorry and its variants, 53–5
speech act typology, 26–39, 40, 41, 76, 92, 93, 99, 100, 105, 112, 113, 128, 131, 135, 175
strong contrastive hypothesis, 27

Su, Yunwen, 129
supportive move, 17

Taguchi, Naoko, 22, 41, 109
Tell, 98, 99, 101, 104, 105, 131
Tertium comparationis, 21
Thanks, 22, 74–89, 137, 138, 162
thank you and its variant, 74–89
Turner, Victor, 35
typological distance, 174

Vanderveken, Daniel, 31, 128

wei 喂, 74–89
Welcome, 136
Wish-Well, 114
Wittgenstein, Ludwig, 12

xiexie[ni] 谢谢[你] and its variant, 74–89

zaoshang/xiawu/wanshang hao 早上/下午/晚上好, 140, 141
zhuyi 注意, 96

EU representative:
Easy Access System Europe
Mustamäe tee 50, 10621 Tallinn, Estonia
Gpsr.requests@easproject.com

www.ingramcontent.com/pod-product-compliance
Lightning Source LLC
Chambersburg PA
CBHW051125160426
43195CB00014B/2352